# STUDIES

## AND

# ESSAYS

KEATS SHELLEY AND SHAKESPEARE

# STUDIES

&

# ESSAYS

## IN ENGLISH LITERATURE

BY

S. J. MARY SUDDARD, L.L.A.

FELLOW UNIV. GALL.

Cambridge :

at the University Press

1912

# CAMBRIDGE
## UNIVERSITY PRESS

University Printing House, Cambridge CB2 8BS, United Kingdom

Cambridge University Press is part of the University of Cambridge.

It furthers the University's mission by disseminating knowledge in the pursuit of
education, learning and research at the highest international levels of excellence.

www.cambridge.org
Information on this title: www.cambridge.org/9781316509623

© Cambridge University Press 1912

First published 1912
First paperback edition 2015

*A catalogue record for this publication is available from the British Library*

ISBN 978-1-316-50962-3 Paperback

# CONTENTS

## KEATS SHELLEY AND SHAKESPEARE STUDIES

## ESSAYS IN ENGLISH LITERATURE

# CHRONOLOGICAL TABLE

| *Abridged Title* | *Date of Composition* | |
|---|---|---|
| Versification of *Romeo and Juliet* . | November (?) | 1905 |
| Shakespeare's *Sonnets* . . . | " | — |
| *Astrophel and Stella* . . | . December | — |
| Swift's Poetry . . . . | . February | 1906 |
| *Hymn to Intellectual Beauty* . | . March | — |
| John Inglesant . . . . | . May | — |
| *Hellas* . . . . . | . Spring | — |
| Keats's Evolution . . . | . " | — |
| Keats's "*Prelude*" . . . | . June | — |
| *Measure for Measure* . . | . February | 1907 |
| Addison's Humour . . . | . March | — |
| Keats's Style . . . . | . May | — |
| Chaucer's Portraiture . . | . Spring | — |
| *The House of Life* . . . | . " | — |
| Ben Jonson and Shakespeare . | . " | — |
| Wordsworth's "Imagination" . | . Autumn | 1908 (?) |
| Shelley's Transcendentalism . | . " | — (?) |
| Shelley's Idealism . . . | . (?) | |

SARAH JULIE MARY SUDDARD, b. May 13, 1888, d. May 29, 1909

# THE EVOLUTION OF KEATS'S MIND

THE story of the "pang-dowered poet whose reverberant lips And heart-strung lyre awoke the Moon's eclipse" is the story of a soul working out its own salvation in unswerving obedience to its own laws of development, against the painfully degrading accidents of its fate.

Keats's was a lethargic sort of mind borne down by the weight of its own riches, one that, in a normal way, needed much sunlight and manuring before putting forth its blossoms—"a complex mind, imaginative and yet careful of its fruits, who would exist partly on sensation and partly on thought," and to whom "it was necessary that years should bring the philosophic mind[1]." Such a nature required more than common soil, sturdy props, liberal but sympathetic pruning, more than the average warmth of exposure, above all plenty of time to strike deep roots and gather strength before the season of production began. As he well knew, what he wanted was "a free and healthy and lasting organisation of heart, and lungs as strong as an ox, so as to be able to bear unhurt the shock of extreme thought and sensation

[1] *Letters*, November 1817.

without weariness[1]," a thorough mental training to fortify his instincts and correct their occasional tendencies to go astray, judicious criticism to lop the luxuriance that retarded his growth while cherishing and bringing the most promising buds into light, first and foremost a long life in which to shoot up to his full height, spread out to his full girth unchecked.

But fate was against him from the first hour of his birth. A constitution, sound to all outward appearance, but doomed in advance by a disease which literally ate him away before the age of twenty-six—such was the body that was to contain the throbbings of the great poetic heart; a scanty education supplemented by the pernicious influence of Leigh Hunt—such the preparation for the mind; the taunts of political antagonists, or at best the reluctant and measured admiration of brother-poets—such the criticism to encourage and direct his efforts. A brief span of life was allotted, and that brief period filled with anguish both physical and mental such as few have undergone. Under such treatment many a mind would have pined away unexpressed. "For the best of men," he tells us, "have but a portion of good in them; a kind of spiritual yeast that creates the ferment of existence, whereby a man is propelled to act and strive and buffet with circumstances[2]." Fortunately for Keats, the proportion of yeast was large. His intuitive knowledge of what his own nature required led him to create within himself a kind of second world that counteracted the chilling influences of the

[1] *Letters*, August 1819.    [2] *Ibid.* January 1818.

world outside. He developed like a double, triple, multiple rose, planted in a sandy soil, exposed to every blast, yet by virtue of its royal breed opening out leaf after leaf, the first petals curling off as the new ones unfolded, to leave the heart supreme in its delicate odour and flame.

Into eight years (from seventeen to twenty-five) were compressed the aspirations, doubts, triumphs of a lifetime. The struggle, becoming more and more intense as he felt his physical strength slipping away, was, in its main lines, that of many a far inferior soul, redeemed into tragedy by its untimely end. Keats began in utter darkness as to his object and, having found his way, was in no undue haste to see whither it was leading. Content to know the sunset skies were glowing radiant down the long, dark, tangled alley, he went quietly along, never swerving into a side-path, but clambering over every obstacle as it came, with many a fall and bruise in the process. Convinced that "nothing is finer for the purposes of great productions than a very gradual ripening of the intellectual powers[1]," he allowed his mind to evolve of itself, "capable of being in uncertainties, doubts, mysteries, without any irritable reaching after fact and reason[2]." He took his soul as he would a bottle of rich red wine, and shook it up, and held it against the light to watch it settle down. No hurry, no worry; a deliberate intensity. No fear of public opinion either; no terror and trembling before any judge but his own conscience. He cast his verse upon the world and let it take its chance:

[1] *Letters*, January 1818.     [2] *Ibid.* February 1818.

> Sang his story up into the air,
> Giving it universal freedom.  There
> Has it been sounding for those ears
> Whose tips are glowing hot,
>
> > (*Endymion*, Bk. II)

and for those ears alone.

Keats's unfeigned indifference to achieving aught but the final truth gradually concentrated his powers more and more upon one form of the truth, beauty in art.  The intensity with which he wrought, as a necessary consequence, circumscribed the range of his mind.  Its limitations are no less astonishing than its depth.  All the ordinary interests of humanity were to him unknown.  Religion, without scepticism or hatred, he simply ignored.  Philosophy, to whose charms he was far from indifferent, as is shown by his letters, despite the famous tirade in *Lamia*[1], never stirred his curiosity far enough to divert him for a moment from art.  Science, though through his profession he was fairly well versed in one of its branches, proved an object first of distaste and later of indifference.  Never in his own soul did he go through the conflict of incompatible duties which mars the life of a Cowper from the poetical point of view.  His very limitations as an all-round man favoured his development as an artist.  All the "terrier-like resoluteness of character," conspicuous even in the schoolboy, was bent on the pursuit of poetry—"the best sort of poetry, all I care for, all I live for[2]."  Cruelly bruised and mangled as his lot may seem, it was perhaps in some

[1] Do not all charms fly At the mere touch of cold Philosophy?
[2] *Letters*, August 25, 1819.

respects the best for the special end in view. It led him to shut himself up in a "tower of ivory" where he might live out his life in sensation and thought rather than in action. His moral nature, unimpaired by the excesses which sapped the mind and constitution of Byron, unembittered by the constant struggle with social conventions which tainted the life of Shelley, up to all but the very last retained the requisite vigour for urging on the weary flesh through doubt, disappointment and failure, whether in the eyes of the world or his own. The exquisite sensitiveness of his whole organisation sent him through many a fiery ordeal before reaching the philosophic content only the anguish of disease could disturb. Fits of dejection, crises of despair in which the ideal was for a moment half-forsaken he was continually passing through. Now and then he may have asked himself:

> Were it not better done, as others use,
> To sport with Amaryllis in the shade
> Or with the tangles of Neæra's hair?

but soon the steadfast answer came: No, the supreme mistress was still the Moon, the passion Poesy.

We may follow the pilgrim in quest of his poetic Zion through all the earlier stages of his progress. First the sense of sinfulness and possible salvation when the young soul wakes up in the City of Destruction, groaning under the burden of conventions. Then the wandering in the fields without the city, crying upon the Book whose spirit is as yet but dimly felt. Then the setting-forth, passing through many a Slough of Despond, threatened by many a flaming hill, till he knocks at the gate of Interpreter Nature.

Thereupon the burden rolls off and the Shining Ones bestow on him the scroll—his passport to the Eternal City. Then, after a long struggle up the Hill Difficulty, the entrance into the Palace Beautiful. There he sojourns awhile and arms himself in shield, All-prayer and coat of mail for the coming fight with Apollyon, the Prince of the World. On leaving the palace of early hope, the passage through the bitter Valley of Humiliation, healed, after many a wrestle with the giant, by the leaves of the far-off Tree of Life. Last of all, his figure fades and is lost in the Valley of the Shadow of Death.

We awake and, behold, it was a dream. For the progress of the pilgrim was ended. Save in thought he was never to roam on the Delectable Mountains or in the land of Beulah fall asleep.

The study of Keats's whole artistic existence is but as the study of one cycle in a longer life. But this cycle forms a continuous and rounded whole. His first ideal evolved through every phase, slowly waxing into the full splendour of triumph before as slowly waning into death. And thus it was that Keats while

> turning grandly on his central self
> Ensphered himself in twenty perfect years,
> And died—not young—the life of a long life
> Distilled to a mere drop, falling like a tear
> Upon the world's cold cheek, to make it burn
> For ever.    (MRS. BROWNING: *Aurora Leigh*, Bk I.)

No formal account has been left us of this self-education. Keats has favoured us with no *Prelude* in which to follow out step by step the growth of his

poetic mind. His ideal of poetry—that it should be
"great and unobtrusive, a thing which enters into
one's soul and does not startle or amaze it with itself
but with its object"—would have received a painful
shock at the very notion of systematizing his struggles, his yearnings, his hours of triumph into anything
bearing the remotest resemblance to a treatise of his
art. Ostentatious confession and theorizing on a subject to him so sacred seems to have sent a little quiver
of indignation through all his sensitive nerves. "Every
man may have his speculations, but every man does
not brood and peacock over them till he makes a false
coinage and deceives himself." His feeling of the
utter helplessness even of the highest among mortals
before the Unattainable put him on his guard against
taking any gleams of truth that here and there broke
in upon the general dark for revelations to be recorded
for the enlightenment of ages yet to come. "Many
a man may travel to the very bourne of Heaven and
yet want confidence to put down his half-seeing."
And the letter ends on a flourish of defiance to the
modern poet's over-conscious reduction of sensation
to precept and rule. "We need not be teased with
grandeur and merit when we can have them uncon-
taminated and unobtrusive. Let us have the old
poets and Robin Hood. Your letter and its sonnets
gave me more pleasure than will the Fourth Book of
*Childe Harold* and the whole of anybody's life and
opinions." (Letter to Reynolds.)

But if we have not the chaptered history we have
all its substance in the diary. So spontaneous a mind
could not pass through eight years of such earnest

struggle in the conquest of a single love, without
expressing, however unpretentiously, his varying conception of the ideal.   If Keats wrote no *Prelude*, it
was, in truth, because he had no need to.  The growth
of his mind is told in every page of his letters, in every
line of his verse.   In these unbroken records, verse
condensing prose, prose explaining verse, the slightest
fluctuations in the soul's atmosphere are registered as
on a barometer.   What to the cursory reader must
often seem an aimless and inharmonious succession
of zigzags, to the initiated reveals the mutation of
all the interdependent elements of the mind.   Keats
possessed to an eminent degree the power of self-
analysis.   This faculty, one of the earliest to come
out in his nature, went on developing into subtler
complexity as his own mind ripened and his psychological intuition evolved into consciousness.   "Grant
me," he cries in one of his last letters, "that I always
strive to know myself."

He succeeded, for allied to this power of self-
analysis was the rarer power of self-criticism.   What
we know so far of Keats's character shows him to
have been singularly modest in his own estimation.
"My greatest elevations of soul leave me every time
more humbled[1]."   He defines himself with truth as
"a man whose love of Beauty in the abstract makes
him a severe critic on his own works."   In the progress of his art this critical perception is felt throughout, testing the relation of achievement to ideal with
the sensitive accuracy of a spirit-level.   This ever-
watchful Mentor, his infallible guide through life, has

[1] *Letters*, October 29, 1818.

become our infallible guide through the pages of the dead.

The story of the development, while complete, is by no means obvious. The tale stands written on asbestos-paper, only legible in the flame of a mind heated to sympathetic communion with his own. In his earlier days, he is labouring under a double disadvantage: the problem is too near to be viewed round on all sides and he has not yet learnt to express his half-conscious ideas with fluency in a language still new to his tongue. In *Endymion* and *Isabella* the explanations, while copious, are conveyed through the medium of obscure and not always self-consistent symbolism. In the later works, with their higher artistic self-restraint, we are left to judge rather from changes in the general tone than any direct confession. Nor is the gloss afforded by the letters conspicuous for that lucidity the impatient twentieth-century reader requires. The signs which show the way his mind is taking are like finger-posts along a forest-road muffled up in leaves and trailing creepers from the eyes of those who would run while they read. To disentangle, without snapping, the tendrils that curl round the letters is a labour of love but of infinite patience.

My object would be to present a continuous account of the evolution of Keats's artistic mind, based entirely on his own confessions and told over again, as nearly as possible, in his own words. The diffused rays might be focussed to a round image by passing through the lens of a second mind. My sole ambition would be to furnish this lens.

# KEATS'S "*PRELUDE*"

## A STUDY OF THE POEMS OF KEATS
## UP TO *ENDYMION*

"NOTHING is finer for the purposes of great
productions than a very gradual ripening of the
intellectual powers[1]," writes Keats in 1818, just on
emerging from the first period of darkness we are
entering into, and what constitutes the true greatness
of Keats's mature work, its power of suggestion beyond
all possible expression, may be ascribed to the gradual
unfolding to their inmost depths, the gradual filling
to their utmost capacity, of heart, senses, and
imagination. If we take the general law of Keats's
development to stand as follows—great faculty for
absorbing and, through the heaviness ensuing on this
over-repletion, great difficulty in reproducing—the two
conditions for Keats's work will be extra tranquillity
to take in, extra stimulus to bring forth. Therefore
he was not meant to be precocious, he was meant to
come late, comparatively speaking, to a consciousness
of his own power and, after the ideal had dawned
upon him, before even attempting to display this

[1] *Letters*, January 1818.

power in definitive work, to pass through a laborious
process of self-education.

The first awakening is usually supposed to have
come at fourteen, after reading the *Faery Queen*,
perhaps because the instinct for beauty that lay
dormant in the hidden depths of the boy's nature
could only be roused by the poet in whom, almost
alone before Keats, the love of beauty truly "obliterated
every other consideration." Yet Keats cannot be said
to have formulated any approach to a personal conception of beauty before the age of twenty-two. The
workings of his mind during these eight years of
search for the ideal are involved, from the nature
of the case, in an obscurity to be dispelled rather by
inference from the course of its later development
than from any positive data. *Endymion* gives the
first approximately coherent and intelligible account
of "Imagination's struggles far and nigh" to reach an
object already felt, already possessed, if still nameless
and unknown ; but the struggles of imagination, before
conceiving of its object, to define its own existence
who shall describe?

Nothing but a study of this first inarticulate
struggle can show how far the "yearning fondness
and passion for the beautiful" was for Keats an acquired, not a natural, inclination. Nothing indeed
can be further removed from "fondness and passion"
than his first attitude towards beauty. Yearning there
was, the yearning of helplessness for power, intensified
by the exquisite susceptibility of his nerves, but,
through his pleasure-loving languor, accompanied by
a reluctance, almost a dislike, to the means that might

lead to this power.   The two combined to plunge his
whole being in a kind of aching torpor.   A habit of
mind was at this time formed from which he could
never after rouse himself but by an intense effort
of will.   As soon as the will gave way it developed
into a chronic morbidity of temperament.   Its first
effect, when still in its mildest form, was to delay him
several years on the threshold of art.   He describes
himself as having been long "addicted to passiveness."
The hesitation he shows to throw himself into the
active struggle and joy of artistic production is a sign
of abnormal and to himself inexplicable numbness.

   In a letter written soon after the plunge had been
taken, while the impression was still fresh in his mind,
Keats compares human life to a large mansion of
many apartments[1].   "The first we step into we call
the Infant or Thoughtless Chamber, in which we
remain as long as we do not think.   We remain there
a long while...."   Beyond the Thoughtless Chamber
lies a second, full of light and perfume and every
æsthetic delight that can appeal to the senses, the
chamber through which his own mind had to pass before emerging into the luxuriant garden of *Endymion*.
This he christens the Chamber of Maiden Thought.
Now "notwithstanding the doors of the second chamber
remain open, showing a bright appearance, *we care
not to hasten into it*."   Indeed the cause that over-
came the first lethargic indifference to him still
remains a mystery.   He can give no explanation of
the transition from the first chamber to the second.
He only knows that, after long delay, he was at last

[1] *Letters*, May 3, 1818.

"imperceptibly impelled" by the awakening of what he calls "the thinking principle" in him.

Without attempting to define the thinking principle more precisely than Keats, we may ask under what influences it was awakened. Through Spenser he presumably caught the first glimpse of the Chamber of Maiden Thought. This first initiation into the mysteries of beauty was followed up by a diligent if incomplete and fragmentary study of those predecessors in whom the same spirit might be recognized. However tardy the personal effort at production, he was not slow to learn by proxy "all the sweets of song"—

> The grand, the sweet, the terse, the free, the fine,
> What swelled with pathos and what right divine[1],

showing already the tendencies of his own mind by the choice of favourites and yet more by the choice of rarely-recognized characteristics in those favourites. The latent delight in voluptuous sound and concordantly voluptuous emotion is already thrilled by the languor of Spenserian melody,

> Spenserian vowels that elope with ease
> And float along like birds o'er summer seas,

and in Milton, far above the rebellion of the fallen angels, by the fondness of "connubial love,"

> Miltonian storms, and more, Miltonian tenderness.

Mixing with these memories of the past steals in the influence of the living realities by whom the tradition

---

[1] *Epistle to Cowden Clarke*, ll. 54, 55.

is carried on.   Thus we find his heart "brimful" no
longer merely

> Of fair-haired Milton's eloquent distress
> And all his love for gentle Lycid drowned[1],

or else

> Of lovely Laura in her light green dress
> And faithful Petrarch gloriously crowned,

but of something nearer and more tangible:

> of the friendliness
> That in a little cottage he has found,

the master of the cottage being no other than the
author of *The Story of Rimini*.   Through Leigh
Hunt he was gradually drawn into the literary life of
the day, initiated into every side of romantic poetry,
brought into contact with several romantic contemporaries and, a fact of more importance, unconsciously
filled through and through with romantic theories of
art.    There might at first have been a danger of the
principle of beauty being lost or at least the taste for
beauty vitiated among these complex and by no
means equally sound influences.   But if, as he remembered later to his mortification, he used to worship
Beattie and Mrs Tighe, far above these "wallowers
in the bog at the foot of the poetic mountain" rose up

> He of the cloud, the cataract, the lake,
> Who on Helvellyn's summit wide awake
> Catches his freshness from archangel's wing[2].

Keats's taste, cultivated by study of the masters, soon
taught him to feel the best and healthiest in romantic

[1]   " Keen fitful gusts are whispering here and there."...
[2]   " Great spirits now on earth are sojourning."

art, and when once the best had been felt he did not
hesitate to reject all of inferior quality, even though
the rejection included his constant friend and early
idol, Leigh Hunt.

So all these different influences, that at first
threatened discord, gradually settled down into harmony, touched by the tuning-fork of the inborn sense
of Beauty :

> no confusion, no disturbance rude
> Do they occasion ; 'tis a pleasing chime.
> So the unnumbered sounds that evening store;
> The song of birds—the whispering of the leaves-
> The voice of waters—the great bell that heaves
> With solemn sound—and thousand others more,
> That distance of recognizance bereaves,
> Make pleasing music and not wild uproar[1].

The general effect of this purely literary education
was by refining and soothing the mind to make it
receptive of beauty when beauty should come. Beauty
itself remained as yet an abstract ideal. It could not
be felt as a living reality before Keats had made some
active effort to express whatever might as yet be
slumbering in himself. Keats, while ever eager to
drink in, felt the unconquerable aversion of an indolent
nature, as yet unconscious of its own depth, to bring
forth. True, his ambition fired him with an intense
desire to emulate the masters. True, after sailing

> Past each horizon of fine poesy,
> Fain would he echo back each pleasant note[2]

[1] " How many bards gild the lapses of time.". . .
[2] *Epistle to Felton Mathew*, ll. 12, 13.

as on Sicilian seas one gondolier sends back the other's song.    And to the carrying out of this desire we may ascribe the existence of a fair amount of published, and perhaps more unpublished, verse which stands in the same relation to the crudest efforts of his original genius as Chatterton's *London Satires* to the *Rowley Poems*.    They are of interest only as showing the depth of Keats's nature before that depth had been filled.    Shelley's first attempts may be pronounced chaotic, but Keats's are void.    The *Poems of Margaret Nicholson* may seem, as they desire to appear, insane, but into the insanity are wrought Shelley's own opinions at the time; they possess, if nothing else, an autobiographical interest.    Whereas the *Address to some Ladies*, the lines "Hast thou from caves of Golconda a gem," the rondeau "Hadst thou lived in days of old," the apostrophe to Hope, even the *Imitation of Spenser*, to which may be added the Odes to Apollo and several of the Sonnets, while glitteringly correct in expression, display a nullity of thought— worse, an insincerity of feeling—that sufficiently show with what indifference, if not positive dislike, Keats entered upon his poetical career.

An indifference perhaps only relative, after all. An indifference, at any rate, that soon became conscious of itself.    An indifference that throbbed with a very genuine heart-ache at its own cold and factitious impersonality.    For in a sonnet to Spenser[1]—occasioned perhaps by the *Imitation* of that poet, perhaps by the tale of chivalry entitled *Calidore* (though, considering the far superior value of this fragment,

[1] Beginning : ''Spenser, a jealous honourer of thine''...

I should be inclined to place it later than the Sonnet in question), perhaps again by an unsuccessful attempt in the master's manner which has not been preserved— Keats, after an almost abject apology for the sacrilege, proceeds to explain and defend his own case. Crushed by a sense of his mortality, he recognizes the futility of his own efforts. The god-given inspiration will not come:

> 'tis impossible
> For an inhabitant of wintry earth
> To rise, like Phœbus, with a golden quill,
> Fire-winged, and make a morning in his mirth.

The weakness of the flesh must be overcome. Passive indolence must be exchanged for labour— active labour. For

> 'tis impossible to 'scape from toil
> O' the sudden and receive thy spiriting. [inspiration?]

To the poet as to the plant time must be given to absorb in peace the nutriment on which its final splendour must depend :

> The flower must drink the nature of the soil
> Before it can put forth its blossoming.

Acting on this conviction, Keats proceeds to absorb what from previous example, without as yet any personal experience, he supposes to be the materials of inspiration. At this time he approaches art from the outside through the methods, rather than the spirit, of the masters, just as certain unbelievers, wishing to be converted, try to initiate themselves into the mysteries of the faith through strict observance of its external ceremonies. Keats understood vaguely that

the first step in the right direction was to bring himself into a certain receptive frame of mind. And to
bring himself into this frame of mind he considered it
necessary to surround himself with those outward
associations whence his contemporaries seemed to
derive their strength. While the "passion Poesy" was
still for him the alien "Muse[1]" of convention, he suspected she would not condescend

> 'Mid *contradictions* her delights to lend.

In harmonious surroundings alone could the inner
voice of the spirit make itself heard:

> Should e'er the fine-eyed maid to me be kind,
> Ah surely it must be whene'er I find
> Some flowery spot, sequestered, wild, romantic,
> *That often must have seen a poet frantic.*

To Nature forthwith he goes, hoping "to find a
place where he may greet the maid," waiting for her
advent in a state of intellectual abstraction such as
we read of among the mystics waiting for the image
of the god to flash upon them.

"Full many a dreary hour have I past," says
Keats, looking back upon these early communions
with Nature, straining eye and ear by a superhuman
effort to concentrate his wandering senses upon the
objects traditionally supposed to inspire the fine frenzy
of the poet. As yet the only result of the tension is
"a brain bewildered and a mind o'ercast with heaviness," bringing as a consequence the conviction

[1] *Epistle to Felton Mathew.*

No spherey strains by him could e'er be caught
From the blue dome, though he to dimness gaze
On the far depth whose sheeted lightning plays,
Or on the wavy grass, outstretched supinely,
Pry 'mong the stars *to strive to think divinely*[1]....

This mood, though to Keats startling in its novelty,
is not rare, as he was to learn by much bitter subsequent experience, as he might, even at that time, have
learnt from a contemporary and fellow-sufferer, the
author of *Dejection*. Through the limpid clearness of
the latter's long and carefully filtered language seems
to shine a feeling identical with that of Keats. Little
difference could be established between Keats's bewilderment and heaviness and the "wan and heartless
mood" of Coleridge. As Keats to dimness gazes
upon the lightning and the stars, so Coleridge
gazes all the evening long upon the "western sky
and its peculiar tint of yellow green," upon the
clouds, the stars behind the clouds, the crescent
moon "as fixed as if it grew in its own cloudless,
starless lake of blue." Both knew, as either might
have said,

> I see them all so excellently fair,
> I see, not feel, how beautiful they are.

Yet there is one all-important difference which
may help to throw on the cause of Keats's failure the
light in which Coleridge could serenely analyze his
own. The difference lies in the respective periods at
which the two effusions were poured forth. Keats
writes before knowing what inspiration means ;
Coleridge after having lost it. Coleridge therefore

[1] *Epistle to My Brother George.*

can describe, though not apply to his own case, the remedy.   Knowing what Keats has yet to learn:

> He may not hope from outward forms to win
> The passion and the life whose fountains are within,

he feels, while Keats does not as yet even distantly suspect, that

> from the *soul itself* must issue forth
> A light...

and

> from the *soul itself* there must be sent
> A voice...
> Of all sweet sounds the life and element.

That is, Nature cannot directly act but only react upon the soul.   An interchange of sympathy must take place.   Nature will only lend its beauty at a high rate of interest in human emotion.   Therefore passive receptivity must develop into active proffer of love. When this interpenetration of the inward and external is complete, inspiration will descend under the form of Joy,

> Joy such as ne'er was given
> Save to the pure and in their purest hour.

Yet even to Keats at this early period, unanalytical and unconscious, there comes a time when, after patient waiting through the objects of his contemplation steals a feeling not far, in appearance, from the pure Joy of Coleridge.

> There are times, when those that love the bay,
> Fly from all sorrowing far, far away;
> A *sudden glow* comes on them, nought they see
> In water, earth, or air but poesy.

In this "glow" of "poesy" all the objects before so
vacantly gazed at seem to be transposed into another
region. The skies seem to divide and open out into
long vistas of superhuman splendour :

> And what we, ignorantly, sheet-lightning call
> Is the swift opening of their wide portal.

Only the Poet's eye can reach those golden halls
where every common thing is changed under the
touch of an unearthly light, till even the lustre of a
falling star is but the stream of nectar that pours
from an enchanted goblet.

Keats evidently looks upon this "glow" as a sign
of genuine inspiration and indeed calls his masters to
vouch for its truth [For knightly Spenser to Libertas
(= L. Hunt) told it], but it seems to me to be removed
from the Joy of Coleridge by just so many degrees as
Fancy is distant from Imagination. Keats, living
through the struggle of his age, was sure to fall at
the beginning into the traps that beset the path of
every young romantic. An almost inevitable mistake
was to confound the false dawn of Fancy with the
sunrise of Imagination. Even the steadfast intelligence of Wordsworth, when his eye was fixed on such
objects as Keats, out of respect for tradition, had
chosen as food for "poesy," was apt to be led into
a similar delusion. Wordsworth, instead of lightning,
was content with "a diamond light" seen "whene'er
the summer sun, declining, smote A smooth rock
wet with constant springs[1]," yet even this comparatively prosaic phenomenon, from its unquiet, formless

---

[1] *Prelude*, Bk VIII.

vagueness gave ample scope to the inferior faculty
of Fancy.

> Often and long
> Upon this restless lustre have I gazed
> That made my fancy restless as itself,

subjecting it to the same process of transformation as
Keats :

> 'Twas now for me a burnished silver shield
> Suspended over a knight's tomb who lay
> Inglorious, buried in the dusky wood :
> An entrance now into some magic cave
> Or palace built by fairies in the rock.

Wordsworth in this amusement, which by Keats
was taken seriously for poetic ardour, recognized the
touch of " wilful Fancy "

> Engrafting far-fetched shapes on feelings bred
> By pure Imagination.

Having known " pure Imagination," Wordsworth
could afford to indulge in Fancy and even to call it
" hurtless," but for Keats there was a danger it might
usurp the place of true poetic feeling.   It had done
its duty, which was to rouse his mind, if only for a
moment, from the lethargy in which it lay, but now it
was of the utmost importance the objects magnified
by this over-excitement should be reduced to their
due proportions.   Keats seems to have found instinctively the same corrective Wordsworth, on principle,
administered to his own mind.   As soon as the emotion had subsided, he, like Wordsworth, sought for

> forms distinct
> To steady him.

Those weary hours of watching before the "sudden glow" were not lost; for, during this time of apparently fruitless effort, he was training his senses to concentration. They acquired a sharpness which, in calmer moments, allowed them to interpret into the conceptions of over-heated Fancy the reality it disdained. Keats now brings the glorified vision down to its humble counterpart upon earth.

While listening for "spherey strains," Keats was revolving in his mind the prose libretto to which the music might be set. "Knightly Spenser" had suggested a subject on which he meant to turn the inspiration, whenever it should come. In a vague way, he thought of choosing, for his first theme,

> Some tale of love and arms in time of old.

And, if the visions perceived during the "sudden glow" be closely analyzed, they will be found to present, much distorted by the flickering of the light in the magic lantern, a succession of dissolving views from the far-off world of the *Faery Queen.* By dint of gazing on the unsoftened glare, five or six situations will be seen to rise out, all meant to be included in the tale : a tournament, a parley at a castle gate, a festival, a glimpse of ladies retiring into their bowers. Now imagine Keats bringing them down out of the sunset skies, where all are lost in the universal blaze, to examine them on earth in the milder light of day : we shall have the *Specimen of an Induction to a Poem.* Here the scenes which before could only be conceived as a series of hallucinations are presented as so many definite realities. Instead of "white

coursers" prancing "in air," "bestridden of gay
knights in gay apparel," the chargers with their
riders are shown to "Leap to the honours of a
tournament" from solid earth.   Instead of the
"glory of the festivals" where wine "pours with
the lustre of a falling star," we have the "splendour
of the revelries" where prosaic "butts of wine are
drunk off to the lees."   And among these significant
changes steal in no less significant additions ; a
number of deft little touches indicative of direct and
intelligently adapted observation : the lady "Who
cannot feel for cold her tender feet," the knight's
lance resting against the boughs of the ash thence
reflected in the lake, the "half-seen mossiness of
linnets' nests," etc.   This change in feeling is of good
omen for the tale itself.   With this genuine, if rudimentary, delight in Nature for itself and in itself, the
true inspiration has come, though in an unambitious
form,—the Joy Coleridge had known and lost, a state
of mind to which Keats had trained himself by a
painful effort of will, and in which, with lapses into
indifference, when the will is overtaxed, he for the
future will remain.   Into Nature, as the first object
of his love, is thrown all the newly-discovered power
of emotion.   He wanders out in the declining day, no
longer straining his senses, no longer bewildered and
weighed upon with heaviness, but with

> His healthful spirit *eager and awake*
> *To feel* the beauty of a silent eve[1],

yea, and not only eager but able to feel, because he
comes

[1] *Calidore: A Fragment.*

> With a *warm heart* and eye *prepared* to scan
> Nature's clear beauty.

Now bringing the overflowing heart and carefully
trained perceptions to the contemplation of familiar
things, before passed by without a thought, he feels
a human joy, a human sorrow throbbing through
their new-known beauty. As Keats clings fondly
to the " silent eve," the eve, in mute harmony with
his desire, itself seems " loath this *happy* world to
leave," the dwindling light he would delay " dwells
o'er the scene so lingeringly," to lengthen out the
joy it feels in giving joy by touching all things into
beauty.

By instinct for the law of compensation, Keats is
already beginning to require a return for the emotion
poured forth without reserve. He " receives but what
he gives." The life he feels in Nature is his own.
Therefore the stock of feeling can only be paid back,
it cannot be increased. Nature has not sufficient
vitality to do more than develop and objectify
the emotion latent in himself, it cannot expand
that emotion beyond its own limits. When by
contemplation of Nature " his heart is well-nigh
overwound," he feels it fill with emotion to the
bounds of its present capacity. For that capacity
to be widened and deepened, another and different
emotion from an external and living source must be
poured in.

Wordsworth, when passing through the same stage,
remembers to have felt

> Distinctly manifested at this time
> A human-heartedness about his love,

and Keats, anything but distinctly, while sending out
blind feelers on every side, seems, unawares, to have
touched the same remedy.

The needful supply of emotion to Keats as to
Wordsworth was transmitted through the medium of
man, or rather, as more accessible to his half feminine
nature, through the gentler sympathy of the " milk-
white lamb that bleats For man's protection[1]."

When the heart has exhausted its emotion on
Nature, the voice of human affection brings news of
fresh emotion, unfathomed, still in store.  The evening
dreamer is roused from his meditation by a "trumpet's
silver voice...fraught with many joys for him."  These
joys are those of waking tenderness for woman—
accepted and returned—rising on neither side to love,
yet even now "thrilling him with pulses new."   In
this first gush of new blood through his veins, the
rapt senses seem to transpose the soul into another
sphere estranged from common life, where impressions
before felt as familiar now seem alien, where the sound
of another's voice comes to his ear

> like something from beyond
> His present being.

Soon, however, these common impressions re-
assume their sway.   Keats did not long remain in
this trance.   There was no necessity as yet for
drawing heavily on the newly discovered store.   We
know through what gradual, if certain, process impressions settle down in this slow-moving and retentive

---

[1] Last of three Sonnets beginning :
  " Woman, when I behold thee, flippant, vain "...

mind.   The love of humanity for itself takes as long
to wake up as did the love of Nature.   So far, it only
plays a subsidiary part.   By giving a fresh impulse
to the whole man, it quickens feeling and refines
perception.   But both quickened feeling and refined
perception return, throbbing with a new power, to the
study of Nature.

No longer to the external forms of Nature, or, if
to her external forms, less for themselves than for the
undefined half-human life underlying each one and
binding all together.   Slowly, very slowly, through
the precise, literal transcription of sights and sounds a
subtler feeling steals.   Coming, full of the new emotion,
to " watch *intently* Nature's gentle doings[1] " Keats, if
but in far-off gleams, in sudden flashes, seems to catch
sight of a single principle, the common origin of all.

A new organic life runs through the stream.   The
silent water, placid on the surface, heaves with an
undercurrent vigour that bears along the blades of
grass into the swarming minnows, before breaking
into ripples, again to swell into the coiling weeds
which, catching the new life, "keep up an interchange" of verdure and coolness with the sun-warmed
water.   Since that first season when he gazed on
Nature, trying to extract the unknown inspiration
from the most distant and, for him, unrelated phenomena,—sunset, stars and lightning,—the waking heart
and senses from the sky have brought him down into
sympathetic contact with the most earthly things of
earth, all distinct to eye and ear, yet through a
thousand unseen ramifications interwoven in feeling.

[1] " I stood tip-toe upon a little hill."

In the former mood, to listen for "spherey strains"
was of little avail, but now, in this state of self-
restrained yet intensely throbbing concentration,
trying to define the blind motions of universal life,
in the silence he seems to hear a voice.   A sound
"softer than ring-dove's cooings," the very inmost
tone of the Spirit of Nature.   A voice that can only
appeal to a newly recognized spiritual perception.
Inaudible to the "sensual ear"

> The *inward ear* will hear her and be blest[1].

This still small voice has already taught him to
know "glories That smile on him to tell delightful
stories."   In Nature, understood in this new spirit,
Keats recognizes the primary impulse of man's
creative power:

> For what has made the sage or poet write
> But the fair paradise of Nature's light?

Nature, as the recipient of all his emotion, has become
so intimately a part of him that, except through her
medium, he is incapable of conceiving the abstract
life peculiar to man's intelligence.   The creations of
this abstract intelligence can only spring from direct
contemplation of Nature.   So perfect, for Keats, is
this interpenetration of Nature and the soul, that in
the purely intellectual, therefore human, processes of
art he traces the same spirit, if not the same forms, as
in Nature.   Even when not borrowed in substance
from Nature, all poetry, for him, is necessarily the
outcome of an impression produced by Nature.   That

---

[1] Not included in the ordinary editions.   Printed by Lord Houghton.

is, Nature induces a certain frame of mind ; the poet,
working in this mood, unconsciously translates into
his art the impression produced by the object of his
inspiration. With sufficient insight, the spirit of each
artistic creation may be followed up to its source
in a natural phenomenon. What reason must we
give for

> the calm grandeur of a sober line,

for such a line, say, to take an example from Keats's
own maturest and most chastened style, as

> Thou foster-child of silence and slow time...?

It was the result of a moment when the poet had felt

> the waving of the mountain pine

sink down deeper than the sense into the soul. Whatever its apparent meaning, the inmost spirit expressed
through its moral tone or sensuous rhythm was the
impression produced on the creator's mind by the
moving of the boughs. Not only does it resemble
a mountain pine, it *is* the waving of the mountain
pine in sound. In the same manner, every emotional
effect is but a humanized sensation. Staidness in
feeling for him becomes synonymous with the shelter-
ing warmth of a hawthorn glade :

> And when a tale is beautifully staid
> We feel the safety of a hawthorn glade.

Voluptuous imagination, however human it may seem,
finds its food, again, in the commingling of many
kindred sensations arising from Nature :

> When it is moving on luxurious wings,
> The soul is lost in pleasant smotherings, etc.

In order to understand the essence of poetry we must then go back to its origin. Civilisation looks upon art as the expression of humanity, but, to reach the truth, we must drop these civilized illusions and return to the primitive state in which, for man in general, as for Keats in particular, as for every poet according to his conception, the feeling for Nature preceded the feeling for the kind. Where indeed the apparent expression of interest in humanity is only the supreme form of passion for Nature. Where man attributes to Nature not only his own feelings, but his whole being and, in giving Nature his own shape, annihilates himself. Just as among certain tribes the highest mutual token of regard between friends is to exchange names, so, in this peculiar relation to Nature, the most perfect way in which man can express his identification in feeling with the object of his worship is to give her his own form. Only in the intensest glow can this transfiguration take place. When the Spirit of Nature has filled the souls of her beloved till they

> Walk upon the winds with lightness (SHELLEY)

or, as with Keats, feel

> uplifted from the world
> Walking upon the white clouds wreathed and curled,

man, having poured his whole vitality into Nature, spontaneously sees her rising into his own shape, because born of his own life, before his eyes.

> So felt he who first told how Psyche went
> On the smooth wind to realms of wonderment;
> What Psyche felt and Love when their full lips
> First touched...

and, after thus symbolising the passage of the human soul through Nature to Love or inspiration, Keats develops the effect of this new love on the study of Nature. In the myth of Pan and Syrinx the poet, in the passing fit of inspiration, is represented as coming to feel Nature so intensely as to re-create it after his own image. But, as if in warning of Nature's incapacity to satisfy the soul for ever, the illusion is shown to fall with the falling emotion. Nature will not keep the form it has assumed.

> Poor Nymph,—poor Pan—how did he weep to find
> Nought but a lovely sighing of the wind
> Along the reedy stream...

after the heated chase in which imagination seemed to see, fleeting and glancing on before, a living Syrinx to answer his desire.

To modernize the process thus discovered in the ancient myths and adapt it to his own mind is for Keats, at this stage, as instinctive a tendency as the direct perception of Nature to most men. Thus we next see him giving out of his own experience the origin of the tale of Narcissus and thence working out the symbol till it becomes as much his own property as that of the original creator.

> What first inspired a bard of old to sing
> Narcissus pining o'er the untainted spring?

Through the intuition gained by his previous education Keats feels it to have arisen from a scene such as he may have witnessed a thousand times himself:

> In some delicious ramble he had found
> A little space with boughs all woven round...
> And in the midst of all a clearer pool...
> And on the bank a lonely flower...
> Drooping its beauty o'er the watery clearness
> To woo its own sad image into nearness....

Out of these simple, realistic facts the poet's
emotion, whether the anonymous " bard of old " or
Keats here matters little, evolved an imaginative
creation, endowed with human feeling and thence
with human shape :

> Nor was it long ere he had told the tale
> Of young Narcissus and sad Echo's bale.

As a proof of the completeness with which he
enters into the universal spirit of poetry, thus illustrated from the ancients, Keats proceeds to re-create
an old myth after his own fashion. Above all the
" glories that smile on him to tell delightful stories "
one shines serenely on the rest, the fountain-light of
inspiration. " With a gradual swim Coming into the
blue with all her light " he sees the Moon, the Moon
already identified, if not in word, at least in feeling,
with the " passion poesy." She changes into Cynthia,
not Cynthia chaste and cold, but Cynthia leaning
down, enamoured, over the shepherd-king. He, the
modern shepherd, under her smile feels himself slowly
waking from the immemorial slumber of the soul.
Though not yet ripe to sing the story of their budding
love, her influence, even at this early stage, sends
swimming through his brain the moonlit splendour
of *Endymion.*

How modest Keats's estimate of his own accomplishment is as yet may be seen from his disclaiming all but the most distant knowledge of the goddess, from his not daring to celebrate the " sweet close " of Endymion and Diana :

> Cynthia ! I cannot tell the greater blisses
> That followed thine and thy dear shepherd's kisses.

But while he makes no pretension to the name of Poet, the feeling for the possibility of being a Poet is awake. The pilgrim in his progress through the House of Life has left the Thoughtless Chamber far behind ; the thinking principle has impelled him forward on to the very threshold of the Chamber of Maiden Thought. There he stands wondering whether he shall enter in, already faint with whiffs of perfume coming through the door, already dazzled with glimpses of the light. This first ecstasy is far above the triumph of actual accomplishment, for it contains in itself untold possibilities of accomplishment. The bondage of indifference has been exchanged for the liberty of delight, a delight as yet undiminished by the pangs of creation. The aching void is filled to overflowing; with repletion comes the sense of power, power that can believe itself infinite through not attempting to express itself through finite form. For Keats, by definition, poetry is

> the supreme of power[1],

and the supreme of power is power so confident that it can sleep upon its strength:

> 'Tis Might half-slumbering on its own right arm.

[1] *Sleep and Poetry.*

In this great reaction after the tension, his attitude towards life is changed from resigned, almost sullen, submission, into cheerful, nay eager, acceptance. With the new conception of art comes a new conception of life, if not the first true comprehension of its meaning. As the guerdon of his efforts is bestowed, along with the promise of reward to come in art, a philosophy of life, sunny, breezy, ringing, rippling and rebounding. The past is dreary, the future uncertain, the present full of pleasure. Uppermost in his Epicurean nature lies the enjoyment of the present. To all pessimistic restrictions he turns a deaf ear. Sad warnings like distant rumblings of thunder may be heard, but the light still remains serene. Perhaps true as a general theory:

> Life is but a day, etc.

but of his special life at that special moment, of the life of twenty-two,

> Why so sad a moan?

For him

> Life is the rose's hope while yet unblown,
> The reading of an ever-changing tale,
> The light uplifting of a maiden's veil,
> A pigeon tumbling in clear summer air,

last, best, truest of all, as most completely expressive of himself:

> A laughing school-boy, without grief or care,
> Riding the springy branches of an elm.

Thus, starting off in search of an unknown ideal, his faculties, under a single influence opening out one after the other, have found their equilibrium. To

their perfect balance is due the sense of untainted
vitality tingling through his whole being, physical
and moral. Now if he seeks the special artistic aim
on which to concentrate the new-found power he will
find it already contained in the general philosophy.
With this hearty hold on life in every form, the object,
before so vague, shapes into precision. The sense of
*life*, awakened in the pursuit of art, pours all its complex and accumulated vigour into art. Art, in fact, is
only the expression of the general spirit of vitality
in concrete form. Its aim is to communicate the
originator's optimism to his fellows.

So without premeditation, out of the general
superabundance of strength, rises to his lips the
definition of

> the great end
> Of poesy—that it should be a friend
> To soothe the cares and lift the thoughts of man.

The next question is, how to carry out this end.
At this stage, Keats takes a review of the means at
his disposal in the present and their development in
the future. Allotting himself, with alas! unprophetic
liberality, a span of time in which to complete his
education, he takes in with the eye the different
materials through which the ideal is to be realised:

> O for ten years that I may overwhelm
> Myself in poesy; so I may do the deed
> That my own soul has to itself decreed.
> Then I will pass the countries that I see
> In long perspective....

Before him stretches an avenue, broad, flooded
with sunlight from where he stands, but gradually

narrowing into shadow-haunted shade, to lose itself
at last in almost total gloom.

First...

To soothe the cares of men, the most obvious
course is to set them the example of absolute enjoyment in pleasure which through its æsthetic refinement
may elevate their thoughts.   The object of man's life
being pleasure, the present task of poetry is to free
the soul from all earthly bonds, in order to make
it receptive of unadulterated beauty.   To bring all,
in fact, to feel happiness most perfectly attained in
freedom with delight:

> What more felicity can fall to creature
> Than to enjoy delight with liberty?
>
> (SPENSER: *Fate of the Butterfly*.
> Chosen by Keats as the epigraph to the volume of 1817.)

The key-note of his first conception is struck in the
two lines drawn from his beloved master.   Spenser's
hero young Clarion, the butterfly, sets off in coat of
mail and shimmering wings to seek delight with
liberty among the countless flowers of every clime
and season which his creator brings together for his
benefit.   Insect-pleasure humanized only means the
development and extension of the objects to satisfy
man's many faculties and capacious senses; the spirit
is essentially the same.   To Keats the liberty attained
gives leave to roam with ever new delight the "realm
of Flora and old Pan," where he may "choose each
pleasure that his fancy sees":

> sleep in the grass,
> Feed upon apples red and strawberries...
> Catch the white-handed nymphs in shady places...etc.

In this spirit he feels quickening into shape the formerly vague conception of his "first-born song," in this spirit he begins the prelude of his passion for the Moon.

But Clarion's delight is short-lived, and with a man who worshipped art as earnestly as Keats the butterfly conception could not last. Even when immersed in sensuous delight he had a feeling that the task he had set himself to do was only half-fulfilled. For poetry to soothe with tact the cares of men, to raise their thoughts to purpose, she must descend into close contact with those cares, learn how to analyze those thoughts. To set before them, without knowledge of their wants and sympathies, an unprepared ideal he had himself only reached after the severest struggle, would prove a vain endeavour. The incorporation of those wants and sympathies into the beauty which at first seemed to completely ignore them, he felt to be the next stage in his art.

"Can I ever bid these joys farewell?" asks the lover of simple beauty looking back with reluctant fondness at the "store of luxuries" which completely satisfy his own desires.

"Yes," replies the larger lover of humanity in whom the former is included,

> Yes, I must pass them for a nobler life
> Where I may find the agonies, the strife
> Of human hearts.

Probably about this time the Chamber of Maiden Thought began to "become gradually darkened and, at the same time, on all sides of it many doors are set open" or rather ajar, "—but all dark—all leading to dark passages." No proof of psychological power had he given as yet, but vague yearnings of sympathy towards human life in its happiest aspects, and the emotion thence derived, as has been seen, immediately returned to Nature. He might well call the study of agony and strife "dark."

Yet for this further labour he intended to prepare himself through the first stage of seemingly self-concentrated enjoyment. Wordsworth, in *Tintern Abbey*, explains the preparation of one mood through the other, and in *Tintern Abbey* Keats recognized a correct analysis of a state he had passed through himself. To the contemplation of those "beauteous forms" which now fill Keats's senses through and through, Wordsworth owes not alone "sensations sweet," but "another gift of aspect more sublime," which is

> "that blessed mood
> In which the burthen of the mystery,
> In which the heavy and the weary weight
> Of all this unintelligible world,
> Is lightened..."

lightened because gazed on

> with an eye made quiet by the power
> Of harmony and the deep power of joy,

and more than quiet, acute enough

> To see into the life of things.

The first bewilderment of joy in sensuous delight in reality prepares the soul for finer spiritual perception. "No sooner do we get into the second chamber ...than we become intoxicated with the light and atmosphere. We see nothing but pleasant wonders and think of delaying there for ever in delight." This first period of simple pleasure may seem to bear fruit insufficient for the highest purposes of art. "However," notice, "among the *effects* this breathing is *father* of, is that tremendous one of *sharpening one's vision into the heart and nature of man*, of convincing one's nerves that the world is full of misery and heartbreak, pain, sickness and oppression."

Keats seems to have felt that the development of his present all-absorbing passion for sensuous beauty, if consistently pursued, would react even upon the faculties not directly involved in the development, thereby fitting them to carry out the distant psychological ideal when it should become a living reality. He thinks it wiser to advance by easy stages from the first to the second. For the first he considers his training complete; for the second he has only just arrived at a sense of his deficiencies. He frankly confesses that, having hardly yet felt the full weight of the "burthen of the mystery," its solution lies far beyond his present grasp. In the three requirements he conceives to be necessary,—power of generalisation, thence feeling for the historical reasons which condition the great changes in humanity as a whole, last, out of this general knowledge answer to the riddle of each individual life,—as yet he is not equipped :

> I am not wealthy in the dower
> Of spanning wisdom...
> >              ...I do not know
> The shiftings of the mighty winds that blow

> Hither and thither all the changing thoughts
> Of man...
>       ...No great ministering reason sorts
> Out the dark mysteries of human souls
> To clear conceiving...

Best, therefore, improve the present opportunity to the utmost; best write down on the tablets of the mind

> All that is for our human *senses* fitted,

then, when that store is exhausted, grown to muscular power in the effort, seize "the events of this wide world"

> Like a strong giant, and his spirit tease
> Till at its shoulders it should proudly see
> Wings to find out an immortality.

So having reached this point, Keats paints for himself in perspective the state of his mind, past, present and to be. He represents its progress in an allegory. From the height on which he now stands, looking back to his earliest efforts, he sees the Chariot of Imagination coming from afar down to the point which he has reached, and again sweeping on into the future. Imagination first seeks its way among the clouds; then with

>                                     sprightly
> Wheel downward comes it into fresher skies,

ever nearer and nearer to the earth.

> Still downward with capacious whirl they (=steeds) glide.

It touches earth upon a mountain, close to the beholder, where for a while it will remain

> In breezy rest amid the nodding stalks.

Imagination enters into communion with the objects all around:

> The charioteer with wondrous gesture talks
> To the trees and mountains...

But in the midst of their converse, breaking in upon their peace,

> there soon appear
> Shapes of delight, of mystery, of fear,

sweeping in a phantom-train out of the gloom. These shadows "muffled to the ear" engage the charioteer's attention. From where the poet stands, he cannot so much as divine the meaning of their inaudible replies. He can only watch the attitude of Imagination:

> Most awfully intent,
> The driver of those steeds is forward bent
> And seems to listen.

While listening, he writes down the answers of the ghosts upon his tablets. The poet, still completely in the dark as to their meaning, can only express the wish he may come to share the knowledge of the charioteer:

> O that I might know
> All that he writes with such a hurrying glow.

Keats, when he has risen to this degree of detachment, may be said to have, at last, come to a consciousness of himself. More, to a consciousness, one-sided, of course, and incomplete, as was inevitable in a contemporary, of the age, in whose struggle he saw the reflection of his own, or, from an objective standpoint, through whose evolution he himself was evolving. But, while recognizing his natural affinities

with his fellows and the superadded debt of education
he owes his seniors, in one respect he claims distinction
as an innovator.   One principle he brings with him to
add to the general store, one corrective for the defects
which, according to him, the romantic movement was
developing, one incitement to development in a new
direction.   This innovation touches the very heart and
core of all.   It offers an unhesitating answer to the
ever open question of the end and aim of poetry.
The whole of Keats's self-education has led him up,
as we have seen, to the conviction it is

> a friend
> To soothe the cares and lift the thoughts of man.

Having struck his formula for himself, he would
turn it into current coin.   Counting on the influence
of his own projected work and the contagion of
example, he foresees a time when it may give, what
had been rather lacking in romanticism, a unity of
purpose to the whole movement.

> All hail, delightful hopes

of that coming day when by all, as by himself,

> they shall be accounted poet-kings
> Who simply tell the most heart-easing things.

Unpretending as the formula may seem, it expresses
for the first time the inmost need of his nature, the
craving for pleasure, as extended to art.   For him the
end of art is pleasure, a conception, if not new, so
completely renovated as to have the value of novelty,
especially coming as it did in an age which had not
yet decided on the goal towards which it was tending.
Keats brings the first draft of the conception which

was gradually absorbing his own life as his personal contribution towards the progress of the whole. " Pleasure as the end" required only to be supplemented by "Beauty as the means," in order to form a complete theory which should give a new impetus to romantic art. He was himself to prove by consistent example what Shelley had stated in words,— that the function of poetry was to "turn all things into loveliness"; having proved it, he could develop his first conception into the maxim, true without reserve for himself and, in spite of its passionate exclusiveness, true for all art:

> Beauty is truth, truth beauty—that is all
> Ye know on earth and all ye need to know.

Keats then, having discovered the ideal for himself, now purposes bringing it home to the conviction of others as surely as to his own. In his present state of inexperience he confesses his ignorance of the means through which the project may be realised:

> An ocean dim, sprinkled with many an isle
> Spreads awfully before me. How much toil!
> How many days ! What desperate turmoil !
> Ere I can have explored its wildernesses.
> Ah what a task !

A task indeed, whose full complexity he could not estimate. The difficulty he deplores arises from a cause he could not, at that stage of development, suspect. In the present conception of the ideal itself there was something which deprived Keats of the power of transmitting it.

If we go back to Keats's plan of self-education, as analyzed above, we shall see his intention is, for a

time, to give himself up to indulgence in sensuous
delight from which all psychological interest in
humanity is excluded.    Art, for the present, is to be
the expression of that delight in a form that may
appeal to the minds of others as to his own.

But where shall he find a form of expression to
appeal to the minds of others while himself ignorant
of the workings of those minds ?   A certain knowledge
of psychology is indispensable even for the expression
of unpsychological delight.   If art is to appeal to
the human mind, it must base on knowledge of the
human mind.    Now the acquisition of that knowledge Keats had put off indefinitely as a thing of the
future.

Because this lacuna in his knowledge nowise inter-
fered with his personal enjoyment, he did not see it
was the one thing which would always prevent the
enjoyment from being transmitted.   For the poet's
success in communicating with the reader depends on
his power of adaptation to the reader's mind.   Power
of adaptation depends on a knowledge of the reader's
power of receptivity.   This knowledge is the outcome
of psychological analysis, whether conscious or intuitive.   When Keats shrank from undertaking this
analysis, in order first to pour into his art his store of
sensuous beauty, he was, through the very act, con-
demning the beauty to remain imperfectly expressed.
Nor does Keats, in any prolonged attempt at
expression of beauty, find this adaptation throughout
to the reader before *Isabella*—the first poem showing
signs of interest in psychology.   At the time when
he draws up his plan, on account of this deficiency,

his power of transmission is distinctly inferior to his power of retention.

The truth is, the process of absorbing on his own account, and the process of communicating the result are not kept apart. It has been seen in a general way by what method of training he had brought his mind to its present state of repletion. Whatever the stimulus chosen, he was always working it up to a certain pitch of emotion in which it became receptive of sensation. Now, for the inspiration he requires his heart should be

> warmed luxuriously by divine Mozart,
> By Arne delighted, or by Handel maddened,
> Or by the song of Erin pierced and saddened[1];

it is under the influence of music "wandering round his ears" that a train of celestial visions sweeps into his mind:

> Pink robes, and wavy hair, and diamond jar,
> And half-discovered wings and glances keen[2];

now, a succession of thoughts arranged themselves in his brain excited and bewildered by the sharp air blowing from the sea:

> These things I thought
> While in my face the freshest breeze I caught[3];

now, it was as he stood tip-toe upon a little hill, open to every wave of light and sound, that "many pleasures to his vision started"; last, it was in that state preceding sleep, when the soul, on the confines of swoon and

---

[1] *Epistle to Cowden Clarke.*

[2] "Give me a golden pen and let me lean."...

[3] *Epistle to my Brother George.*

dream, losing hold of reason, sways backwards and
forwards on the billows of emotion, that the end and
aim of all his life rose up before his eyes.   We know,
from his own testimony, that in every one of these
cases the expression was begun either before the
sensation was completed or immediately on its com-
pletion.   In the very act of listening to the music
that brings with it the heavenly apparitions, he is
noting down the impression they produce:

> The while let music wander round my ears,
> And, as it reaches each delicious ending,
> Let me write down a line of glorious tone
> And full of many wonders of the spheres.

The thoughts that came wafted on the breeze are
written down as fast as they are blown into his brain:

> E'en now I'm pillowed on a bed of flowers
> That crowns an ocean-clift which proudly towers
> Above the ocean-waves ;

nay, so instantaneous is the reproduction that we see
the stalks and blades, shaken by the wind,

> Chequer his tablet with their quivering shades.

When the pleasures awakened by the summer day had
started to his vision he

> *straightway* began to pluck a posey
> Of luxuries bright, milky, soft and rosy.

Lastly, on rising from the trance in which he had felt,
rather than thought, out his career, he resolved

> to begin *that very day*

the definitive expression of all his aspirations, entitled
*Sleep and Poetry.*

This method of creation is the logical outcome of the way in which he had trained himself to absorb. On account of the general slackness of his nature it was necessary he should be keyed up very high before he could vibrate. Only when the latent emotion had been stirred to its depths could he respond to an external influence. Therefore the work of conception with him must necessarily take place in a state of abnormal excitement. In order it should lose none of its intensity during the dead lapses into languor ensuing on the fits of inspiration, he imagined expression should be as nearly as possible simultaneous with conception. Not till two and a half years later did he recognize effective expression could only arise from emotion mellowed at leisure in the "peaceable and healthy spirit[1]" in which he had elaborated that little masterpiece of presentation, the *Ode to Psyche*.

Keats's ignorance of psychology at this time, preventing him from analyzing his own sensations or divining the attitude of the reader, retarded the progress of his artistic growth. While painfully alive to the general defect of his own work at the time,

> my thoughts were never free and clear
> And little fit to please a classic ear[2],

he seems never to have suspected that the remedy lay in a complete change of method.

His present mode of working in itself excludes the two processes through which art becomes transmissible, analysis and preparation. When the artist contents himself with playing stenographer to improvising

---

[1] *Letters*, April 1819.     [2] *Epistle to Cowden Clarke.*

emotion, the emotion is seized before it has had time to come to a consciousness of itself and, in this undigested state, is projected on the reader before the reader's mind has been opened to receive it. Thus, at the time when Keats is ready to communicate the beauty he has more than sufficiently absorbed, through confounding the process of production with the process of creation, he fails to give the ripeness of sensation and feeling an adequate ripeness of presentation.

This defect, which applies in general to the expression of his early ideal, gradually disappears with the gradual incorporation of the second into the first. In the first stage, art was conceived as the means of projecting the poet's self on the reader, but, when he had advanced to the second, as the ground on which the reader might project his own individuality. From the time of this change of attitude dates the power of the giver's ideal of pleasure over the receiver. While still immersed in self-centred enjoyment, he had, in *Sleep and Poetry*, set up his conception of poetry for himself alone. Eighteen months later, when, as he had foreseen, this interest in self had expanded into interest in humanity, while engaged in composing the first expression of that larger interest—*Isabella*—he writes the counterpart of his personal creed dramatically, from the reader's point of view.

"In poetry I have a few axioms[1]"...

The first defines the impression the change is intended to produce. "Poetry should surprise by a fine excess and not by singularity." It should not

---

[1] *Letters*, Jan. 30, 1818.

startle by obtruding the unknown, but awaken wonder by refining on the familiar. Instead of requiring the reader to accept an alien ideal, it should set before him his own unconscious ideal incarnate in concrete form. "It should strike the reader as an embodiment of his own highest thoughts and appear almost as a remembrance."

This effect can only be reached by an imperceptible insinuation of the writer's thought into the reader's, till he reaches the point of contact where his own consciousness may flash upon the receiver's reminiscence. The two should close gradually in a mutual clasp till, pressed heart to heart, the tense throbbing of the one may double its intensity by beating against the high-strung throbbing of the other, and unclose again as slowly till each stands independent as before, yet thrilling with the other's life. "Its touches of beauty should never be *half-way*, thereby making the reader breathless instead of content. The rise, the progress, the setting of imagery should, like the sun, come natural to him, shine over him and set soberly, though in magnificence, leaving him in the luxury of twilight."

Keats, even at this point, declares himself " far from the centre " of his axioms, but the precision of the formulæ shows them to be the result of more than an abstract theory. He could not, by anticipation, have condensed into three sentences the secret of all his future success. No more than it was possible to set up pleasure as the end of art, before himself tingling through and through with the pleasure it was his object to transmit, was it possible to base on a

pre-conceived idea the code of technical excellence
by which the pleasure was to be communicated.
These maxims had been displayed in practice before
settling into theory.

Yes, before writing out his axioms he had shown,
in miniature, the possibility of applying them.   Even
at the time when his general work was suffering from
the defect of method contained in his first ideal, under
exceptional conditions he had, by a still unconscious
process, reached that perfect adaptation to the reader
he was to lay down as the fundamental principle of
his mature art.

The "peaceable and healthy spirit" of production
fitted to his own nature he had found, unawares, in an
exceptionally peaceable and healthy mood of conception.   Without external stimulus of any kind, he had,
for once, avoided the excess of emotion which, as a
rule, blurred his vision, by drawing inspiration directly
from his normal state of languor.   In some temper
"indolent and supremely careless" such as that in
which he later wrote the *Ode on Indolence*, a series of
sensations rose up and, as they coincided with the
general tenour of his mind, recurred again and again
till, through constant rumination, they took shape,
fitted into each other and spontaneously evolved into
a little scene.   What had been simply a phase of
feeling developed into a situation.   The subject, as it
now presented itself, was one peculiarly in tone with
Keats's temperament.   It was the first of those
slumber-scenes on which he was to lavish the wealth
of his mature imagination, the prelude of the slumber
of Adonis, of Madeline, of Autumn, of Cupid and

Psyche. The origin lay in the contrast between the
sensations and feelings of the body when awake and
asleep. The waking mood had been conceived to
cast the shadows of its own sensations on sleep, and
then to interpret back into these ghosts their first
reality. All the scene was in the inaudible dialogue
between the two moods, in the efforts of each to
express its meaning so as to reach the understanding
of the other. They took human shape, became no
longer merely moods, but a waker and a sleeper, a
slumbering woman and a waking man. A lover has
left his beloved sleeping. Though outwardly unconscious, with all her senses sealed in sleep, touch, ear
and eye, through the finer perception of sleep she is
made aware that he is gone. The phantom-feeling of
love in slumber longs for his return. Her lips moving
with a noiseless sound attempt to call him back. He,
watching their mute motions, through the imagination divines the unexpressed desire. In response,
though the dawn is blushing at the window, to the
bygone moments of delight he will add one more.

In the transmission of this almost incommunicable
pleasure the giver finds the exact medium between
himself and the receiver. The lover, into whose
mouth the tale is put, sets forth in terms of waking
sense the present situation as it rises out of the past,
already fading into remembrance:

> Unfelt, unheard, unseen,
> I've left my little queen,
> Her languid arms in silver slumber lying.
> Within their nestling touch
> Ah, who can tell how much
> There was for madness—cruel or complying?

the melody of the voice beginning on detached notes in the statement of the facts and lengthening out into reverberant runs with the expansion of the feeling.

The poet, having started from the reader's un-modified sensations, thence leads him up into the sphere of extra-waking sense. The lover looks down at the sleeper's closed eyes and mouth just opening to give phantom-utterance of her desire to the quiet air of early dawn.

> Heard melodies are sweet, but those unheard
> Are sweeter.

The phantom-song is caught by a now etherealized perception, "fancy's ear." Now, when the scene is ripe, upon the mellowness of silence, sense and sleep the last velvet touch of bloom is laid by Love :

> Those faery lids how sleek !
> Those lips how moist ! they speak,
> In ripest quiet, shadows of sweet sounds ;
> Into my fancy's ear
> Melting a burden dear
> How "Love doth know no fullness and no bounds."

To leave an impression of perfectly normal satis-faction, after thus rising for a moment into the senses of the imagination, we are brought back once more into the light of common day:

> True, tender monitors !
> I bend unto your laws ;
> This sweetest day for dalliance was born.
> So, without more ado,
> I'll feel my heaven anew,
> For all the blushing of the hasty morn[1].

[1] The manuscript of this song affords proof of repeated revision. See Buxton Forman, *Works of John Keats*, Vol. I, p. li*.

This tiny gem of presentation, in its rise, progress and setting, completely satisfies, if indeed it did not suggest, the axiom that "it should come natural to the reader, shine over him and set soberly, though in magnificence, leaving him in the luxury of twilight." To see, presented with equal perfection, a subject "striking the reader as an embodiment of his own highest thoughts and appearing almost as a remembrance," we must turn to another, conceived at a higher degree of intensity and therefore requiring a genuine triumph of self-control in the working out.

Keats, through his literary education, deep if not broad, as has been seen, had been led into the study of the native classics, returning time after time to certain sources where his fine perception felt delights not to be exhausted in a lifetime. But, ever eager to imbibe more than he could contain, in the midst of plenty he thirsted after what was to him a spring shut up, a fountain sealed. His imagination had been fired by the report of untold wonders in the Greek of Homer. "Standing aloof in giant ignorance," he waited, wondering and expectant, till that memorable night on which, through Chapman's mouth, the revelation burst upon him. Under the surprise that, like a gathering wind, swept over him with the tenfold force of preparation, all the emotion in him, glowing to the core, burnt itself clear[1]. Spontaneously,

[1] The story of its instantaneous composition has become a legend. Cowden Clarke, who first introduced Keats to Chapman's version, declares it to have been written between dawn and ten o'clock of the same day: "We had parted at day-spring, yet he contrived that I should receive the poem, from a distance of, may be, two miles, by ten o'clock." (C. Clarke's *Recollections of Keats.*)

he flashed the impression of long-expected wonder into an image just in the same degree surprising, in the same degree familiar to the reader. He changed into a Spanish adventurer setting out for El Dorado, into Cortez' self, sailing round and round islands already found before, yet ever longing for the sight of an unknown ocean far beyond. Here is an allusion to an allusion which for no man alive can mean more than a legend, hence one which hardly a reader will have in his mind, yet every one hidden somewhere in the subterranean depths of reminiscence. Its influence, more subtle than any acting on the memory of reality, stirs in the glimmering shades of the memory of imagination the remembrance of the never seen. When this first fusion is accomplished, a further step is taken. Keats, having blended the abstract sense of the unknown into the dreamy unreality of the reader's reminiscence, now brings directly before the latter's wondering eyes the reality of his dream, a traveller sailing round islands held in fee by the vassals of the Father of all verse:

> Much have I travelled in the realms of gold,
> And many goodly states and kingdoms seen,
> Round many western islands have I been
> Which bards in fealty to Apollo hold ;

but ever yearning for the boundless domain of the highest vassal among them all:

> Oft of one wide expanse had I been told
> That deep-browed Homer ruled as his demesne,
> Yet never did I breathe its pure serene
> Till I heard Chapman speak out loud and bold.

Now, the real surprise, having advanced by slow degrees into the foreground, is definitively assimilated to the joy of Cortez on discovering the Pacific, Cortez whose own joy could only find its symbol in the vaster triumph of

> some watcher of the skies
> When a new planet swims into his ken.

All the elements having been wrought up to their acme of intensity, from this point onward all conscious allegory is dropped that the situation may develop for itself. The situation is in reality adapted to the progress of the soul as it climbs up to the highest point of expectation, whence the promised wonder bursts upon the dominant perception with a force that spreads the electric shock of ecstasy, too great to be contained in one, through the subordinate senses, awed into silence by surprise. But all hint of hidden meaning is avoided that the scene may expand into the ocean and slowly rise into the peak:

> Or like stout Cortez when, with eagle eyes,
> He stared at the Pacific—and all his men
> Looked at each other with a wild surmise,—
> Silent—upon a peak in Darien.

Here Might, starting, a perfect architect, from his slumber, in the space of a few hours raised a rounded, sculptured, finely-carved and richly-tinted shrine, through whose echoing vault the inner organ rolled the prelude of the deep-toned harmony of *Hyperion*.

Here, without premeditation, Keats had fulfilled from point to point the laws to be later matured by long months of reflection, even to the last requirement: "that poetry, if it was to come at all, must come as naturally as leaves to a tree." It had come; come from the inmost depths of his own emotion; gone down into the hidden memory of the reader; risen, reached the zenith, set, in ever varying, yet ever equal splendour; and withal "come as naturally as the leaves to a tree."

Keats, at twenty-two, stands instinct with power upon a height. He has discovered his vocation; he has recognized his object; he has drawn up a complete scheme for the future; he has the feelings of a poet, the sensations of a poet and the music of a poet in his being; he knows how to condense the general sense of poetry into definite production; he now prepares to "send his herald thought into a wilderness[1]" to blow its trumpet through *Endymion.* The normal Keats has come to a full consciousness of himself; what still remains to be seen is under what influences he altered in the sequel.

[1] *Endymion,* Bk I, l. 59.

# KEATS'S STYLE AS EXEMPLIFIED
## IN *THE EVE OF ST AGNES*

KEATS'S poetical development may be defined
as a steady, unswerving progress from a sensuous
to a spiritual love of beauty. He possessed, to start
with, a distinctly sensuous nature, not unintellectual
by any means, but rather defiantly anti-intellectual.
" O for a life of sensations rather than of thoughts ! "
is the cry that runs through all his early work.
Acting on this principle, Keats for a time subdued
all tendency to philosophize about his feelings and
surrendered himself to the luxury of enjoying individual impressions as they came. Not till after
the first flush of youth was over did he attempt to
correlate and generalize his sensations. At the beginning he cared for nothing but separate effects
of light, sound, colour, touch and smell. Not till
the *Ode to a Nightingale* did he dream of

> Flora and the country green,
> Dance and Provençal song and sunburnt mirth

all blending into the flavour of one draught of
Hippocrene. When he wrote *Endymion* so intense
was his feeling for every separate manifestation of
loveliness that, lost in the passion for sun, for moon,
for daffodils, for musk-rose blooms, he could conceive
of nothing but the " thing of beauty "—being " a joy

for ever." Not till the *Grecian Urn* did he openly claim for Beauty in the abstract a place beside Truth. In a word, the nature of Keats inclined him to seek for individual and isolated examples of beauty; the result of his self-education was to teach him the connexion or rather the interdependence of all the senses.

The style follows in its main lines, though not in every detail, the lead of the mental development. The groundwork of Keats's style is at all times sensation. Words are treated by him simply as vehicles of sensation or as sensations in themselves. The component elements of his successful style, at whatever period you take it, remain constant. As far as grammar, vocabulary, choice of epithet are concerned, that is as far as mere language goes, all his poems present the same characteristics, somewhat more buoyant and spontaneous in the first, somewhat riper and more deliberate in the last. The language of *Endymion* only differs from the language of *The Eve of St Agnes* or *Lamia* as the odour of wild flowers from perfume, or fresh fruit from preserves. But, in the combination of words into sentences and sounds into rhythms, Keats's method varies with the different periods of his mental growth. The substance does not change, nor does the language properly speaking, but in the *style* three distinct manners may be discerned. *Endymion* represents the first, *The Eve of St Agnes* the second, *Lamia* the third. To begin with, Keats attempts to express his unconnected sensations directly in an equally unconnected, impressionist style; next he tries to introduce into these

disjointed sentences an emotional unity that corresponds to the ever tightening bond between the
sensations themselves ; lastly, by a great effort, he
creates a firm and definite intellectual mould into
which sensation and feeling may be poured. Sensation
forms the basis of his language everywhere, but the
style passes through three stages : first, the directly
sensuous ; then the sensuous-emotional ; and, finally,
the sensuous-emotional-intellectual.

Keats rendered a genuine service to English in
bringing back the fossilized language of the eighteenth
century to a sense of its own meaning.   In this task
he succeeded better than any of his compeers ; better
than Shelley, better than Coleridge, better than
Wordsworth, better than all three together.   For
Keats stands quite alone in his feeling for language.
It was more than a love, more than a passion, an
instinct, a sixth sense as keen as any of his other
five.   " I throw my whole being into Troilus and,
repeating those lines, ' I wander like a lost soul upon
the Stygian bank staying for waftage,' I melt into
the air with a voluptuousness so delicate that I am
content to be alone[1]."   A word for him is never a
conventional symbol, but a living thing replete with
meaning, to be loved for its meaning and, far above
its meaning, for its sensuous sound, for itself.   Opposite that line in *Paradise Lost*,

> To slumber here as in the vales of Heaven,

he writes :

" There is a cool pleasure in the very sound of

[1] *Letters*, Oct. 29, 1818.

*vale.* The English word is of the happiest choice. Milton has put vales in heaven and hell with the very utter affection and yearning of a great poet[1]." And if such is the passion roused by a single word, how much more will be called forth by the musical succession of words the most fruitful and the most fertile, the richest and mellowest in meaning and in sound. " I look upon fine phrases like a lover."

On the casual gazer a fair woman produces no more than a general undefined impression of pleasure. But the lover knows every detail in the beauty of her face; he can interpret the meaning of every motion, every gesture: the change in the colour of the eyes, the raising of the eyebrow, the turn of the neck, the curl of the lips, to him not one of these is unexpressive. And so Keats has weighed and considered the value, not only of every word, but of every syllable and every letter that goes to the making of a fine phrase.

> Let us inspect the lyre and weigh the stress
> Of every chord, and see what may be gained
> By ear industrious and attention meet ;
> Misers of sound and syllable, no less
> Than Midas of his coinage, let us be
> Jealous of dead leaves in the bay-wreath crown[2].

Herein lies the true definition of the reform Keats set himself to accomplish. Through all his tentative and experimental work he was struggling to reach an ideal that never varied. His object was to pull

[1] *Notes on Milton.*
[2] *Sonnet on the Sonnet,* beginning:
   "If by dull rhymes our English must be chained" (1819).

the dead leaves out of the laurel garland; to root
all the weeds out of the language; to deliver English
from all its choking parasites; to throw the ballast
of convention out of every sentence and pack each
single word with meaning. Hence, the first and
fundamental praise to be awarded to Keats is that
of having realised the value of language with an
intensity superior even to Marlowe's, even to Spenser's,
unrivalled except by Milton and hardly surpassed by
Shakespeare.

This sensitive feeling for the component parts of
language lays the foundation of a good style, but it
can do no more. It rather retards than helps forward
the creation of style. For, when every individual
word is required to express sensation, all the conventional, arbitrary links of relation are necessarily
eliminated from the sentence. Without these purely
intellectual symbols, no construction in the usual
sense of the term is possible.

Yet a certain type of mind can, after all, dispense
with these swimming-bladders. Take the following
period from the *Triumph of Life*:

And her feet ever to the ceaseless song
Of leaves, and winds, and waves, and birds, and bees,
And falling drops, moved in a measure new
Yet sweet, as on the summer evening breeze
Up from the lake a shape of golden dew,
Between two rocks, athwart the rising moon,
Dances in the wind, where never eagle flew.

It will be felt that in such a style the individual
value of every syllable is preserved, at the same time

that every syllable contributes to the general effect. The sentences spontaneously cleave to each other. They fit into the paragraph like cells into a honeycomb. Now the ideal for Keats would have been to reach this construction through sense which Shelley so perfectly possessed. But Shelley achieved this triumph not through any superior intellectual power, but through an innate love of motion which kept him always soaring when he sang. Keats, on the other hand, brooded with such intensity over his sensations that he could only sing when on the nest. The deliberate, ruminating, lethargic nature was, of necessity, a little short-winded. No great poet was ever primarily more devoid of feeling for motion than Keats. Of the two supreme qualities of motion, dash and sustained flight, he had not even a suspicion. Seek where you will through Keats, in his very best work, you will never find anything so much as approaching the soar of Swinburne's

> Bird of the bitter, bright, grey, golden morn
> Scarce risen upon the dusk of dolorous years !
> *(Elegy on Villon.)*

Keats felt more than any other the initial difficulty of getting under way. And even when well started, he seems scarcely ever to have wind enough to swell his sails. One never feels oneself carried away by him, as by Shelley, in the enchanted boat scudding along before the full breeze of song. He could not have written the *Ode to the West Wind*. On the other hand, it should be remembered that Shelley could not have written the *Ode to Autumn*. Perhaps this winged speed was incompatible with Keats's finest qualities. One scarcely ventures therefore to denounce a certain want of poetical afflatus as a defect ; one must, at least, admit it to have been his most serious limitation.

How therefore to adjust an intense feeling for the value, in meaning and in sound, of every individual word to the build and swing of the sentence as a whole was the problem Keats had to work out.

Its significance does not seem to have been borne home to him till after much fruitless struggle in the dark. Through his early poems the hunt after the single word was so eagerly pursued as to make him lose sight of syntactical or rhythmical construction. He must have felt his own want of intellectual backbone when attempting the didactic and critical style of *Sleep and Poetry* or of certain passages in *Endymion.* But his chief object was to record sensations, and in the record of sensations all difficulties of construction could be easily evaded. For the purpose of noting down separate impressions a purely enumerative style, such as we find through " I stood tip-toe upon a little hill" or the opening of *Endymion*, was sufficient. A succession of simple sentences, or even verbless phrases, standing each alone or, at the outside, connected only by an "and" or an "or," perfectly satisfies Keats's need of symmetry at this time. If every single word has done duty in expressing the share of sensation assigned to it, he seems quite content. No shading ; no sketching ; nothing but a stippled outline. To feel the charm of this early impressionist style at its best,—and this impressionism, let it be remembered, lays the foundation of his finest verse,—turn to the concluding sestet of the sonnet " After dark vapours have oppressed our plains[1]." With the return of spring, says Keats,

> The calmest thoughts come round us...as,—of leaves
> Budding,—fruit ripening in stillness—autumn suns
> Smiling at eve upon the quiet sheaves—
> Sweet Sappho's cheek—a smiling infant's breath—
> The gradual sand that through an hour-glass runs—
> A woodland rivulet—a poet's death.

Impressionism can go no further.  Language has been brought to a standstill.  The phrases filter through the silence one by one.  At first, they seem quiet as with the calm of locked waters.  Yet under their inviolable stillness will be felt a sense of onward swelling motion.  A current of feeling quivers on below :

> ...leaves
> Budding—fruit ripening in stillness—autumn suns
> Smiling at eve upon the quiet sheaves....

The year passes through two periods of still growth into final harvest and rest, from the budding of the leaves in spring, through the ripening of the summer fruit, to the evening of the year as of the day bathing its bound-up wealth in light.

Then a pause—

> Sweet Sappho's cheek...

Then

> a smiling infant's breath,
> The gradual sand that through an hour-glass runs,
> A woodland rivulet—a poet's death.

[1] Written about the same time as the first books of *Endymion*.

The symbol suggested in the evolution of the year is carried out in the evolution of a life, from the first breath drawn by the new-born child, through the tranquil years of manhood slipping away like sand through an hour-glass or the rivulet through the wood, till the time when the poet lays down his task to die.

Such veiled feeling, such faint suggestion admit of no proof. But in the supreme triumph of the early enumerative style we receive intimations of a coming change. The dying note of impressionism forms the prelude of the second manner.

By the time Keats reached *The Eve of St Agnes*, his mind had so completely assimilated the principle of relation, so far only hinted at, as to feel the need of a more organic style.

Consider the construction of the poem as a whole.

Its object is to convey a certain number of very definite and intense impressions appealing to all the senses in turn. The chilliness of a winter night— the noise and glare of an evening revel—the fragrant stillness of a maiden's chamber—the moon shining through a Gothic window—all enhanced by an atmosphere of mediæval suggestion—form the substance.

Keats, along with his brother-poets, had learnt the great æsthetic lesson of romanticism,—to wit, that sensations need to be combined, in order to bring each other out. Notice how he balances the incidents so as to throw into relief by comparison and contrast the impressions of light, cold, fragrance, etc. He sets off the drunken revelry in the hall by the stillness of Madeline's bedroom. Again, her enforced silence under the spell is supported by Porphyro's breathless watch in the closet. The flourish of trumpets outside is introduced as a prelude to the low throbbing of the lute under the curtain. The fasting which forms the central subject stands out in sharp isolation between the gorgeous feast in the distance and the untouched banquet by the bedside. The applications of this one principle are endless.

The sensations thus brought together are further unified by an emotion just strong enough to sustain without overpowering, to lend vital warmth to the whole without engrossing the attention for itself. To see, from a short example, in what manner sensuous delight may be informed with feeling, take three lines from Victor Hugo :

> L'ombre était nuptiale, auguste et solennelle,...
> Un frais parfum sortait des touffes d'asphodèle,
> Les souffles de la nuit flottaient sur Galgala.
>
> (*Booz Endormi.*)

Imagine this, in the same measure and proportion, expanded into twenty flawless stanzas ; you have the second half of *The Eve of St Agnes,* the most successful illustration of what Coleridge defines as the mark of the born poet, "the power of reducing multitude into unity of effect and modifying a series of thoughts by some one predominant thought or feeling."

As the result of this unifying emotion, add a unique, Keatsian quality, indicative in the highest degree of allied strength and self-restraint. I mean

a steady progress of action which prevents the mind
from dwelling morbidly on any one effect, as a soft
breeze continually keeps the shadows playing over
the light before its brilliancy can strain the eye,
muffles the music before its pathos can excite the
nerves and wafts away the perfume before its intensity
can affect the brain.

It will be readily understood that so highly
complex and subtle a scheme will call for an equally
subtle and complex style. The richness and ripeness
of the individual sensations require a corresponding
mellowness in language; therefore the best qualities
of Keats's early impressionism are brought into play.
On the other hand, the blending of the sensations
one into another of itself suggests a closer interweaving of the words; the dexterous parallels and
sharp contrasts bring with them a finer knowledge
of the music and pauses of the verse; the continued
movement and prolonged strain of emotion spontaneously produce an appearance of continuity in the
style. While his native manner of construction still
subsists, it gradually develops into a living unity, where
its beauties stand out in strong relief; more, where its
very defects are turned into virtues or, at least, so far
toned down as not to jar on the harmony of the
whole.

*The Eve of St Agnes* offers Keats's most personal
and original solution of his initial difficulty. The
poem, if not in its entirety at least in its latter half,
may be regarded as his typical achievement. Anyone

who knows *The Eve of St Agnes* well knows Keats. Accepting therefore this style as representative, we shall examine it in detail.

Its fundamental excellence, as might be expected from his early training, lies in its pervading sense of the value of every single word. In this respect Keats goes back to the Renaissance. The exultation of a young age on discovering its own power seems still to be tingling through his veins. Keats rejoices over a fine word like a navigator over a new island. Into his blood has passed something of Shakespeare's psychological grip and mastery of language, able to thrill every word to the heart with life. "Hark ye, how rich!" exclaims Keats in a letter, quoting from the *Sonnets* :

> When lofty trees I see barren of leaves
> That erst from heat did canopy the herd,
> And summer's green all girded up in sheaves
> Borne on the bier with white and bristly beard...
>
> *(Sonnet* 12.)

He had indeed inherited this peculiar power of arresting every word in its course and weighing it down with sound and meaning, a power still better exemplified in *Sonnet* 73 :

> That time of year thou mayst in me behold
> When yellow leaves, or none, or few, do hang
> Upon those boughs that shake against the cold,
> Bare, ruined choirs where late the sweet birds sang...

or best of all displayed in a quatrain Keats himself might have written—*Sonnet* 102 :

Our love was new and then but in the spring
When I was wont to greet it with my lays,
As Philomel in summer's front doth sing,
*And stops her pipe in growth of riper days.*
............
And lucent syrups tinct with cinnamon.

(*Eve of St Agnes.*)

N'est-ce pas?

To reach his own effects of equally powerful and deliberate beauty, Keats passes his unlimited vocabulary through riddle after riddle, from the coarsest wire to the finest hair sieve, before mind and ear are completely satisfied.

A word is chosen first for its fidelity to fact. From Keats's real style all approximation is banished; in his richly-freighted stanzas no stop-gap, no makeshift can find place. The verb must express the essential action, the epithet the essential quality of the object. The *essential*—that is, distinctive and inmost,— characteristic in the faces of the angels supporting the cornice is their rapt gaze into futurity:

> The carved angels ever *eager-eyed*
> *Stared....*

The *essential* characteristic of the festival music is, through its apparent gaiety, the undertone of sorrow:

> The music *yearning* like a God in pain....

The *essential* characteristic of Samarcand was its silk-mart, the *essential* characteristic of Lebanon its cedars. The epithets "silken" and "cedared" of themselves suffice to suggest the whole moral and religious atmosphere of town and mountain:

> From silken Samarcand to cedared Lebanon.

Fidelity to fact will not suffice, unless borne out by fidelity to the emotion each word arouses through its associations. Few have felt like Keats the slight shades of meaning by which usage marks off one from another words of the same import. Take for example the two adjectives "hearty" and "cordial." Their sense may seem the same, yet none can fail to feel the delicate difference between the familiar and more learned word. Any bluff, outspoken impulse may be expressed through a "hearty grasp"; only a refined and self-restrained sentiment can be conveyed through a "cordial squeeze." Consider the amount of cultivation and reflection necessary before knowing where to use the class of words typified by *hearty* and where the class typified by *cordial*. And then consider how Keats differentiates the word Madeline dares not speak aloud from the inner whispering of the heart she is unable to repress:

> No *uttered* syllable, or woe betide!
> But to her heart her heart was *voluble*,
> Paining with eloquence her balmy side.

Nor will it suffice the word should be faithful to feeling, unless equally faithful to impression. The sound of the word must present the object to the senses long before the mind has fathomed its meaning. To satisfy this æsthetic requirement all rules of etymology may be broken. "The jelly was so smooth it seemed to soothe the throat as it went down," says ordinary prose. Poetry can, by elimination and transposition, blend the two *impressions* of "smooth" and "soothing" into the single epithet *soother*. "Lucent syrups tinctured with cinnamon" might seem a phrase limpid enough to please any other ear. But Keats knows the second syllable of *tinctured* to be super-fluous; he therefore cuts it off, in order not to dim the sparkle of the "lucent syrup."

These examples are only chosen as indicative of a power which, everywhere apparent, through the last twenty stanzas never flags, proving a faculty of hypnotizing language and suggesting into the most unpoetic words a passion and a beauty they do not of themselves possess. Keats's one object through all his experiments and innovations is to freshen up English, so as to bring back its primitive vividness and depth of colour. Every time he adopts a word he tries to peel off the soiled bark of convention, that it may stand out again, clean, white and glossy like birch-wood underneath.

And now perhaps it will be understood out of what a long process of selection and rejuvenation such a volume of sound has arisen as the description of the Gothic window:

A casement high and triple-arched there was,
All garlanded with carven imageries
Of fruits and flowers and bunches of knot-grass,
And diamonded with panes of quaint device,
*Innumerable of stains and splendid dyes*
*As are the tiger-moth's deep-damasked wings;*
And in the midst, 'mong thousand heraldries
And *twilight saints* and dim emblazonings,
*A shielded scutcheon blushed with blood of queens and kings.*

To feel the multitude of individual impressions that have blended into its gorgeous confusion, turn to the next stanza, where the compact mass splits up into fragments, each of which may be studied in all the intricacy of its translucent, lustrous, veined and variegated beauty:

> Full on this casement shone the wintry moon,
> And threw warm gules on Madeline's fair breast,
> As down she knelt for heaven's grace and boon;
> Rose-bloom fell on her hands together prest,
> And on her silver cross soft amethyst,
> And on her hair a glory like a saint.
> She seemed a splendid angel newly drest,
> Save wings, for heaven:—Porphyro grew faint,
> She knelt, so pure a thing, so free from mortal taint.

Finally, to feel how this synthetic style, where the sentences still hang heavy in the stanza like waves lifted by the wind, may dwindle into another, where the words quiver on the rhythm like dew-drops on a gossamer-thread, at every moment ready to break the line, pass on to the banquet-stanza:

> And still she slept an azure-lidded sleep,
> In blanched linen smooth and lavendered,
> While he from forth the closet brought a heap
> Of candied apple, quince, and plum, and gourd,
> With jellies soother than the creamy curd,
> And lucent syrups tinct with cinnamon,
> Manna and dates in argosy transferred
> From Fez, and spiced dainties, every one,
> From silken Samarcand to cedared Lebanon.

Of course, the underlying sensation dictates the order of the words and frames them into sentences, just as in the early impressionist style, but now comes the crucial question: Out of detached sentences how can the period be built up?

This question had not assumed any vital importance in Keats's eyes while working in the couplet

form of his early poems. The six-line stanza of
*Isabella* must first have led him to reflect on the
necessity of a certain pre-ordained plan for every
group of ideas or impressions. The long nine-lined
Spenserian stanza, the most ample and majestic fixed
form in the language, required him to put forth an
effort, considerable for any man and for him peculiarly
strenuous, on account of a constitutional defect, before
referred to.

The Spenserian stanza depends for its effect on
two qualities: an ear for the relations of sound, to
throw its triple system of rhymes into relief, and a
sense of regular progression, to carry the weight of
sound through two interwoven decasyllabic quatrains
up to its climax in the final Alexandrine. Take, as
a typical example of both qualities in equilibrium, the
opening stanza of the "Hymn to Venus"—*Faery
Queen*, Bk IV, Canto 10:

Great Venus! Queene of beautie and of grace,
The joy of Gods and men, that under skie
Doest fayrest shine and most adorne thy place;
That with thy smiling looke doest pacifie
The raging seas and makst the stormes to flie:
Thee, Goddess, thee the winds, the clouds doe feare,
And, when thou spreadst thy mantle forth on hie,
The waters play and pleasant lands appeare,
And heavens laugh and all the world shews joyous cheare.

As far as sonority went, Keats was fully equipped;
perhaps better than Spenser, for sonority was entirely
a matter of sensation. But to a love of sound, somewhat formal but none the less sincere, Spenser added
a sense of motion, more deliberate than Shelley's, but
no less powerful and sustained. It has already been

seen that in this department Keats could not vie with
Shelley.  Not even the Spenserian stanza could inspire
his verse with the afflatus in which it was, by nature,
deficient.

But the character of the subject helped Keats
to disguise his fundamental defect; indeed, by an
exquisitely skilful manœuvre, to convert it into one
of his most approved beauties.

The impression to be produced by the complete
poem is a sense of fluctuating stillness, a kind of
pulsation in quiescence, as of

> a throbbing star
> Seen 'mid the sapphire heaven's deep repose.

The long strain of Madeline's fast and Porphyro's
watch strings the nerves up to a tension which the
faintest sound or movement startles.  A uniformity
of impression must be sustained, yet at every moment
broken by an imperceptible stir, like a calm sheet of
water ruffled by the slightest thrill of air.

Now the impression of uniformity is conveyed
through sound and the impression of variety through
motion.

For the first Keats was qualified by his positive
virtues; in the second he turned to account what
threatened to prove his most serious failing.

The Spenserian stanza, with its lingering, overlap-
ping rhymes, appealed to Keats's *ruminant* nature, if it
may so be called.  Keats, like Jaques, spent his whole
life chewing the cud of sweet and bitter fancy and, still

more, of sweet and bitter sensation. This tendency
chiefly accounts for the limited range and corresponding depth of his poetry. It comes out in nothing
more than in his melody, sweet almost to excess,
mellifluous as a blossoming willow, yet never palling
on the taste like weaker verse, always saved from
cloying by the poignant intensity he himself discerned
through

> The music yearning like a God in pain.

Through *The Eve of St Agnes* the music was
to remain in the same key, at the same pitch, in a
*piano* tone, to be saved from monotony by an occasional
swell or discord. Speaking of the banquet-stanza,
Leigh Hunt remarks:

"Wordsworth would have said the vowels were
not varied enough, but Keats knew his vowels were
*not* to be varied." (*Recollections of Keats.*)

But the remark applies to more than one stanza.
Its force may be felt in reading such lines as:

> It *seemed* he *never, never* could re*deem*
> From such a *stea*dfast *spe*ll his lady's eyes.

It comes out still better in the stanza on Madeline's
waking dream, where Keats actually sacrifices a correct
rhyme to the general uniformity of tone. The note
of the whole is set by the vowel *ee*.

> .   .   .   .   .   .   .   .   .
> Of all its wreathed pearls her hair she frees,
> Unclasps her warmed jewels, one by one,
> Loosens her fragrant bodice; by degrees,
> Her rich attire creeps rustling to her knees;
> Half-hidden like a mermaid in sea-*weed*
> Pensive awhile she dreams awake and sees
> In fancy fair St Agnes in her bed.

Can *weed* rhyme with *bed*?    No, but the vowel of
" frees," " degrees " and " knees " had to be carried
over to " sees " before being dropped.    Keats had
brooded and ruminated over *e* as giving the true
impression of the reverie, and no change could be
introduced before the girl's sudden start at seeing, as
she thinks, St Agnes in her bed.

From another point of view the false rhyme has the
further advantage of expressing the shock of surprise.
The same device recurs with still more marked effect
in Stanza 36.    The lover's bodily presence mixes
with Madeline's drowsy image of him in trance :

> Into her dream he melted as the rose
> Blendeth its odour with the violet,
> Solution sweet: meantime the frost-wind blows
> Like Love's alarum pattering the sharp *sleet*
> Against the window-panes: St Agnes' moon hath *set*.

Indeed, nothing brings out better the general
uniformity of tone than these perfectly timed devia-
tions from the norm.    The one discord in *The Eve
of St Agnes* serves to mark its sustained sense of
harmony.    How deep seems the stillness and the
calm of Madeline's chamber before and after the one
dissonant note, the sudden explosion of the brass
instruments in the middle of her dream :

> O for some drowsy Morphean amulet !—
>
> The boisterous, midnight, festive clarion,
> The kettle-drum and far-heard clarionet,
> Affray his ears, though but in dying tone:
> The hall-door shuts again and all the noise is gone.—
>
> And still she slept an azure-lidded sleep....

In the same manner, nothing more conduces to
the effect of lulling, languid, unchangeable sound,
than these semi-rhymes, not to be confounded with
false rhymes, as they appear in the sudden expansion of

> But to her heart her heart was volu*ble*
> Paining with eloquence her balmy side,
> As though a tongueless nightingale should *swell*
> Her throat in vain, and die, heart-stifled in her *dell*....

or in the faint echo of

> Affray his ears, though but in dying *tone*;
> The hall-door shuts again and all the noise is *gone*.

The subdued hum of the melody is, at every
moment, relieved by the break of pause and overflow.
If Keats could not rival Shelley or Swinburne in
movement properly speaking, he surpassed them
both in the art of placing

> the grand orchestral silences
> In pauses of the rhythmic sound.
>
> (Mrs BROWNING.)

A secret, learnt probably from Milton but made
entirely his own in appropriation, had very early
enabled Keats to do justice to his beloved, far-sought
single words or phrases by position. In the *Sonnet
on Chapman's Homer* he had already shown how to
isolate or, as Matthew Arnold would say, to "enisle"
the important word in the surrounding seas of sound.
Consider, as indicative of this underlying power, how,
all through *The Eve of St Agnes*, Keats contrives
to hold the essential verb, noun, or adjective *in
suspense*:

The carved angels, ever eager-eyed,
Stared, || where upon their heads the cornice rests,
With hair blown back and wings put cross-wise on their
        breasts.

(Stanza 4.)

But soon his eyes grew brilliant, when she told
His lady's purpose ; and he scarce could brook
Tears, || at the thought of those enchantments cold,
And Madeline asleep in lap of legends old.

(Stanza 15.)

            he from the closet crept,
Noiseless as fear in a wide wilderness,
    And over the hush'd carpet, | silent |, stept,
And 'tween the curtains peeped, where lo! how fast she slept.

(Stanza 28.)

This power displayed in the suspension of the single word, when applied to sentences, gives the impressionist construction we know Keats to have instinctively employed the appearance of an artistically chipped and splintered period.

Come back, for a moment, to his first style. We know Keats wrestled, all through *Endymion*, with the difficulties of construction. We know that the sentences under his hands did not instinctively form themselves into periods as with Shelley. (Contrast the stanzas that seem spontaneously to grow out of the couplet-form in the *Epipsychidion* with Keats's short-winded use of the same form in *Endymion*.) We know that when Keats succeeded in a fine effect it was through two or three dotted lines without the least attempt at shading, as in the tale of Pan and Syrinx :

Poor Nymph—poor Pan—how did he weep to find
Nought but a lovely sighing of the wind
Along the reedy stream ;—a half-heard strain,
Full of sweet desolation—balmy pain.

> (" I stood tip-toe upon a little hill.")

To understand *The Eve of St Agnes* this previous
knowledge must be recalled.    Bear this early style
in mind, fairly balancing its clear-cut beauty at its
best with its tremulous hesitation at its worst.    And
now say whether this unconnected impressionist style
does not form the basis of every stanza in *The Eve
of St Agnes*, whether in action :

—Out went the taper as she hurried in.
—Its little smoke in pallid moonshine died.
—She closed the door,—she panted—all akin
  To spirits of the air and visions wide.—
—No uttered syllable, or woe betide !

or in apposition :
                    [her soul]
—Flown like a thought until the morrow-day ;
—Blissfully havened both from joy and pain ;
—Clasped like a missal where swart Paynims pray ;
—Blinded alike from sunshine and from rain,
As though a rose should shut and be a bud again.

or in description :

Down the wide stairs a darkling way they found.
—In all the house was heard no human sound.
—A chain-drooped lamp was flickering by each door ;
—The arras, rich with horseman, hawk, and hound,
  Fluttered in the besieging wind's uproar ;
—And the long carpets rose along the gusty floor.

Here one recognizes the early style at its best,

with its limpid simplicity and straightforwardness
of thought.    But a difference has crept in.    The
sentences are still distinctly stippled,—only, a line
has been drawn through the dots.   The progress of
the action carries on, without effort, one sentence
into the other; the accumulation in idea piles up
the component phrases to the climax.

In this way, I think, Keats solves or, at any rate,
eludes, the chief difficulty he encountered in form.
His fundamental love of sensation had led him first
to weigh the value of words in themselves, apart from
all connection; this love of the single word in the
sentence develops into a love of the single phrase
or sentence in the period; the blending of the
sensations into one another produced a spontaneous
interweaving of the sentences in feeling; this feeling,
being purely a matter of sensation or emotion, comes
out, not in any intellectual construction, but in the
imbrication of rhymes afforded by the Spenserian
stanza.   Now, to realise how perfectly the modulation
of the music succeeds in impressing the dominant
feeling of repose, while the series of simple sentences,
here and there broken by an artful pause, sends
through the whole the required throb and tremor of
life, read the stanza on Madeline's reverie, above
quoted, or, perhaps still better, Porphyro's watch
beside his sleeping bride:

> Thus whispering, his warm, unnerved arm
> Sank in her pillow.  Shaded was her dream
> By the dusk curtains:—'twas a midnight charm
> Impossible to melt as iced stream:

The lustrous salvers in the moonlight gleam ;
Broad golden fringe upon the carpet lies :
It seemed he never, never could redeem
From such a steadfast spell his lady's eyes.
So mused awhile, entoiled in woofed phantasies.

Through all this variety of method, without a
shadow of artifice, Keats achieves a triumph that
can be most fitly expressed in the words of the one
poem *The Eve of St Agnes* most nearly approaches
in sweetness of feeling and sensuous beauty : " like
the best wine for the beloved it goeth down sweetly,
causing the lips of those that are asleep to speak."

Taken in itself, the second half of *The Eve of
St Agnes* presents scarcely a defect in form that the
minutest inspection can discern. It everywhere meets
the requirements of its own inner law. But the first
part, despite certain passages which for sober magnificence Keats never surpassed, reminds one almost at
every step that the poet is working in a borrowed
form. And his treatment of this form is based on
a misconception of its first principle.

In their rebellion against the cut and dried poetic
diction of the eighteenth century the romantics went
back in search of beauty and spontaneous emotion
to the Renaissance. But, absorbed in this pursuit
of emotion and beauty, they overlooked or failed to
perceive the existence of a quality the Renaissance
shared in common with the eighteenth century. Its
clear-headed love of order and symmetry seems never
to have struck them. Poems like *Hero and Leander*
or *Venus and Adonis* may seem at first to appeal

to the senses alone, yet a little analysis reveals the presence through Marlowe as through Shakespeare of the coolest self-control and intellectual grasp. Spenser, in this respect, excelled all his contemporaries. Keats and Shelley both adopted the Spenserian stanza, yet neither realised the first condition of success in such a form was a well-defined syntactical framework round which the whole rhythmical and sonorous edifice could be built up. Neither instinctive movement nor instinctive melody sufficed to swell the slow majestic period of the " Hymn to Venus," quoted on page 73. Each stanza, for Spenser, is a graded development of one idea or of several closely related ideas, so branching out or so crossing and intertwining as to weave all the sentences firmly together. This strong intellectual unity forms so indispensable a condition in the eyes of the creator that the type, once fixed, recurs in all the stanzas alike, whatever their value as sound or meaning. Take an average stanza from the *Faery Queen*, one which would never be quoted as a favourable illustration of Spenser's pictorial or melodic power—part of the description of the House of Temperance: *Faery Queen*, Bk II, Canto IX, Stanza 24:

> Of hewen stone the porch was fairly wrought,
> Stone more of valew and more smooth and fine
> Than Jett or Marble far from Ireland brought ;
> Over the which was cast a wandering vine,
> Enchaced with a wanton yvie twine ;
> And over it a fayre Portcullis hong,
> Which to the gate directly did incline
> With comely compasse and compacture strong,
> Neither unseemly short, nor yet exceeding long.

Set over against this a stanza neither better nor
worse as a whole than twenty others in *The Eve of
St Agnes*:

> So, purposing each moment to retire,
> She lingered still. Meantime, across the moors,
> Had come young Porphyro with heart on fire
> For Madeline. Beside the portal doors,
> Buttressed from moonlight, stands he, and implores
> All saints to give him sight of Madeline,
> But for one moment in the tedious hours,
> That he might gaze and worship all unseen;
> Perchance speak, kneel, touch, kiss—in sooth such things
> have been.

The difference between the master's well-knit
periods and the loose, flimsy texture of the disciple
might be pointed out in every stanza uninspired
by imaginative or sensuous charm. Through want
of preparation and firm connection many a fine
cumulative effect is lost; many a powerful rhythm
dispersed in spray that might have rolled up in a
long Spenserian billow.

The comparison with Spenser simply reveals a
defect prevalent in all Keats's work at this time.
He has achieved supreme triumph in his own mellow,
deliberate, sensitive style, all sensation and emotion;
what still remains to be acquired is a practical style
whose value, as form, may remain constant, to whatever subject it may be applied. Before the end, he
realised the necessity of exchanging, once for all,
his early impressionism for a more certain and solid
intellectual construction. His study of Milton and
Dryden helped him finally to overcome his most

serious defect, without sacrifice of sensuous or
emotional depth.

To be convinced how successfully the one deficiency which impairs the value of *The Eve of St
Agnes* could be supplied, read the opening paragraph
of *Lamia*. The subject possesses little intrinsic
beauty or passion, but precisely on that account
consider the advance it marks in sustained intellectual power:

> Upon a time, before the faery broods
> Drove Nymph and Satyr from the prosperous woods,
> Before King Oberon's bright diadem,
> Sceptre and mantle, clasped with dewy gem,
> Frighted away the Dryads and the Fauns
> From rushes green, and brakes and cowslip'd lawns,
> The ever-smitten Hermes empty left
> His golden throne, bent warm on amorous theft:
> From high Olympus had he stolen light
> On this side of Jove's clouds, to escape the sight
> Of his great summoner, and made retreat
> Into a forest on the shores of Crete.
> For somewhere in that sacred island dwelt
> A nymph to whom all hoofed Satyrs knelt;
> At whose white feet the languid Tritons poured
> Pearls, while on land they withered and adored.
> Fast by the springs where she to bathe was wont,
> And in those meads where sometime she might haunt,
> Were strewn rich gifts unknown to any Muse,
> Though Fancy's casket were unlocked to choose.
> Ah, what a world of love was at her feet!
> So Hermes thought, and a celestial heat
> Burnt from his winged heels to either ear
> That from a whiteness, as the lily clear,
> Blushed into roses 'mid his golden hair
> Fallen in jealous curls about his shoulders bare.

From vale to vale, from wood to wood, he flew,
Breathing upon the flowers his passion new,
And wound with many a river to its head
To find where this sweet nymph prepared her secret bed.

A man who can write purely expository style with such sinewy strength for thirty lines running has conquered every difficulty and divined every secret of his art.

The possession of this new power gives Keats a new command over his own special domain of sensuous and sonorous language. For after all, if, as he himself recognized, the value of the single word depends on its position in the sentence, it stands to reason that the value of the sentence will depend on its position in the paragraph. He could not display his full wealth of sensation before finding his definitive intellectual form. The inmost, central, true Keats does not put forth his reserve of steady, glowing splendour till the vision of Lamia's spirit-wanderings

Whether to faint Elysium, or where
Down through tress-lifting waves the Nereids fair
Wind into Thetis' bower by many a pearly stair ;
Or where God Bacchus drains his cups divine,
Stretched out at ease beneath a glutinous pine ;
Or where in Pluto's gardens palatine
*Mulciber's columns gleam in far piazzian line.*

# THE *HYMN TO INTELLECTUAL BEAUTY*

THE *Hymn* records Shelley's first attempt to sum up the complex aspirations of his nature in one all-embracing formula. But the formula itself must be looked upon as provisory. It does little more than foreshadow the possibility of a final solution, like the cadence of a phantom-melody that will not settle into sound or the silent motions that hover about within the mouth before they cross the lips as words.

Shelley at twenty-three stands out, to use his own favourite image, like a young Mænad of the intellect, dizzy with the intoxication of new thought. Five years before he had driven out of his breast the devils of established prejudice, law, and order, and adjured his fellow-sufferers to follow his example (*Queen Mab*). While meditating on the means of filling up the vacuum left in universal thought by the abolition of religion and morality, the void in his own mind was being unconsciously absorbed by a new principle, recognized three years later as the spirit of Beauty (*Alastor*). The opening hymn to the " Mother of

this unfathomable world" expresses the first positive
doctrine of Shelley's life, the belief that in Nature his
own soul would find a satisfactory guide.    But while
the opening of *Alastor* represents this Nature-worship
simply as a personal intuition, the end hints at the
possibility of a development :

> O, that God,
> Profuse of poisons, would concede the chalice
> Which but one living man has drained

to humanity in general.

> O, that the dream...
> Were the true law of this so lovely world.

He has discovered the solution of the problem in his
own case and now flashes across his mind the thought :
Cannot this individual solution be generalised ?  What
if in the æsthetic ideal of Beauty the world might find
a standard including and surpassing the moral ideal
of Christianity ?  Beauty, from an egotistic enjoyment
of the senses, may be raised into an agent of the
intelligence.    As such, it might perhaps give the
answer to the question asked in *Queen Mab*.  Perhaps...
for Shelley still feels the hesitation of inexperience
in extending the personal ideal to mankind.  He puts
forth the idea simply as a working hypothesis whose
value still remains to be tested by a long series of
experiments.

The characteristic of the *Hymn* then will be the
somewhat premature translation of personal feeling
into a general theory.

From the poet's boyhood, his mind has been
haunted by the shadow of an unseen Power, the same

"shadow" that rested on the opening of *Alastor*[1].
Not on him alone has the shadow fallen. It
floats, although the Power itself remains unseen,
"among *us*,"

> visiting
> This *various world* with as inconstant wing
> As summer winds that creep from flower to flower.

The Spirit behind the shadow may be identified
with the Being met in his visioned wanderings "in
the clear golden prime of his youth's dawn" (*Epipsychidion*). But there, as here, she was "robed in
such exceeding glory That he beheld her not." The
Spirit of Beauty, for ever invisible, can be felt only
through its sensuous manifestations. And as, in the
story of his soul, her voice came to him through the
whispering woods, the fountains, the odours of the
forest, the breezes, the rain of every passing cloud...
(*Epipsychidion, passim*), so in the early *Hymn* the
Spirit had descended in the likeness of the most
transient and fugitive of natural phenomena: moonbeams that behind some piny mountain shower,...hues
and harmonies of evening,...clouds in starlight widely
spread,—in the likeness of "aught that for its grace
may be dear, and yet dearer for its mystery." But
what the *Epipsychidion* represents merely as a personal
intuition the *Hymn* attributes to humanity. Beauty's
"inconstant glance" visits "*each* human heart and
countenance." This Beauty, mysterious and evan-
escent as its manifestations may seem, is yet supposed

---

[1]      Mother......
> I have watched
> Thy shadow, and the darkness of thy steps.

to contain in itself a power of universal appeal on which Shelley bases his first argument in its favour.

The truth behind the shadow, now hailed as the Spirit of Beauty, through these sensuous manifestations may communicate to the beholder the moral perfection which forms the object of every creed. Wordsworth's doctrine of the educative power of Nature gives the clue to this development in Shelley's theory. Wordsworth had shown the action of Nature upon the spirit of Lucy, moulding the moral character till the beauty mirrored upon the soul was thence reflected back upon the outward form (e.g. "...till beauty born of murmuring sound Should pass into her face"). Shelley simply extends the application of this theory not only of the universal but universally purifying influence of Beauty: it "consecrates with its own hues all that it shines upon Of human thought or form." But Beauty may appeal to all, may sanction all, yet none can bid it stay. Even while he sings has it not fled? "Where art thou gone? Why dost thou pass away?"

Here arises the first objection. How shall the multitude be brought to put firm faith in a power so fickle, so fleeting, so inconstant, which from the very exquisiteness of the joy it brings when present only increases the blank gloom of reality when gone, leaving the world, "this dim, vast vale of tears," vacant and desolate? But, on investigation, it will be seen that this reproach is shared by every creed. Mutability is not special to Beauty. No argument strong enough to impugn its right can be brought against Beauty by faiths still subject to the universal law.    Rather than ask why Beauty dies away

> Ask why the sunlight not for ever
> Weaves rainbows o'er yon mountain-river,
> Why aught should fail and fade that once is shown,
> Why fear and dream, and death and birth
> Cast on the daylight of this earth
> Such gloom; why man has such a scope
> For love and hate, despondency and hope?

No solution has been found by the moral or religious creeds men have accepted as their standards. If the poet receives no reply to his eager questioning neither does the philosopher:

> No voice from some sublimer world has ever
> To sage or poet these responses given.

The difference lies in this: Out of their very ignorance the apostles of religion have built up a specious system of theology:

> Therefore the names of Demon, Ghost and Heaven
> Remain the records of their vain endeavour—

a system on examination proved to be hollow, for these words are but the meaningless incantations of a wizard:

> Frail spells, whose uttered charm might not avail to sever
> From all we hear and all we see
> Doubt, chance and mutability.

Whereas the poet frankly admits the instability of Beauty, only now and then felt in the mist flying over the mountains, or the strains of the Æolian harp, or moonbeams glancing on a midnight stream.    Yet fleeting as we know the Spirit to be, when it does descend it can confer the sanction wanting in the other creeds.  It can harmonize life's unquiet dream into grace and through grace into truth.

In this connexion of grace (i.e. attractiveness) and truth, or rather translation of one term into the other, is contained the very essence of Shelley's theory.  For him "Beauty is truth, truth beauty."  Here he expresses for the first time his conviction that mankind can only be brought into contact with moral truth, as he himself was, through sensuous beauty.  Here, for the first time, he sketches the plan

> Of *charming* the minds of men to truth's own sway.
> (*Revolt of Islam.*)

But the high moral feelings inspired by Beauty, the gentle passions,—Love of humanity, Hope in the future, Esteem for ourselves,—on account of the transient character of the motive power, come and go "like clouds for some uncertain moments lent." Yet if such is its influence on the mind even now, what were its continued presence?  Without clearer definition, its continued, if unconscious, sojourn, with all its train of associations, in the human mind could raise man to immortality :

> Man were immortal and omnipotent
> Didst thou, unknown and awful as thou art,.
> Keep with thy glorious train firm state within his heart.

Is there no hope this endless union of the mind with the Spirit of Beauty may be realised after death ? In life its very mystery forms the food of human thought[1], as darkness throws into relief a dying flame.

[1] I have omitted the first apostrophe to Beauty:
Thou messenger of sympathies That wax and wane in lovers' eyes !
not understanding its connexion with the rest of the *Hymn.*

But could the mind forsake every other hope of
immortality for a Power that might desert it at the
tomb?   O Spirit of Beauty, depart not (after life)—
"lest the grave should be, Like life and fear, a dark
*reality*."

Shelley clings to this hope as the only one remaining.   The promises of immortality held out by
Christianity are by him rejected with the bitterness
of one who had tried to believe and been thrust back:
For

> when yet a boy he sought for ghosts and sped
> Through many a listening chamber, cave and ruin
> And starlight wood, with fearful steps pursuing
> Hopes of high talk with the departed dead....

He too

> had called on poisonous names with which our youth is fed.

But the powers turned a deaf ear in his hour of
need:

> I was not heard—I saw them not
> When musing deeply on the lot of life—

that is just at the crucial moment when he was to
decide his fate.   Then it was that Beauty came to fill
the vacant place.   As it saved him then, so it will
save him hereafter.   It is in the name of this first
meeting that he conjures it to remain faithful.

> Depart not as thy shadow came!

How did the shadow come?

> I do remember well the hour which burst
> My spirit's bonds....

he tells us in the Dedication of the *Revolt of Islam*,
the clearest commentary on this stanza of the *Hymn*.

To him, as to Wordsworth, the revelation came on
"a fresh May-dawn" (*Revolt of Islam*) "when winds
were wooing All vital things that wake to bring News
of birds and blossoming" (*Hymn*).

> Sudden the shadow fell on me,
> I shrieked and clasped my hands in ecstasy.
>
> > (*Hymn.*)

From henceforth he felt, like Wordsworth, "a dedi-
cated spirit."

> I vowed that I would dedicate my powers
> To thee and thine...                (*Hymn*)

and, to learn the precise words of the vow, we may
turn again to the Dedication :

> ...I spake: "I will be wise
> And just, and free, and mild, if in me lies
> Such power, for I grow weary to behold
> The selfish and the strong still tyrannise
> Without reproach or check."

Has he not kept the vow? Even now the emotion of remembrance is so strong as to make him live
over the whole scene again. As then he "clasped his
hands," as then "his streaming eyes poured forth
their warm drops on the sunny ground" (*Revolt...*)—
even now, "with beating heart and streaming eyes,"
he calls "the phantoms of a thousand hours, each
from his voiceless grave," to justify the boast. For
from that hour he "heaped knowledge from forbidden
mines of lore...working linkèd armour for his soul"
(*Revolt...*). The thought haunted him not only
through nights of studious zeal, but into the very
"bowers of love's delight" (*Hymn*)—mixing "awful

talk and asking looks With his most innocent love"
(*Alastor*).   In a word, the thought had sunk so deep
into his soul as to have become a part of him.

The account of the vow given in the *Revolt of
Islam* shows the idea of generalising the personal
revelation, noted all through the *Hymn*, to have been
in Shelley's mind from the beginning.   The sudden
expansion of thought :

> They (i.e. phantoms of the hours) know that *never* joy
>   illumed my brow
> Unlinked with hope that thou wouldst free
> This world from its dark slavery...

forms the logical climax of the whole *Hymn*.   May
not the Power that burst his spirit's bonds burst those
of universal thought, sunk in the night of superstition
and tyranny?   May it not exercise upon humanity
the same effect as on himself?   Is not the feeling for
Beauty an intuition common to all, which it is the
poet's mission to develop?   At this early stage in his
experience Shelley can do no more than express the
hope his hypothesis may come true,

> That thou, O awful loveliness
> Wilt give whate'er these words cannot express.

The calm of certainty is still lacking.   Will future
experience bring this calm?

> The day becomes more solemn and serene
> When noon is past; there is a harmony
> In autumn and a lustre in its sky
> Which through the summer is not heard or seen
> As if it could not be, as if it had not been....

So may the power of Beauty, which in the likeness
of unadulterated Nature descended on the expectant

youth, supply to the mature years of the man a calm
as deep as Nature's own.    May the boon be granted
in the name of his all-absorbing worship of the Spirit
of Beauty and its every incarnation, a worship which
bound him first to fear himself (that is, his own power
of carrying out the ideal) and next "to love all
humankind."

How far was the prayer answered?

Shelley, having formulated his ideal, proceeds to
put it into practice with burning zeal.    The *Hymn* of
1816 forms the prelude to the colossal *Revolt of Islam*
of the following year, based upon the inseparable
companionship of Philanthropy and Poetry, Laon and
Cythna, the sister and the brother.    The two go forth,
Laon inspiring the songs of Cythna, Cythna voicing
the theories of Laon, bent on turning the world into
a kind of Garden of Adonis, simply by appeal to the
most exalted feelings of æsthetic morality.    But their
ardour is quenched or, rather, damped at the outset by
the scepticism of the wise.    The old Hermit shakes
his head:

> he had beheld the woe
> To which mankind was bound, but deemed that fate
> Which made them abject would preserve them so.
>
> (Canto IV.)

Still Laon and Cythna put out to sea on the frail
hope:

> "great is the strength of words."
>
> (*Ibid.*)

Alas! the Hermit's predictions come true.    The
abject multitude can be roused to no permanent
action.    The strength of words may be great, yet

it cannot prevent Laon and Cythna being burnt together on the funeral pyre.

If within a year of the *Hymn* Shelley can so far doubt the stability of his own theory, it will be understood that, as time goes on, the sense of discord will increase.   Beauty in itself becomes more and more of an absorbing worship, but in proportion as it grows more and more subtle, complex and refined, diminishes the chance of bringing it into contact with the multitude.   Upon the cry of despair follows a period of exhaustion, when the mind that had appeared so full of indomitable resolve simply drifts away on the current of imagination into a fairy El Dorado where fancy builds a windless bower

> In a dell mid lawny hills
> Which the wild sea-murmur fills,
> And soft sunshine and the sound
> Of old forests echoing round
> And the light and smell divine
> Of all flowers that breathe and shine.

There, basking in the luxury of the most delicate sensations, Shelley sends through the "Spirits of the air" a contemptuous message to the "polluting multitude" to come and heal their rage "in that clime divine and calm."

> They, not it, would change and soon
> Every sprite beneath the moon
> Would repent its envy vain
> And the earth grow young again.
>     (*Lines written in the Euganean Hills*, 1818.)

But, it must be admitted, this lazy tolerance contrasts almost painfully with the zeal of the opening cantos of *Laon and Cythna*.   As early as 1817

Mrs Shelley informs us he had "lost that eager spirit which believed it could achieve what it projected for the benefit of mankind." From this time a kind of languor spreads over the ideal, soft and silent as a film of breath over a mirror. Nothing can be more indicative of the change than the *Prometheus* of the year after (1819). The Titan on the recovery of his liberty, with his old enemy at his feet and the universe at his command, no longer seeks the salvation of the world with the enthusiasm of the days when he stole the fire from Jove. His first care is to retire into a haven where his memory throbbing with past pain may be soothed into oblivion by sighs and smiles and fragments of sea-music and sweet tears. Only as an after-thought does he bid the Spirit of the Hour blow through the magic conch the strain that shall transform the earth.

Shelley is simply wearying of his ideal. The blow he has received by coming into contact with reality has stunned him. Yet he has cherished the ideal too dearly ever to outwardly break with it, too much also, ever in his own heart to forgive the disappointment. Ever, as Beauty soars further and further above the earth, increases the unexpressed conviction of its unfitness to play the part of social regenerator. A year more brings us to a most unequivocal burlesque of his own early faith: *The Witch of Atlas* (1820). Shelley seems to take a pleasure in tantalizing common sense with the pranks and caprices of the Spirit of Poetry, daughter of one of

those mysterious stars
That hide themselves between the Earth and Mars,

whom hereditary taste leads "up the serpent lightning's winding track" to "run upon the platforms of the wind," etc. Only as a passing freak does she descend upon the earth to write "strange dreams" upon the brains of men, these dreams being so many parodies of Shelley's once beloved projects of democracy, universal peace and free love.

These hysterics of the imagination only serve to hide the depth of Shelley's grief at the destruction of all his early schemes. The true clue to his state of mind is given in the preface to the *Epipsychidion* of 1821, where, under the transparent allegory of the youth who died in the attempt to realise "a scheme of life suited perhaps to that better and happier world of which he is now an inhabitant but scarcely practicable in this," Shelley finally confesses the futility of his own first ideal. "He had framed to himself certain opinions," says Shelley in a cancelled "Advertisement" to the same poem, "founded no doubt upon the truth of things, but built up to a Babel height; they fell by their own weight, and the thoughts that were his architects became unintelligible to each other, as men upon whom confusion of tongues has fallen."

Yes, founded on the truth of things, in this sense that the theory started from a correct assumption which the whole of Shelley's work justifies: viz. that for a certain class of mind a system of life could be constructed on principles of æsthetics not only containing but surpassing those of common morality. Therefore based upon the truth of a personal experience. But built up to a Babel height through an over-hasty generalisation which had supposed in the minds of the multitude the capacity of response. Shelley had gone wrong simply through attributing to the common mind a sort of æsthetic acoustic which was entirely lacking.   If his music found no echo, it was because there was no power of resonance in their souls.   This truth he was finally to recognize, too late, in his last poem, where the fair shape of Poesy wanes in the icy splendour of the coming car of Life :

> For deaf as is a sea which wrath makes hoary,
> The world *can hear not* the sweet notes which move
> The sphere whose light is melody to lovers.
>
> > (*Triumph of Life*, 1822.)

In one sense the prayer of the *Hymn* was answered.   Beauty endured, though Beauty Intellectual was a dream.   Its calm descended on his onward life, but, as through the harmony and lustre of the autumn moans and darkens the sense of coming change, so through incommunicable Beauty, however perfect, Shelley ever felt the sadness of an unsatisfied ideal.

# SHELLEY'S TRANSCENDENTALISM

UPPERMOST in Shelley's mind lay an innate love of union and harmony, which struggles for expression through his philosophical and sentimental as through his socialistic verse. Shelley felt, as all under the habitual sway of intense emotion must, the falsity of the divisions, conventional, social, political, rhetorical, logical, etc., introduced by man's understanding into

> the web of being blindly wove
> By man and beast and earth and air and sea.
>
> (*Adonais.*)

His object everywhere is to remove the barriers set up by tradition, to remind us of our inability to gauge incommensurable feeling and, consequently, to define its limits. If we will give our sensations and emotions liberty to transcend their artificial boundaries, to come together, recognize their own affinities, overlap, and finally coalesce, all the discords created by the isolating power of the understanding will be lost in the primal harmony man has, for centuries, been labouring to destroy.

> All things together grow
> Through which the harmony of love can pass.
>
> (*Witch oj Atlas.*)

This object has in the sphere of social reform been too clearly set forth by Shelley even to require illustration. But the same tendency may be felt, though in a more unconscious and intuitional form, in his purely poetical work. In intellect and sensation he required the same absorption of divisions into unity, which I take to be the fundamental law of his mind.

The organic unity of life, lost sight of by the unthinking because too complex to be comprehended and retained, may be first discerned in sensation. For convenience' sake the intellect divides the senses into five, without connexion, and we, disregarding our own feeling which would teach us their relation to each other, look upon these divisions as absolute. But, for Shelley, the slightest impression made upon one sense sends an electric shock through all the others. Sometimes the connexion is only hinted at; the sensations co-exist, but do not yet overlap:

> Music, when soft voices die,
> Vibrates in the memory—
> —Odours, when sweet violets sicken,
> Live within the sense they quicken—
> —Rose-leaves, when the rose is dead,
> Are heaped for the beloved's bed....

A stage higher in complexity the different sensations are grouped round a central idea. The singing of the lark, after

> Like a poet hidden   In the light of thought,

turns into instrumental music, odour and light...

> Like a high-born maiden   In a palace-tower...
> Like a rose embowered   In its own green leaves...
> Like a glow-worm golden   In a dell of dew...

This connexion however is as yet only dimly perceived. The sensations, without the intervention of
a unifying idea, should spontaneously suggest each
other. The dying music of the nightingale

> Is scattered in a thousand notes,
> And now to the hushed ear it floats
> *Like field-smells known in infancy.*
>
> > (*Rosalind & Helen.*)

Or, again, the "soft and glowing light" lining the
magic conch

> Looks like lulled music slumbering there.

Or, conversely, the Spirit of the Hour approaches

> Wrapped in sweet sounds as in bright veils.
>
> > (*Prometheus Unbound.*)

And so on. But the recognition of this interdependence between the senses will not yet suffice. To satisfy
Shelley's capacity for sensation, even the distinctions
presupposed by the transposition felt through the
metaphor must be overcome. All must be present
simultaneously, and all borne in at once upon one
general "sense" into which all the others have been
merged: the light of the brook, the "wild odour of
the forest-flowers," "the music of the living grass and
air," "the emerald light of leaf-entangled beams"

> Seem kneaded into one aerial mass
> Which drowns the sense.
>
> > (*Prometheus*, Act IV.)

In the yet more fluid region of feeling, the distinctions usually recognized are so far from absolute
that, at a certain point of intensity, they positively

contradict each other. As, in physical sensation, intense cold turns over into intense heat, so any moral feeling, if only carried far enough, will turn over into its opposite. Joy, when too acute, is felt as pain. Sorrow, when brooded over undisturbed, comes to be regarded as a luxury. The sensation which should, in a normal way, give pleasure, may, when too exquisite, cause a twinge of pain, and conversely:

> Weeping, till sorrow becomes ecstasy.
> > (*Epipsychidion.*)

> And from the moss violets and jonquils peep,
> And dart their arrowy odour through the brain
> Till you might faint with that delicious pain.
> > (*Epipsychidion.*)

> Sounds overflow the listener's brain
> So sweet that joy is almost pain.
> > (*Prometheus.*)

Now, if this passage from one sensation to another, this annihilation of the boundaries between the emotions, in the case of one individual proves the factitious character of conventional divisions, how much more convincing a proof may be drawn from the complete surrender of self, the negation of individuality, by which all distinctions whatever are transcended in the act of love—

> the strong control
> Which blends two restless frames in one reposing soul.
> > (*Laon and Cythna*, Canto VI.)

Shelley seems to me to have attached supreme importance to love because, in the unity of sensation and feeling reached in perfect passion, the guiding principle of harmony was realised. Everywhere he dwells on

the theme in almost the same language, insisting on
the value of love, not as voluptuousness or personal
pleasure, but as the negation of egotism in the
*exchange* and *interpenetration* of life.

> I saw not, heard not, moved not, only felt
> His presence flow and mingle through my blood
> Till it became his life and his grew mine.
>
> *(Prometheus*, Act II.)

> ...The fountains of our deepest life shall be
> Confused in Passion's golden purity,
> As mountain-springs under the morning sun.
>
> *(Epipsychidion.)*

> I am as a spirit that has dwelt
> Within his heart of hearts....
>
> *(Wedded Love.)*

You remember? See also

> One soul of interwoven flame
>
> *(Rosalind and Helen)*

and the sixth canto of *Laon and Cythna.*

So far, good. Up to this point Shelley's position
can scarcely be disproved. But the royal ease with
which Shelley "overleaps all bound" raises a little
doubt as to the validity of the means by which he
reaches his final union. A mind filled with the love
of harmony may at the same time be a mind without
compartments. The individuality which can be so
readily sacrificed was perhaps not too clearly defined
and conscious of itself at the beginning. This want
of feeling for boundary and limit, which in the realm
of sensation and emotion appears as comprehensive
unity, in his more pretentious philosophy leads Shelley
to take up an untenable position.

You remember the general tenour of Shelley's doctrine. He believes in the existence behind every form of reality of a motive power appearing under different names as

(1) The Spirit of Nature

[The Eternal whose own smile
Unfolds itself and may be felt, not seen,
O'er the grey rocks, blue waves and forests green.
(*Epipsychidion.*)

Mother of this unfathomable world...
I have watched
Thy shadow and the darkness of thy steps.
(*Alastor.*)

Life of life thy lips enkindle, etc.
(*Prometheus.*)]

(2) The Spirit of Beauty

[The awful shadow of some unseen power.
(*Hymn.*)

Shadow of Beauty unbeheld.
(*Prometheus.*)

There was a Being whom my spirit oft
Met in its visioned wanderings...
(*Epipsychidion.*)]

(3) The Spirit of Love

[The shadow that doth float unseen
But not unfelt o'er man's mortality.
(*Laon and Cythna.*)

The shadow of fire surrounding me.
(*Rosalind and Helen.*)]

(4) In poetry, that "deep music" with which all things are in unison—

The soul within the soul.
(*Epipsychidion.*)

Shelley's true desire is to carry all feeling, all sensation, all thought to that pitch of intensity where, all divisions having been overcome, reality may enter into union with the ideal. The higher the stage reached, the more completely the sense of separation will be lost. Emilia Viviani, as most perfectly embodying ideal beauty, will herself be

> lost and in that Beauty furled
> That penetrates and clasps and fills the world.
>
> *(Epipsychidion.)*

Helen, as still of the earth, unable to rise to the height of truly ideal passion, still feels the obstacles and "exclusive bars" of mortality, but Lionel, as nearer immortality, has already reached in love his future perfect freedom:

> HELEN: Alas, the unquiet life did tingle
> From mine own heart through every vein,
> Like a captive in dreams of liberty
> Who beats the walls of his stony cell.
> But his, it seemed already *free*
> *Like the shadow of fire surrounding me.*
>
> *(Rosalind and Helen.)*

Now, at this supreme moment of union with the ideal, you expect a clear remembrance of the divisions which have been gradually absorbed. Had Shelley retained his full consciousness to the end, the harmony at last reached would have been true, for it would legitimately have reduced discord into unity. But you must have noticed in Shelley a certain tremulousness at the highest point of intensity, an unsteadiness of vision which only perceives the ideal in blurred outline, a quavering in the voice when it rises to the highest notes.

When all the sensations have been "kneaded" into unity, the "aerial mass"

> drowns the sense.
>> (*Prometheus.*)

When the souls of those whom the Spirit of Nature loves "walk upon the winds with lightness," that is, when they enter into communion with the Life of life,

> Then they fail as I am failing,
> Dizzy, lost, yet unbewailing.

When he wanders out in quest of Ideal Beauty he finds her, but

> Robed in such exceeding glory
> That I beheld her not.

And even Emilia Viviani [who, by-the-bye, is so far from being truly an incarnation of Ideal Beauty that she stands on the same level with the visionary Being, the description of the ideal and the description of the real Lady almost exactly tallying, one neither more nor less intangible than the other,]—even Emilia Viviani is

> Scarce visible from extreme loveliness.

When, in the excess of passion, the poet reaches "the height of Love's rare universe"

> I pant, I sink, I tremble, I expire !

Even in the *Lines to an Indian air*

> I die !  I faint !  I fail !

But, as most characteristic of this dissolution to which
the attempt at union leads, take *Laon & Cythna*:

> What are kisses whose fire clasps
> The failing heart in languishment?...
> ........................or the quick dying gasps
> Of the life meeting, when the faint eyes swim
> Through tears of a wide mist boundless and dim
> In one caress? What is the strong control
> Which leads the heart that dizzy steep to climb
> Where far over the world those *vapours* roll
> Which blend two restless frames in one reposing soul?

And the lines following show that Shelley looked
upon this state of swooning dissolution as the true
union with the ideal, for in answer to the question
comes the assurance:

> It is the shadow which doth float unseen
> But not unfelt o'er blind mortality....

You see what union without difference results in.
It leads to a purely negative conclusion. In these
trances Shelley grasps nothing but the phantom of
the ideal. The final outcome of all the process of
unification is blank nothing. And Shelley recognizes
as much himself in the paradox contained in those
lines of *Rosalind and Helen*, the summary of all his
fits of passion, meditations and poetic ecstasies:

> Heard'st thou not......
> That love when limbs are interwoven,
> And sleep when the night of life is cloven,
> And thought to the world's dim boundaries clinging,
> And music when one beloved is singing
> *Is death*?

# SHELLEY'S IDEALISM

ALL the unessential aspects of Shelley's poetry may, at the present time, be left out of account. Much that was due simply to accidents of training and surroundings may be excluded, or just glanced at in passing when it serves to explain some difficulty, contradiction, discord.—A large proportion, even after this preliminary sorting, still remains to be considered. The best criterion to apply, after these ephemeral interests have passed away, is the following: What is generally recognized to contain Shelley's finest verse and what are its constituent qualities? Judged by such a test, much of his most ambitious work will give place to slighter trifles.— The twelve cantos of the *Revolt of Islam*, with the exception of perhaps a dozen stanzas, would be easily outweighed by " Music when soft voices die...." The whole of *Hellas* sinks into insignificance before " O world, O life, O time ! "

A natural tendency to metaphysics, developed by a certain amount of philosophical training, supplied Shelley with the materials of his genuine verse. It taught him to look on all things from a new point of view. The results which the poet usually reaches through feeling were reached in his case by a process which, while still pervaded by sensation and emotion, yet approximated to pure thought. The question is to follow out one by one the several stages which must be gone through before Shelley's method can be understood.

Shelley seems to me to have been guided throughout by a correct idea which never attains quite satisfactory expression. This idea I would like to explain first in my own way from my own point of view.

Our life in its main lines is a fact which we have never yet been able to realise. No power from the outside compels us to understand its object. Our free-will consists precisely in this,—that our consciousness of life, our comprehension of its meaning, is biassed by no external necessity. The choice lies before us. We may go through all the forms of life in a perfectly mechanical fashion, looking upon ourselves all the while as the victims of a scheme external to ourselves which has been forced upon us. This is the attitude of what is usually called the natural man. Or else, our free-will may, *of its own free will*, bring itself into union with laws which are no longer felt to be at variance with our spirit, since they are nothing but emanations from itself. This is the attitude of what is called the idealist. But this terminology implies a distinction which does not, in truth, exist. It presupposes an opposition between our nature and our ideal. No such opposition should be made. If by nature we mean the average standard which has hitherto been reached, the ideal must, by force of contrast with reality, strike us as a paradox. But if by Nature we mean the norm, then nature is identical with the ideal. The singular sense of satisfaction and familiarity which fills the spirit on the discovery of a new truth, the rapidity with which it settles down and makes itself at home in the truth, the amazement, the feeling of estrangement and repulsion with which it looks back upon its former self, should suffice to convince us of this identity.

Now, in order to understand Shelley, you must admit and yourself be permeated with the sense of this identity. You must learn to look upon the ideal we are struggling forward to as not only more true, but as more natural and more normal than the reality we have reached. All idea of paradox must be banished. For the mere fact of feeling a contrast would prove you to be still moving in a lower plane of thought. The child-like innocence of Shelley's mind allowed him to accept the ideal in all simplicity, without a trace of the astonishment it would have roused in a worldling bound down by the actual forms of reality. The absence of all constraint in expression, the ease of his language, which seems to increase in proportion to the subtlety of the theme, offers the surest guarantee of this conviction.

I really think the only difficulty in Shelley lies in the mode of approach.

You must put aside all the conceptions formed in the "dark reality" of "life" (*Hymn to Intellectual Beauty*) and try by intuition to reach the "Life of

life" (*Prometheus*), the "unseen power" whose very
shadow remains unseen (*Hymn*). This faith in the
ideal and normal "Life of life" as contra-distin-
guished from "life," its artificial imitation, forms the
first article of his creed. He starts, as we must start,
with the Platonic doctrine of the pre-existence of the
idea ever trying to realise itself in the forms of matter.
Shelley seems in every act and emotion of life to
have been haunted by the presence of this Idea in
various shapes hovering above the particular realisa-
tion in question. It appears now as the shadow of
Nature, now as the shadow of Beauty, now as the
shadow of Love, the smile of the Eternal "felt not
seen" (*Epipsychidion*), present to intuition, though
hidden from the senses.

# THE IMAGES IN SHELLEY'S
## *HELLAS*

THE most intense craving of Shelley's nature
was for liberty. With him liberty is the first, as the
last, note heard. Liberty is the theme of *Queen Mab*,
liberty the theme of *The Triumph of Life*. If we
look through a list of Shelley's works, we shall see
that they may all be classed as so many different
manifestations of this one principle, in every sphere
of moral, political and religious life. Liberty in
politics is the theme of *The Revolt of Islam*; Liberty
in Love the theme of *Rosalind and Helen*; Liberty
in religion the theme of *Prometheus Unbound*. Herein
Shelley is at one with nearly all his poetical contemporaries. Remember that nearly all the great
romantic poets began their career as extreme radicals:
all started with the eighteenth-century ideal of political
liberty.

Wordsworth was a radical, so was Coleridge,
so was Byron, so was Leigh Hunt, nay, even Keats
himself. All began as partisans of liberty in politics,
but, in the case of nearly all the men enumerated,
the political was soon exchanged for the poetical

career: while their abilities seemed to be concentrated upon a different object, in reality the guiding principle of their lives remained the same.

The ideal, first conceived as the supreme object in politics, became the supreme object in Art. In fact we may define the romantic movement as an attempt to reform literature through the same means the eighteenth century had employed in reforming society. Shelley, as the most ardent partisan of liberty in politics, was also sure to be the most ardent partisan of liberty in Art; and, to the list of those works in which liberty is represented as the guiding principle in politics, religion and morality, we may now add another in which the claims of LIBERTY IN IMAGINATION are upheld, that is *The Witch of Atlas*. So intense was the need for liberty in Shelley's imagination that he alone among the romantics seems to have conceived the idea of expressing this same craving for liberty through an imaginative medium entirely disconnected with form. Now it is precisely the function of imagination to express abstract ideas through form, to embody an abstract idea in a concrete shape; but form immediately limits the liberty Shelley is striving to attain: therefore, if we study Shelley's imagination throughout its various manifestations in logical not chronological order, we shall find his imagination seeking the first expression of liberty in a medium detached from form.

I. Shelley understood that form to a certain extent must limit liberty; therefore he discovered the possibility of exchanging form for motion, in which liberty can develop untrammelled. The most

complete expression of this conception of imagination
detached from form is the *Ode to the West Wind.*
In the *Ode to the West Wind* Shelley seems to have
felt that his liberty had found its fullest expression,
for, in the wild spirit that is moving everywhere, he
seems to have recognised a fit symbol of his own
imagination.    Here Shelley identifies himself with
the object of his thought.

> Make me thy lyre......
> .   .   .   .   .   .
> .........Be thou, Spirit fierce,
> My spirit !   Be thou me, impetuous one !

he cries to the West Wind, but there is a reserve.
The West Wind is, in reality, not a fit symbol of
Shelley's imagination, and he seems to have felt the
difficulty immediately.   The defect of motion detached
from form lies in the fact that motion is more than
free: it is uncontrollable, and Shelley stops short.
"Be thou me; would I were as thee, only less free
than thou, O uncontrollable."    But why less free?
Because Shelley immediately feels the necessity of
limiting the excessive liberty he has now attained.
Liberty is now on the verge of anarchy, and notice
that, through Shelley's work, liberty is not only represented as the opposite of tyranny, but also, perhaps
more so, the enemy of anarchy.   If we proceed to
limit our first definition, we shall see that Shelley's
guiding principle was liberty, liberty versus tyranny
on the one hand, versus anarchy on the other.

We are told in the first chorus of *Hellas* that
"when the Spirit of God unfurled the flag of freedom

over chaos, all its banded anarchs fled," and throughout, in his attempt at regenerating the world through
liberty, it must have been noticed that liberty is
carefully distinguished from licence.

Liberty after all must be contained within certain
bounds, and what is true in politics will be no less
true in imagination.

II.   Liberty can only show its strength when it
has to work in material to a certain extent refractory.
Now motion is not refractory, therefore the next
stage in Shelley's imagination is the attempt to
create a medium where form is at least beginning
to be recognised.   At this second stage Shelley
adopts the solution already found before by the
earlier romantics.   The romantics seem to have
recognised that their imagination would find its
freest play in sensation.   Romantic imagination has
always been defined as sensuous, and the reason is
that the senses easily merge into each other.   There
are no hard and fast lines of distinction drawn
between the various senses : music passes into light
or light into fragrance without incongruity.   For a
poet of 1820 it had become almost impossible to
conceive of any one sensation save through the
medium of another.   A man, we will suppose, is
watching the waving of ash-boughs in the wind.
If he is an ordinary man, this will suggest no
more than motion to his mind, but, if his name is
Wordsworth, this motion will be immediately translated into sound, and the impression described as
that of " A soft eye-music of slow-waving boughs."
Here the method is conscious, for the visual sensation

is directly translated into an auditive sensation. But the same principle was at work in the minds of nearly all the young romantics, so much so that, by at least one, the sole food of poetry is held to be sensation. "Oh, for a life of sensations, rather than of thoughts," cries Keats, and when Keats comes to his own ideal of poetry, when he comes to embody the spirit of poetry in the witch Lamia, notice that this spirit is represented as existing entirely on sensation. When the mortal Lycius begs Lamia to come down on earth and live with him, her first question is "What serener palaces hast thou, where I may all my many senses please?" In the same manner, Shelley's Lamia, the lady who for him embodies the spirit of poetry, the Witch of Atlas, is represented as keeping in her magic cavern— here symbolising the mind of man—certain treasures which, on analysis, turn out to consist entirely of sensations; in the cavern she keeps "Sounds of air folded in cells of crystal silence, visions swift and sweet and quaint, odours in a kind of aviary of ever-blooming Eden trees and, lastly, liquors clear and sweet and bright." In sensation Shelley's liberty could develop unimpeded, yet there was in matter the possibility of resistance, therefore the possibility of discord, hence the possibility of harmony, a possibility excluded in pure and simple motion. Already in sensation matter was attempting to reduce liberty to certain laws of its own, for, if we take such an image as this from *Hellas*, we shall see that the sensations are graded in a rising scale of emotional complexity:

> Through the sunset of hope,
> Like the shapes of a dream,
> What Paradise islands of glory gleam!
>    Beneath Heaven's cope
> Their shadows more clear float by—
> The sound of their oceans, the light of their sky,
> The music and fragrance their solitudes breathe
> Burst, like morning on dream, or like Heaven on death,
>    Through the walls of our prison;

but here, in this example, it will be understood the sensations are graded according to a certain arbitrary disposition of the poet's own. Their progression depends upon the poet's will; could not a higher harmony be attained, in which the same complexity might be preserved and the same order introduced through a guiding principle inherent in the object itself?

III.   Perhaps by combining motion and matter this desired harmony could be attained; for in this lies the secret of Shelley's preference for a certain image that recurs more frequently in his work, in *Hellas* in particular, than any other—the image of the Cloud.

> With wings folded I rest on mine aëry nest
>    As still as a brooding dove.
>
> That orbèd maiden with white fire laden,
>    Whom mortals call the Moon,
> Glides glimmering o'er my fleece-like floor
>    By the midnight breezes strewn;
>
> And wherever the beat of her unseen feet
>    .    .    .    .    .    .    .
> May have broken the woof of my tent's thin roof,
>    .    .    .    .    .    .    .
> ...I widen the rent in my wind-built tent
>    .    .    .    .    .    .    .
> And bind the Moon's throne with a girdle of pearl.
>                    (*The Cloud.*)

Three images in *Hellas* :

(1)    Would I were the wingèd cloud
    Of a tempest swift and loud !

    ·     ·     ·     ·     ·      ·      ·

    To the rocks that gird th' Ægean

    ·     ·     ·     ·     ·      ·      ·

       I would flee.

       ·     ·     ·      ·

       My golden rain

       ·     ·     ·      ·     ·

    Should mingle in tears with the bloody main,
       And my solemn thunder knell
       Should ring....

(2)  Four hundred thousand Moslems......
                     irresistibly
    Throng, like full clouds at the Sirocco's cry,
    But not like them to weep their strength in tears.

(3)        the fierce shout.........
    Rose like the war-cry of the northern wind
    Which kills the sluggish clouds, and leaves a flock
    Of wild swans struggling with the naked storm.

The Cloud is represented as possessing a certain
shape of its own, apparently fixed when at rest, but
a shape which the slightest breath of wind, the
slightest manifestation of internal motion may transform. If we turn back to Shelley's great lyric we
shall find that the Cloud carries with it a higher
form of imagination : it bears along with its own
individuality another—that of the " Orbèd maiden
with white fire laden, Whom mortals call the Moon."

It might be supposed then that at last Shelley's
imagination was fixing itself in definite form, since
it has advanced as far as personification, but notice
that the Orbèd maiden is unseen. Shelley can
conceive of a definite reality fixed in form, but he

will not perceive it. As soon as the personification has been admitted, a veil is thrown over it : the Orbèd maiden is not seen directly, but guessed at through the cloud that hides her.

IV. Then it is on this principle of unperceived personification that the whole of the imaginative value of the *Skylark* depends.

Example in *Hellas* :

> A power from the unknown God,
> A Promethean conqueror, came ;
>
> .    .    .    .    .    .
>
> A mortal shape to him
> Was like the vapour dim
> Which the orient planet animates with light.

It will be understood now that, when Shelley comes into contact with a definite reality that can no longer be avoided, he will not reproduce it directly. When all veil has been withdrawn, when the reality stares him in the face, how is he to escape from the bonds already imposed by the precision of this reality ? He will not reproduce it, he will transform it ; for in personification Shelley feels that both motion and form are limited ; in fact the form here limits the motion.

V. Example of the actual presence modified : the meeting with Emilia Viviani.

> She met me, Stranger, upon life's rough way...etc.

He tells us that throughout his life he has been seeking the embodiment of the mighty abstract idea of the beautiful, and after many unsuccessful attempts has at last discovered this concrete embodiment in the person of Emilia Viviani. Here it will be supposed that Shelley's imagination would be forced by the very nature of the subject to work in fixed and concrete form. Nothing should logically be more concrete and more tangible than Emilia Viviani, but immediately Shelley's fear of being in the least limited by the medium he has chosen leads him to change her into an intense diffusion, a serene omnipresence whose flowing outlines mingle in their flowing till they are lost, he tells us, and " in that beauty furled which penetrates and clasps and fills the world."

The reason must be sought not only in Shelley's personal temperament, but deeper in the general principle of romantic imagination. What is the reason of the quality of suggestiveness attributed to the poetry of the romantics? Every beautiful object for a romantic poet is valuable only on account of its associations, it is valuable as suggesting the other manifestations of beauty throughout the world. In fact an object is no longer clearly seen in itself, but merged in all its relations. A thing of beauty only becomes beautiful in virtue of its associations.

If Emilia Viviani's outlines were not so flowing they could not have been furled in the beauty that clasps the world. She might have possessed more individual beauty, but her beauty would not have been of a suggestive character, and in suggestion the whole charm of romantic imagination lies. Shelley has taken the trouble to describe the process by which his imagination transforms its objects in the lyric of *Prometheus Unbound* entitled " On a poet's lips I slept."

He will watch from dawn to gloom
The lake-reflected sun illume
The yellow bees in the ivy-bloom,
Nor heed nor see what things they be ;
But from these create he can
Forms more real than living man,
Nurslings of immortality !

But now we are reaching the limit of Shelley's imagination. Then at this point it may be said that Shelley's liberty is beginning to feel the impossibility of proceeding further, of binding itself down to any concrete form, of fixing itself under limits, and from this point forward we may expect in the work of Shelley nothing but more or less signal failures. All his experiments in definite form from this point onwards only serve to demonstrate the impossibility of such a conception of liberty as Shelley's, the impossibility of its fixing itself in the precise form of personification, and so we may study out the various attempts, through *Hellas*, at embodying the idea in personification simply as a sign of the inability of the liberty to develop in precise form.

VI. We may study it out (1) through an attempt at discovering another outlet for his liberty in the image of Revenge and Wrong:

Revenge and Wrong bring forth their kind,
The foul cubs like their parents are,
Their den is in the guilty mind,
And Conscience feeds them with despair ;

(2) through an attempt to apply to personification the same laws which hold good in sensation. The mixture of sensation and personification :

> from Time's tempestuous dawn
> Freedom's *splendour* burst and shone:

.    .    .    .    .    .

>         ...The wingèd glory
>     On Philippi half-alighted,
> Like an *eagle* on a promontory.

Or the personification within the personification:

> wolfish *Change*, like winter, howls to strip
> The foliage in which *Fame*, the eagle, built
> Her aerie....

The same without any transition:

> O *Slavery*! thou *frost* of the world's prime,
> Killing its flowers and leaving its thorns bare!

The truth is that at this point a change in method is required. Shelley's method is radically wrong. It is here that Shelley's great quality, the quality he possessed in common with all the romantics, turns against him. The effect of suggestiveness, sought by the romantics in general, as we have seen depends on the recognition of certain unsuspected relations between objects in appearance dissimilar, but when this method is carried too far, when the relations only are insisted upon, there is a danger of the limits being obliterated. And what precisely gave all the value to Shelley's imagery in sensation, or in motion, or in the combination of the two, as in *The Cloud*, turns against him in the realm of personification. The proof that a change is required lies in the fact that forty years before, another poet, having to solve the same problem as Shelley in *Hellas*, solved it successfully, simply because his mind had been trained in a different school of logic:

LEICESTER.  How's this my friends! is't thus your new-
                fledged zeal
            And plumèd valour moulds in roosted sloth?
            Why dimly glimmers that heroic flame,
            Whose reddening blaze, by patriot spirit fed,
            Should be the beacon of a kindling realm?
            Can the quick current of a patriot heart
            Thus stagnate in a cold and weedy converse
            Or freeze in tideless inactivity?
            No! rather let the fountain of your valour
            Spring through each stream of enterprise,
            Each petty channel of conducive daring,
            Till the full torrent of your foaming wrath
            O'erwhelm the flats of sunk hostility.
SIR WALTER.  No more!—The freshening breath of thy rebuke
            Hath fill'd the swelling canvas of our souls!
            And thus, though fate should cut the cable of
            Our topmost hopes, in friendship's closing line
            We'll grapple with despair, and if we fall,
            We'll fall in glory's wake!  (SHERIDAN'S *Critic*.)

For Mr Puff had been brought to recognise the limits he was describing, to the complete exclusion of their relations with each other.  The faculty of isolation, that was the characteristic of the eighteenth-century mind in general, was entirely lacking in the romantics.  It is here that the romantics might have taken a lesson from the much despised poets of the eighteenth century.

We could not expect Shelley so completely to raise himself above his surroundings as to attain the logic here displayed, but without deserting his own fixed principles, without in the least trying to abstract from the tendencies of his age, there was a second way out of the difficulty.  His liberty, now limited in the materials in which it sought expression, might from the very nature of its subject have developed in another direction.  In personification motion and

form are both limited; in these living, in these
animated objects a new possibility of change could
be developed. The animals are endowed with instinct,
man is endowed with a soul, and, had Shelley understood the psychological possibilities of the images he
was now developing, he might yet have found an outlet
for his liberty limited in motion and in form. This
was the solution found by a poet who is almost
Shelley's contemporary, the Frenchman Barbier, in
*L'Idole.* But the same tendency which had led
Shelley to ignore the external limits of form, the same
tendency in which he had gloried in "On a poet's lips
I slept" here again turns against him in psychology.
If he could not recognize the external limits, still
less could he recognise the internal limits. Shelley
as we know was no psychologist. The reason again
may be found in his resolution to ignore the limits
of the soul as well as the body. Therefore in all
those images where it is important that the psychology
should be accurate, we shall find a want of logic, an
incoherence in Shelley's treatment that, after this
study, will be no surprise. We may trace up through
these images a constant effort of Shelley's to attain
his liberty in his own way, in material that excludes
the possibility of this liberty developing.

yon crescent moon......

(1)  ·    ·    ·    ·    ·    ·    ·

> trembles in the blood-red air
> And like a mighty *lamp* whose oil is spent
> Shrinks on the horizon's edge, while, from above,
> One star with insolent and victorious light
> Hovers above its fall, and with keen beams,
> Like arrows through a fainting *antelope*,
> Strikes its weak form to death.

(2)    Nor.....................less exultingly
       Than *birds* rejoicing in the golden day,
       The *Anarchies of Africa* unleash
       Their tempest-wingèd *cities of the sea*,
       To speak in thunder to the rebel world.
       Like sulphurous *clouds*, half-shattered by the storm,
       They sweep the pale Ægean....

Lastly

(3)    One half the Grecian army,...

       .       .       .       .       .       .       .
                                       ...*Islanded*
       By victor myriads, formed in hollow square
                               and thrice flung back
       The deluge of our foaming cavalry;

       .       .       .       .       .       .       .
                           till, like a *field of corn*
       Under the hook of the swart sickleman,
       The band...
       Grew weak and few....

The dangers of this style of imagery are now
apparent. This style of imagery contradicts the
very object of the image. The object of an image
is to make an abstract idea concrete, but it has been
shown that the abstract idea can embody itself in
anything and everything, which comes to the same
as if it were embodied in nothing. Flaubert's theory
of the single word that alone expresses the author's
meaning has been much ridiculed, yet it contains in
itself an element of truth: it is based on the great
principle that a work of art should produce on the
reader's mind a sense of inevitableness, not only as
a whole but in every one of its parts.

Now it is this need for inevitableness that is not
satisfied and that requires satisfaction in this style

of imagery. Shelley has himself recognised this to be the weak point in his own imagination, for, in a drama written a few years before *Hellas,—Swellfoot the Tyrant,*—where he seems to have started with the project of turning into ridicule all his own sentiments and aspirations both political and moral, his own versification, his own vocabulary, he has taken care to allot a special portion of the drama to his own imagination, and it is precisely on this weak point that he insists: the tendency, by embodying the abstract idea in too long a succession of incoherent images, to reach the result with which he started,—by embodying it in anything to embody it in nothing.

| | |
|---|---|
| *Second Boar.* | How glorious it will be to see her Majesty |
| | Flying above our heads, her petticoats |
| | Streaming like—like—like— |
| *Third Boar.* | Anything. |
| *Purganax.* | Oh no ! |
| | But like a standard of an admiral's ship, |
| | Or like the banner of a conquering host, |
| | Or like a cloud dyed in the dying day, |
| | Unravelled on the blast from a white mountain; |
| | Or like a meteor, or a war-steed's mane, |
| | Or waterfall from a dizzy precipice |
| | Scattered upon the wind. |
| *First Boar.* | Or a cow's tail. |
| *Second Boar.* | Or *anything*, as the learned Boar observed. |
| | (*Swellfoot.*) |

It remained for a poet coming about thirty years after Shelley to discover the final harmony Shelley had been vainly seeking, to attain his liberty in every sphere of imagination, with a logic as precise as that of Puff, through a psychology more delicate than Barbier's—for the Pre-Raphaelite Rossetti.

# THE BLENDING OF PROSE, BLANK VERSE AND RHYMED VERSE IN *ROMEO AND JULIET*

THE question, to be fully treated, would require a survey of all Shakespeare's technique. In a study of his evolution *Romeo and Juliet* might be placed at the exact centre. Coming after *Love's Labour's Lost*, after *Venus and Adonis*, presumably after the *Midsummer Night's Dream*, contemporaneous with the *Sonnets*, just before the chronicle plays, one degree removed from the romantic comedies, fifteen years anterior to *Antony and Cleopatra*, twenty to *The Tempest*—there is hardly a single principle hinted at or developed in any one of these which may not be traced up or back to *Romeo*. On the one hand it sums up all that preceded, on the other it prophesies all that is coming. That is, it may be looked upon as the great transition play of Shakespeare's life

In *Romeo* is accomplished the transformation of all the old materials, hitherto kept apart, through a long series of experiments, into a whole, under the inspiration of a new psychology.

Throughout his attempts at blending Shakespeare is actuated by one motive,—to discover which of the three forms could most easily absorb the other two. The search for the dramatic dominant will lead him to the creation of a new form into which the quintessence of all three has entered.

Imagine one unique medium, allowing of every inward change of feeling with no outward change of form.   Imagine something which combines the freedom of prose with the sonority of rhyme, produces the effect of neither and is called blank verse.

Blank verse was supposed to have a normal type : the stopped, decasyllabic line.   Blank verse was supposed to exclude the final consonance of rhyme.   On these two principles its existence was supposed to depend.   Blank verse can exist without a rhythmic norm of any description and it can so exist by calling in the assistance of rhyme incognito.   That is, blank verse can turn over into *vers libre* with pause anywhere and everywhere according to the necessities of the feeling, taking as its only unifying principle the reminiscence of a sound heard before upon the pause.

Shift the barriers of pause from the end of one line into the body of the next, shift the barriers of rhyme so that the primary sound shall not be repeated in the second but reproduced in echo, you will have the double principle on which this new prosody is built up.

Instead of saying with Mercutio :

And in this state she gallops night by night
Through lovers' brains and then they dream of love,
O'er courtiers' knees who dream on court'sies straight,
O'er lawyers' fingers who straight dream on fees,
O'er ladies' lips who straight on kisses dream,

say with Perdita:

| PAUSE AFTER | | O Proserpina, |
|---|---|---|
| 4TH SYLLABLE | | For the flowers now \| that frighted thou let'st fall |
| 5TH | ,, | From Dis's waggon: \|\| daffodils |
| 8TH | ,, | That come before the swallow dares \| and take |
| 7TH | ,, | The winds of March with beauty \| |

you will have changed the guiding rhythmic principle from the final stop to the ubiquitous pause.

Instead of reproducing an initial sound "flourished" in its exact counterpart—"nourished" for instance— say with Catherine:

Like the lily
That once was mistress of the field and flourished,
I'll hang my head and PERISH—

you will have changed the principle of rhyme from repetition to echo.

Then the parallel of the ubiquitous pause will be the ubiquitous echo, late rhyme. Its primary function is to produce in rhythmic prose the unifying effect of rhyme without impressing the duality of form upon the listener's consciousness. Therefore it follows the lead of the pause as rhyme followed the lead of the stop. But, from the suppleness of its principle which is not to reproduce but to remind, it can glide in and out through the line to fulfil a variety of subordinate functions rhyme could not even attempt.

As well as to mark the pause it can serve to

counteract its effect, to join together what a strong pause has put asunder :

> I will o'ertake thee, Cleopatra, and
> Weep for my pardon.  So it must be, for now
> All length is TORTure; ‖ since the TORCH is out
> Lie down and stray no farther.

That is, it can serve to construct the blank verse paragraph.

It can extend the impression of reminiscence, unperceived, by following up the primary echo on the pause with a second fainter, in the run of other notes:

> This is an aspic's trail and these fig-LEAVES
> Have slime on them such as the aspic LEAVES
> Upon the CAVES of Nile;

or gliding away from the pause altogether melt into the body of the verse :

> Give me some music, music MOODy FOOD
> Of us that TRADE in love.

Just as the ubiquitous pause has given the liberty of prose to the paragraph, so the ubiquitous echo has washed the stain of rhyme into the texture of the whole.

The combination of these two principles, or rather the application of this double principle with all its manifold possibilities, will be the final result of Shakespeare's efforts through *Romeo* to blend the quintessence of prose and rhyme into the dominant blank verse.  This form proves the highest from the

dramatic point of view, because it throws each word
important psychologically into relief, the ubiquitous
pause giving the full value in position and the echo
the full sensuous value in sound.

Out of these two principles and these two principles alone, combined in obedience to this higher
law, will arise the supreme harmony of the drama:
Romeo's soliloquy over the body of his love.

The whole MEDITATION is a monody upon the
theme: This is the last of earth, and the response:
This is the first of death. The problem is to interchange the wail and counterwail of "last" and "death."
All the art will be to let the rhythm fall and swell under
the words, and on the rhythm to modulate the echo.

The key-note struck in

> O my love, my wife,
> *Death* that hath sucked the honey of thy breath
> Hath had no power yet upon thy beauty,

sounding again in

> Ah, dear Juliet,
> Why art thou yet so fair?...

after " here, here will I remain," will rise with " last "
into a free and echoed ode:

| SYLLABLES | | ECHOES |
|---|---|---|
| —12 | O, here will I set up my everlasting rest, | —REST |
| —10 | And shake the yoke of inauspicious stars | —STARS |
| — 6 | From this world-wearied flesh. | —FLESH |
| — 4 | Eyes, look your last! | —LAST |
| — 6 | Arms, take your last embrace! | —EMBRACE |
| — 8 | And lips, O you the doors of breath, | —BREATH |
| — 6 | Seal with a righteous kiss | —KISS |
| —10 | A dateless bargain to engrossing death! | —DEATH |

All distinctions of form have melted into one. All type, all pattern is forgotten in the one question of how the wave that rose in " everlasting rest " shall break on " death." The whole strain opening and closing like a great accordion, drawn out to twelve without a stop and coming down to four, drawn out once more, closed and drawn out again, obeys no rule except that on each pause the echo of a pause before shall ring. The vowel of "rest" will faint into a softer sibilant in " flesh," " flesh " in its turn be muted into " breath"; then when the sound is nearly lost, to close the whole, "breath" is caught up as conscious rhyme to "death." Again, in the cross-echoes of the intervening lines, the natural note of *e* the vowel of "rest" will change to *ă*, its flat, with softened sibilant in "stars," to sound again, mingled with "rest," in "Eyes, look your *last*." Again, the under-echo of "embrace " will hiss, though with a different vowel, in " kiss." Under the play of the great waves, under the rush and backwash of the pausal echoes, add the bubblings and boilings of explosive sound, the flow and ebb of " *shake* the *yoke* " and " ever*last*ing *rest*." And, under all, the *s*'s through " engrossing," " righteous," " dateless," " inauspicious " lap on in a low monotony. And out of the arrangement of the echoes will arise the construction of the ode. After each pause in sense, echo will come, not to annul the silence, but to carry on the broken strain. When the tired thought has fallen upon "world-wearied flesh," the transition to " Eyes, look your last " will be in the reminiscence of " ever*last*ing *rest*."

The combination of these two principles in verse forms the counterpart of the dying fall in music, which comes o'er the ear "like the sweet south that breathes upon a bank of violets, *stealing* and *giving* odour." When the wind blows over the bed it comes laden with the scent of other blooms, transfuses it into the flowers in passing and again wafts on their perfume to the next. So the wind of rhythm pauses, rich with music, upon echo, sends through its soul the gathered wealth of sound and in return absorbs its sweetness for the coming rhyme.

This free rhythm borne up on echo is not blank verse, is not prose, is not rhyme. All rivalry of forms has been subdued to give the single word its full psychological effect. Now it will be seen how the free pause allows the meaning of the word to be placed in relief, while the echo allows its sound to be prepared and remembered. The word or words ("last," "death") through echo will be prepared to stand out on the pause with the value of novelty (since their sound is not consciously recognized), yet radiant with the halo of association. The word standing in flesh and blood upon an eminence, under a thousand different lights, is made to cast around a thousand different shadows, transparent, dark, opaque, that, while they do not reproduce, prepare. Each sound, from the depths of reminiscence, flashes up into the light for the twinkling of a star, and slowly sinks again into the deep, never forgotten yet never consciously remembered. Now the word, while coming upon the consciousness as a novelty, is at the same moment recognized by what Shelley calls the soul within the soul, already reverberant as with "echoes of an antenatal dream."

Here at last the music of the form is drawn from the very heart-strings of the feeling.   Here, in truth, the dyer's hand is subdued to what it works in.

## MEASURE FOR MEASURE AS A CLUE TO SHAKESPEARE'S ATTITUDE TOWARDS PURITANISM

THE great wave of the Renaissance, having spent its force, ebbed slowly back, leaving behind an ever-rising heap of slime. Now that the age of Elizabeth was drawing to its close, its unrestrained liberty of life began to lose itself in excesses. At its best it had, if not encouraged, at least allowed of, a laxity of principle which among the lower minds degenerated into licence. Among a certain class, ever increasing in numbers, the voluptuousness of the Renaissance assumed uglier forms than Sybaritism. Its laugh had turned into a grin, its sparkling glance into a leer, its impulsive passion into deliberate foulness. However judgments might differ as to the moral gravity of the offence, there could be but one opinion on the danger of its practical consequences. Cressida found her counterpart in Mistress Doll; the pleasure of the libertine had to be paid for in disease. Debauch threatened death to the material as well as intellectual vigour of the nation. It called as urgently for a hygienic as for a moral reform.

A change was close at hand. A new generation was being trained up in the sound, if narrow, principles on which society might be re-organised. With the

Puritans, as the apostles of law and order, the ultimate salvation of the country lay. They themselves adopted and, if they came into power, would enforce a system of discipline which, whatever its limitations, would at least deliver England from the abuses that were sapping the life as well as corrupting the moral sense of the nation. Any thoughtful observer might recognize in them the future rulers of England. Shakespeare had too thoroughly entered into the spirit of his time not to be, in a certain sense, ahead of it. Quick as he was to feel the very pulse of Renaissance thought he was equally quick to note all symptoms of decay and signs of coming change.

Idealists might dream of a time in the near future when all the artificial restraints and restrictions of society would be suppressed, a time that should "excel the golden age." The Utopian visionary might say with Gonzalo:

> In the commonwealth I would by contraries
> Execute all things; for no kind of traffic
> Would I admit; no name of magistrate;
> Letters should not be known; riches, poverty,
> And use of service, none; contract, succession,
> Bourn, bound of land, tilth, vineyard, none;
> No use of metal, corn, or wine, or oil;
> No occupation; all men idle, all,
> And women too, but innocent and pure;
> All things in common nature should produce
> Without sweat or endeavour; treason, felony,
> Sword, pike, knife, gun or need of any engine
> Would I not have; but nature should bring forth
> Of its own kind all foison, all abundance,
> To feed my innocent people.
>
> > (*Tempest*, Act II, Sc. I.)

But Shakespeare blows away the bubble with a sigh of impatience.   He well knew that the coming age was more likely to prove the age of iron than the age of gold.   Instead of relaxing the bonds of society its first care would be to draw them closer.   Gonzalo's "commonwealth" might stand for an exact picture "by contraries" of the Puritan Commonwealth.   Such a commonwealth, with all the terms reversed, had Shakespeare represented by anticipation in *Measure for Measure.*

*Measure for Measure* might indeed be looked upon as a precursor of those bold and often hazardous prophecies with which our modern socialistic literature is overrun.   The poet had here undertaken to deliver a message from "the prophetic soul of the wide world dreaming on things to come."   It seems hardly reasonable to doubt that in the corruptions of Vienna "that boil and bubble till they o'errun the stew" Shakespeare meant to depict the licence of London under its most loathsome aspect; that in the ill-judged leniency of the Duke, who actually bids vice prosper—"for we bid this be done When evil days have their permissive pass And not the punishment," he meant to censure the slackness of that morality which could not correct the excesses of its own adherents; finally, that in the sudden exaltation of Angelo to the post of governor he meant to show the passage of supreme power into the hands of the Puritans.   The play may be safely accepted as a forecast of the effects of Puritan rule on England.

What gives it its abiding value is its extremely solid basis.   Shakespeare does not dive at haphazard into the future, he develops the future out of the present. The corruptions described are those he had witnessed with his own eyes in many a flourishing house of ill fame, corruptions to whose actual existence in the present many another passage in his works bears witness; the Puritans brought on the stage are still children of the Renaissance, though in process of transformation; the only respect in which he may be said to have anticipated the course of events is in attributing to the Puritans at this stage a political power that only developed fifty years later. However, it may be that the accession of James I to the English throne (taking the play to have been written about 1603–4) led him to expect a sudden inroad of reforming zeal from Puritanic Scotland. Shakespeare exposes with unsparing severity the corruption of Renaissance life among the frivolous middle classes; he admits, in fact insists upon, the necessity of a reform; he already foresees from what quarter it will come; now the question arises: How far is Puritanism fitted to play the part it seems to be on the point of assuming? how far would it be expedient to entrust it with supreme power? He now examines the validity of its titles to authority. In order to remain just, he takes it on its own ground. Puritanism is studied as much in its effects on its own disciples as on outsiders. Shakespeare, with his usual impartiality, continually changes the touch-stone applied. To get an all-round view of the question, he adopts now the stand-point of the initiated, now that of the unbeliever. He investigates now its effect on the individual, now its effect on society. The different methods employed in this psycho-sociological study all, however, as usual in Shakespeare, lead to the same result.

Puritanism is treated by Shakespeare essentially as a moral discipline, divested of all religious peculiarities. None of its distinctive doctrines, opinions, or dialect, varying from sect to sect, from generation to generation, are insisted upon in *Measure for Measure*. He left its transient aspects to be depicted by the author of *Bartholomew Fair*, he himself was concerned only with its underlying principles. And all its principles, from an ethical point of view, may be summed up in one,—the establishment and maintenance, at any price and under any circumstances, of hard and fast lines of distinction between good and evil, virtue and vice, the saint and the sinner. In this inflexibility, now rising into heroic constancy, now hardening into rigidity, lies its saving strength as well as its fatal weakness. On the one hand it prevents all compromise with sin, on the other it denies all possibility of redemption. The effects of this training on the individual, as displayed in the two main types of mind to which it can appeal, are exemplified on the one hand in Isabella, on the other in Angelo.

Isabella represents Puritanism under its most favourable aspect. Puritanism from the beginning seems to have exercised upon the women of England the same fascination Jansenism, its Continental congener, exercised upon the women of France. Had Isabella been allowed to follow out her self-appointed course she would have developed into an Angélique

Arnauld. All woman's yearning devotion and self-sacrifice, absorbed by passion in Italian Juliet, are absorbed by principle in Isabella. Her intellect delights in vanquishing the difficulties of Puritanic (in the play symbolised as conventual) discipline, her heart delights in offering itself up, unrewarded and unrepulsed, to an unattainable ideal. As St Simeon Stylites exulted in straining the cord of penance round his waist "as tight as he could knot the noose," so Isabella, the young disciple of a young religion, exults in multiplying the restrictions of Puritanic rule. Her very first words strike the key-note of her character, so intense in its moderation, so passionate in its self-control:

ISABELLA. And have you nuns no farther privileges?
NUN.      Are not these large enough?
ISABELLA. Yes, truly; I speak not as desiring more,
          But rather wishing a more strict restraint
          Upon this sisterhood, the votaries of St Clare.

A generation of such women would soon ensure the triumph of Puritanism in England. The chief object of the new discipline was to establish law, and the very mainspring of Isabella's nature is obedience to law, whatever suffering such obedience may imply: "I had rather my brother die by the *law* than that my son should be *unlawfully* born."

This obedience to the external law is only the outward sign of obedience to the moral law within. No considerations of human affection can weigh against principle. Rather than violate the virginal ideal of purity imposed by principle, Isabel will stifle the voice of feeling, sacrifice her brother without a tear: "More than our brother is our chastity"; indeed, at the very thought, inspired principle puts into her mouth the language of the Christian virgins fifteen hundred years before. To repel the attacks of the tempter her voice thrills with the ecstasy of martyrdom:

> Were I under the terms of death
> The impression of keen whips I'd wear as rubies,
> And strip myself to death as to a bed
> That longing have been sick for, ere I'd yield
> My body up to shame.

Contrast this unflinching adherence to principle with the yielding of Isabella's prototype, Cassandra, in the original play, you will have caught the difference in spirit between the Renaissance ideal of mercy to the individual and the Puritanic ideal of obedience to the law. Isabella, for the first time perhaps in English literature, displays the wonderful power of Puritanism in conquering nature, that strength which has become the backbone of the Englishwoman's character, that implicit obedience to the laws of truth and chastity which silences alike the casuistry of conscience and the promptings of passion in Jeanie Deans and Jane Eyre.

And yet has Isabella so completely broken with the tradition of the Renaissance? In truth, this strength of principle had always lain dormant in the Englishwoman's nature. The frankness and fidelity of Chaucer's Dorigen needed little transformation to develop into the Shakespearian heroine, and Shakespeare's women are all Puritans at heart. The latent tendencies of all are simply brought to consciousness in Isabella. She is first cousin, if not sister, to Imogen and Desdemona.

As the highest type of Renaissance woman shares Isabella's austerity of principle, so Isabella shares the other's impulsiveness of emotion. As live water may be seen dashing and dancing along under thin ice, so feeling in Isabella seems always on the point of bursting through the set coldness of Puritanic or conventual reserve. Puritanic principles merely fit over the more delicate impulses of her own nature to shield their purity from harm. Puritanism for her meant no more than a moral discipline; it served simply to protect the feeling it could not repress. When the time comes the husk slips off like the sheath off a catkin, leaving a silken tenderness beneath, soon to blossom out in fragrant, tremulous beauty.

Had Isabella always remained a voluntary prisoner in her convent, wrapt in silent meditation, only peeping out at the world through a grating,—in other words, could she have held fast to her Puritanic principles without bringing them to the test of fact, — the slumbering warmth of her nature could only have been divined from an occasional flash; it would never have burnt through to a steady glow and shone out in its own eventual radiance. But Isabella is brought into contact with real life, and with life in the form her training teaches her to most abhor. She is forced to plead for sin, to become the apologist of human frailty and human passion. The first moral crisis of her life reveals to her the inadequacy of her principles to cope

with problems whose magnitude she had never before
realised. Her icicles of logic, which seemed before
so fair and firm, thaw, dwindle, melt away at the first
warm breath of feeling. Or, to be more just, the
logic of the intellect is transcended by the logic
of emotion. In Isabella, as in most women, the
logic of the intellect moves in extremely narrow
grooves. It had sufficed to regulate her own personal
judgment, opinions and conduct. But a finer intuition
tells her it will no longer apply to the case she has
undertaken to defend. This new need calls forth the
supple logic of emotion, reaching the right solutions
by the wrong means, ignoring all the process of
formal reasoning, yet instinctively working itself out
to a result no formal reasoning could have given.
The struggle between the two and her fruitless efforts
to reconcile them are what confer its half-pathetic,
half-humorous interest on her first interview with
Angelo:

> There is a vice that most I do abhor,
> And most desire should meet the blow of justice;
> For which I would not plead but that I must;
> For which I must not plead but that I am
> At war 'twixt will and will not.

This contention of principle and feeling, at which
she herself seems frightened and abashed, is leading
her into a higher sphere. In Shakespeare's women
feeling always carries principle along with it, not
denying its validity, but extending its application.
Struggle as she will, "a something wild within her
breast, A greater than all knowledge" beats her down:
not love, but charity, the divine Amor. It takes her

back to the gracious mercy, the infinite forgiveness
of the Redeemer:

> Why, all the souls that were were forfeit once,
> And he who best the 'vantage might have took
> Found out the remedy....

From such a height, she may look down with an
indignation, too holy to be scorn, on the petty rules
and regulations of "proud man drest in a little brief
authority" as no better than the gambols of an
"angry ape"

> Playing such fantastic tricks before high heaven
> As make the angels weep.

But what has become of her Puritanism? In her
highest, most heroic burst, her early training has been
not only transcended, but unconsciously condemned.
Contact with real life has thrown her back on
Christianity; before the sorrow and suffering of
humanity, Puritanic morality she had thought so
lofty now seems narrow; its solutions she had thought
so just seem almost flippant. Through Isabella the
Renaissance pays Puritanism a magnanimous tribute,
and takes at the same time a worthy and magnificent
revenge.

Shakespeare is, however, very far from wishing to
prove the inability of Puritanism to retain a firm hold
on its disciples. Over against the complex character
of Isabella he sets the more elementary nature of
Angelo. On him Puritanism has set its distinctive
and ineffaceable seal. We have said that Isabella used
the austerity of Puritanism as a moral discipline for
her own passionate nature; Angelo turns this purely

personal and spiritual discipline into a mechanical drill, to be applied to all minds alike. Puritanic principle, as before said, serves rather as a shell to protect her tenderest feelings from injury ; Angelo, carrying his narrow logic to its extreme consequences, tries to assimilate the creature to the shell, to fossilize the living heart within. Puritanism appealed to Isabella through its superhuman difficulty of application ; it appeals to Angelo, on the contrary, through its extreme simplicity. What acts as a restraint on a passionate heart serves as a support to a cold intellect. Live entirely by the brain, suppress feeling, and Puritanic morality becomes the easiest of all to follow. The only penalty Angelo will have to pay for his complete surrender to Puritanic rule is loss of power, under any circumstances whatsoever, to shake off the habits of mind he has acquired.

The difference in the effect of such a discipline on the superior and on the average mind can only be brought out by contact with reality. Angelo, like Isabella, brings his Puritanism to the test of fact and, to the credit of the strength if not the liberality of his training, preserves its logical integrity much longer. The paradox of the situation requires one Puritan to convert the other[1]. Isabella, forced by her instinct to desert her own tenets, beckons to Angelo to follow her up to the summit she has reached. In their first interview the faith of both is shaken. But the result of the crisis is widely different in the complex and the elementary nature. Feeling is in both cases brought

[1] For a development of the relations between Angelo and Isabella see F. V. Hugo's preface to *Measure for Measure.*

into play, but feeling of a radically different character. Departure from Puritanic morality in Isabella meant return to Christian grace, in Angelo it means return to Nature in its lowest form. As in intellect he has never advanced beyond the logic of the understanding, so in emotion he has never advanced beyond animal desire.

The worst feature of Puritanism now makes its appearance. In its anxiety to keep virtue from being sullied by the least contact with vice, it denies all possibility of the two being combined in one,—consequently all possibility of redemption. A false step, once taken, can never be retrieved. At the first offence, the deserter from its ranks is sentenced to be shot. The words of a modern Puritan exactly express the attitude of Puritanism towards the fallen though still believing sinner: "The breach once made by sin in the human soul is never, in this mortal state, repaired" (Hawthorne: *Scarlet Letter*). The knowledge of this essential rule drives Angelo to despair. After the minute and morbid self-analysis Puritanism, to its own great danger, encouraged, Angelo comes to the conclusion he is but as carrion corrupting in the sun. His conduct has always been governed by abstract principle. No sense of human tenderness can restrain him from taking human life. No artistic awe and respect of beauty can prevent him from desecrating Isabella, for the brutality of his proposal is of a piece with the Vandalism which was later to disgrace for ever Puritanic rule. No feeling for "the pity of it," so strong even in uncivilised Othello, can hold him back from shattering the virginal ideal of purity enshrined in Isabella's soul. That is, no consideration but law can keep him from committing the foulest crimes, and Angelo's inner law, once broken, as it admits of no forgiveness and requires no repentance, practically gives the offender scope for all his desires of lust, murder or revenge. With the words

> I have begun,
> And now I give my sensual race the rein,

Angelo curses his better angel from his side and falls to reprobation. His supposed seduction of Isabella, the initial sin, is followed up in quick succession by breach of promise towards his victim, the judicial murder of Claudio, the lie of direct denial to the Duke and the slander of Mariana. Over and above all, may be added the passive hypocrisy of keeping up appearances. Shakespeare takes pains to show that hypocrisy is not the fundamental vice of Puritanism (a necessary warning to the future author of *Hudibras*), but he foresees that, on account of its intangible, indefinable character, it offers Puritanic severity the only means of compounding with human weakness. To such a compromise has the severe and upright judge been brought, not from the sin of following Nature, but from the iniquity of the training which, by cutting off all hope of pardon, has urged him on from crime to crime. For the training of the Puritans leaves as lasting a mark as the training of the Jesuits, and through his worst excesses Angelo remains a Puritan at heart. His rigidity of virtue has simply turned into rigidity of evil. Milton's Satan is a renegade Puritan.

In Isabella and Angelo Shakespeare not only embodies the two main types of Puritan, but sets forth all the advantages and defects of Puritanic training. He does full justice to its abstract loftiness of principle, to its power of resistance, its strength in warding off evil, its straightforward language, its uncompromising divisions between right and wrong, its freedom from all the sophistries of a more indulgent morality. But his praise is emphatically confined to Puritanism in the abstract. Notice that the common test which neither Isabella nor Angelo can resist is coming into contact with real life. Puritanism has done its part as a training and may still last as an ideal; for practical purposes it must give place to a larger and more liberal morality, on pain of falling below itself. Its worthiest disciples will surpass it, its lower ones disgrace it. Different as its result may seem on Angelo and Isabella, the two studies point to the same conclusion: Puritanism, in its present state, unmodified, is unfit to come into contact with society. To borrow the words of Lamb, "it is an owl that will not bear daylight."

Not only is Puritanism unfit to come into contact with society, but society unfit to come into contact with Puritanism. The rigidity of principle in the one case, the terrible elasticity of conscience in the other, makes all hope of a mutual understanding vain.

True, the moral beauty of Puritanism possesses a certain power of appeal even to the most corrupt. The libertine Lucio, for whom no woman is sacred, seems awed into respect and almost into decency in the presence of Isabella. "He holds her as a thing

enskyed and sainted And to be talked with in sincerity
As with a saint." But her influence is not fully ac-
knowledged, nor its power brought to bear directly
on the little feeling his life has not yet beaten out, till
the wonderful scene where the austerity of Puritanism
has been absorbed by the Christian need of mercy.

Puritanism in its logical form, as written on the
settled visage and expressed through the deliberate
word of Angelo, meets with universal hostility and
derision. Blindly conscious of its isolation, secretly
irritated at the resistance it encounters, Puritanism
strikes at random in the dark, with a nervous obstinacy
significant of weakness rather than of strength.
Angelo's administration commits a series of blunders
grotesque in form, but tragic in result. In its anxiety
to tear away the great social fungus which is eating
into the heart of the tree, it pulls down still sound and
flourishing branches. Repenting offenders, willing to
make good the wrong, are sentenced without reprieve;
hardened sinners, who can plead no excuse beyond
antiquity, escape with admonition. Novices must be
prosecuted with the full rigour of the law; all mercy
and tenderness is reserved for procuresses and profli-
gates. For the first slip, scarcely to be termed a fall,
Juliet must be branded with irretrievable disgrace;
Mrs Overdone, "who has worn her eyes out almost in
the service," will be considered. For an informality
Claudio must lose his head, nay perhaps be conducted
to the scaffold by Pompey promoted to the post of
executioner's assistant. Finally, all unprofessional
licence of the Lucio type may be hidden under the
goodly veil of hypocrisy.

All Shakespeare's irony and indignation are summoned up to expose the inefficacy of Puritanism outside its own circle. Its utter ignorance of the temper of the nation, its utter want of tact and sense in its treatment of abuses,—above all, its presumption and self-sufficiency are what call forth his bitterest attacks. How can the general scheme of *Measure for Measure* be interpreted save as an onslaught on Puritanism, if not as an individual yet as a social force? And does not the dénouement mean the downfall of Puritanic rule, the humbling of Puritanic pride, the restoration of the Renaissance? Angelo's delinquencies are all exposed, his decisions all reversed, he himself dismissed with the mercy which he would not show. Like Shylock he is taught "to know the difference of their spirits"; Puritanic, like Judaic morality, with which it shows many points of contact, is absorbed and taken up into Christianity. The Duke, enlightened by his experience, after carrying Puritan logic to its barbarous conclusion, declares the futility in life and before reason of "Measure still for Measure."

But in the course of fifty years a change was to take place. The spirit of the nation was to change. Puritanism was to settle down into English character, chiefly, as Shakespeare seems to have foreseen, through the agency of women. What had been the exception was to become the rule. When the Puritans actually came into power the body of the people went with them. Puritanic rule was no longer imposed as a penance, but exacted as a right. Those fifty years' transition between the death of Elizabeth and the founding of the Commonwealth wrought a change Shakespeare could not have foreseen. Reality would have given his play just the opposite dénouement.

*Measure for Measure* therefore may stand as the supreme study of Puritanism in its essence, detached from all external accidents; to this psychological study it owes its lasting value; it presents the further interest of a record of the reception Puritanism met with from the Renaissance; it must not be accepted on trust as a prophecy of fact.

# CHAUCER'S ART OF PORTRAITURE

IN the *Canterbury Tales* no individual, isolated portrait is to be found. Chaucer does not paint his personages in miniature; he arranges them in groups, in such a way that each may set off the other. It would be quite a mistake to attempt examining them one by one; they can be properly understood, even as individuals, only by studying their mutual inter-connexions. It is not in this or that trait or gesture that the poet's true forte lies; it is in the management of the whole.

The question of the portrait is therefore very closely connected with that of construction. Taking the word " portrait " in its widest sense, it may even be said that the material and psychological presenta-tion of the personages depends, in the first place, on the structure of the poem. Before proceeding to the portraits themselves it is advisable to examine the frames they have to fill.

Chaucer's intention was that the work, as a whole, should start from a Prologue, in which the author in person would supply the data and furnish the indis-pensable information about the narrators, to move on to an Epilogue, in which he would reappear to mete out to each his due and unravel the threads of

interwoven intrigue. Between starting-point and goal
the course was to run, not in a straight line, but in ever
renewed spirals. The work of inner construction was
to start afresh at each articulation of the poem. These
articulations were to be marked by the narrators'
Prologues, which, to avoid confusion in terms, I should
prefer to call the Interludes. Here, the poet was to
keep more or less in the background, so as to allow
the pilgrims themselves to settle the order of the tales.
Lastly, each of the tales was to set off saliently on the
flat surface of the whole the individuality of a narrator, according as his character was holy or profane,
solemn or laughable, chivalrous or facetious.

Such was Chaucer's plan, as it may be divined
amid deficiencies of execution. It matters little
whether he succeeded or not in everywhere shading
in the outlines he drew; the main point is that he
drew them and drew them with a very firm hand.

In accordance with this general arrangement
Chaucer disposes the materials he has collected for
the construction of his personages. To the three
phases the work repeatedly passes through (Prologue
—Interludes—Tales) correspond three modes of presentation which, taken together, make up the complete
portrait. They are: the portrait by description, the
portrait by dialogue and the portrait by monologue.
The characters are outlined in the Prologue, evolve in
the Interludes, and become fixed in the Tales. Hence
results a quite natural division of the work. In the
general introduction the poet depicts the traits that
never vary, in the interludes he watches for changes
of countenance, marks the gestures, records the tone

of the altercations; lastly, in the tales that are told on the way, he leaves each narrator to reveal the dominant preoccupation of his soul.

This is the pattern of dramatic exposition. By its extent this scheme shows each individual under all aspects: hence it does not call for any sacrifice of complexity; by its distribution it arranges in the same plane all the features of like order, thus allowing of taking in at a glance the physical appearance of all the personages in the Prologue, all their gestures in the Interludes taken together, etc.: hence each detail can be elaborated without detriment to the perspective; by the co-ordination of these divisions it slowly develops each individual, showing first his exterior and only disclosing his soul by degrees: hence continuity of interest is at no time interrupted.

Let us see Chaucer at work. Like a discreet artist, he disappears as much as possible behind his personages. He attempts only to set one over against the other, expecting they will be able to complete each other later. In the Prologue, where he speaks in person, almost the sole duty he reserves for himself is that of describing figure, costume and social rank, because they are things that would be difficult to explain in dialogue:

> Me thinketh it acordant to resoun,
> To telle yow alle the condicioun
> Of eche of hem, so as it semed me,
> And which they weren and of what degre;
> And eek in what array that they were inne.

But already in the necessarily superficial description of the Prologue there is observable a love of both accuracy and fairness—accuracy of detail and fairness of arrangement—which is of good omen for the development. Chaucer here shows an impartiality which must be accounted constant, despite the apparent exaggerations or deficiencies that may be noticed in the sequel. He has only known his personages one day, he tells us, and with his usual tact he takes care not to give us too detailed information concerning them. Only the most general intimations as to their rank, trade or profession, or, if details there be, details that he may have learnt from other sources and that apply to all their peers; nothing but their most salient traits : the Monk's shining face and goggle-eyes, the honeyed lisping of the Frere, the irregular teeth and majestic hips of the Wife of Bath, the pimples that adorn the Summoner's red face, etc. (an exception, however, is the Prioress, whose charms are described at length); nothing but the characteristic feature in dress: the supple boots of the one, the red stockings of the other ; lastly, in regard to their soul, he divulges nothing, save for such scraps of conversation or table talk as he may without unlikelihood have noted. We need not be alarmed by this superficiality : it is merely an artistic device of that delightful pseudo-fogey Chaucer was from first to last. The traits will become more marked, the soul be disclosed, the whole personage evolved, but quite gradually and by a far more ingenious method. So far Chaucer has claimed to be an observer, not a psychologist. At every moment, however, there occur, in the Prologue, touches that foreshow with what ease he will be able to assume another part. It is in his capacity of

dramatic observer that he will reappear in the
Interludes.

Before entering upon the study of these, it is well
to realize of what importance grouping is already
becoming as a means of exposition. It is not inconsiderately that Chaucer has assembled his twenty-nine
pilgrims, nor is it inconsiderately either that he distributes them in sets. He knows the picturesque effect
produced by contrast and juxtaposition of colours; he
knows that, in the jumble, the brilliant embroideries
of the Squire, for example, stand out only on the
dark-green background of his companion and servant
the Yeoman; in the moral sphere, he knows also how
important it is to throw into relief the disinterested-
ness, the courtesy of the Knight and his son on the
simpering, hypocrisy and cupidity of the religious
orders, or, again, to contrast the latter with the
surly and threatening masses of the people. In the
Interludes these large groups will draw together in
conflicts that will make more strikingly conspicuous
the members of which they are composed.

To my mind, it is in these Interludes that Chaucer's
genius is best shown. It is a far more delicate matter
to preserve artistic unity amid the jostling of personages of every sort than to trace out the great motionless divisions of the Prologue. The balance of classes
is upset: it is necessary continually to adjust the
balance between individuals. Each one must develop
while developing his neighbour. So the two which
best complete each other must be brought into contact.
Now, besides that the choice of the complemen-
tary colours is fairly difficult, to this first problem is

superadded that of arranging the groups thus formed. It has been said that Chaucer's art oscillates between the knightly ideal and popular realism. It is certain he means to allot parts about equal to nobles and churls, but, to avoid producing an effect of monotony and set purpose, this general division must always be concealed beneath the multiplicity of special divisions. Chaucer does not call attention directly to conflicts between ideals and classes, but to quarrels between individuals. For it is the only way of restoring, without apparent effort, the equilibrium he seeks.

Although the management of these dialogues is very firm, the consequences that spring from them must seem due to accident. If Chaucer places the Miller's interlude after the Knight's tale it is so as to allow each class to appear in turn, but it must not be suspected that this arrangement is preconceived: it must seem due to that drunken churl's uncivil and unexpected intervention. Similarly, if he wishes to show, beneath the main divisions of classes, the jealousy among the corporations—the hostility between millers and carpenters, between freres and summoners, for example—the occasion for doing so must arise spontaneously out of discussions originating mostly in some remark thrown out at random.

It is of this exceedingly difficult part of his task that Chaucer has acquitted himself with most success. While reducing his own part to that of a disinterested chronicler, causing his personages to act solely through their tones and gestures, he manages to order the complex and swarming throng of the Interludes with the same clearness of exposition,

the same balance of parts as he had applied to the
motionless masses of the Prologue. The body of the
Interludes forms a pendant to the Prologue; the next
requirement is that the body of the tales should form
a pendant to the Interludes. The one shows the
personages at rest, the other in action; the third must
enlighten us concerning their inmost soul.

All the Interludes are not devoted to discussions.
There is more than one Interlude in monologue form
that gives a very savoury foretaste of the Tales. As
far as disclosure of character is concerned, there may
be some hesitation between the Wife of Bath's Prologue and Tale, or rather there need be none. The
one serves only to ratify the other. The connexion
is not always so close, but Chaucer mostly makes the
tale result directly from the discussion, for in the
majority of cases the narrator makes his tale into a
sermon on the text he has most at heart. Thus the
Pardoner, being a miser and consummate rogue, turns
his fine subject into a development of the maxim:
"Radix malorum est cupiditas," and many others
follow his example.

This prepares us not to expect of these profane
narrators, all of them "lewed men" in the province
of psychology, the impartiality, the complexity, the
keenness of perception, the perfect grasp of the master.
With him every personal consideration is subordinated
to the great artistic preoccupation of clearness and
accuracy. But for the extempore tale-tellers, not psychologists by profession, it is not the scientific interest
of analysis or the pleasure of construction that is of
moment. They are subjective beings,—men of action

or of meditation, each with his own preferences,
hatreds, prejudices, which he does not mean to
sacrifice for art's sake.  Each of them wants to make
his discourse bear fruit.  He opens his mouth only to
extol the merits of his particular caste, to declare war
on the surrounding castes, to flatter a friend, to damage
a foe, or simply to enjoy the triumph of a general
ovation.  What interests the Prioress in the story of
Hugh of Lincoln is not the little martyr, but the
opportunity of proclaiming the miracle brought to
pass by faith; one degree lower, what interests the
Miller in the merry amours of the clerk and the
carpenter's wife is not so much the motives that impel
the guilty pair, but, along with the delight of describing an improper situation, the keener pleasure of
irritating the Reeve; what interests the Frere in the
legend of the bailiff carried off to hell by the devil is
neither the bailiff nor the devil as individuals, but the
satisfaction of making the Summoner stand up in his
stirrup and "quake for ire"; inversely what interests
the Summoner in his retort is not the psychology of
the couple that come and rob the Frere, but the
pleasure of retaliation.  So here the portraits will be
designedly overdrawn, stumped, blurred, enlarged,
reduced, or incomplete, according to the narrators'
object.  No portrait inside the series is true in the
same way as the Prologue.  For which there are two
reasons, or rather a double reason.  In the first place,
this artistic defect throws the narrator's individuality
into more salient relief.  The leading traits of the tale
betray the leading traits of his mind; so, too, its
deficiencies point to his mental limitations.  At the

same time, they throw into relief the characteristics
of his adversary. Impelled by such practical motives,
each hits hard and hits true, although he only hits in
a single spot. In the next place, the gaps he leaves
are at once filled in by his neighbour. The result is
that through these exaggerations, *which always com-
pensate each other*, the portraits, without becoming
untrue, acquire a relief that the poet could not, as
an impartial observer, have given them directly. The
Frere and the Summoner are clearly shown in the
Prologue, they are seen still better in the Interlude,
but they are really known only after we have read the
unconscious revelations and reciprocal satires of the
tales they hurl at each other like challenges.

Thus general balance is, in the end, restored.

I think Chaucer's real art is negative rather than
positive. It is not in the direct portrait that it must
be sought, but in the portrait by contrast, by anti-
phrasis, by implication. The art lies less in the
stores he accumulates than in the manner in which
he distributes and condenses them. For, in his eyes,
really rich art is not that which lavishes details, but
that which from a single detail causes light to flash
on all sides. Chaucer has not always a very hand-
some stone in his hands, but he always excels in
cutting it on all its faces, so that there shall be
intercrossing, reverberation, and dazzle of light.

# *ASTROPHEL AND STELLA*

MR SIDNEY LEE, after a comparative study of the sonnet in the various European literatures, undertaken for the purpose of determining with more precision than has yet been done the value of the sonnet in England in the sixteenth century, comes to this conclusion: The great lyric wave of the Renaissance, originating in Italy, after having passed over France, only in the last place reached the English shore, there to spend its dying force. The English sonnet, whose vogue has so far been looked upon as a national movement, would, then, appear to be but an artificial product imported from abroad. By thus refusing to recognize any originality in the English sonnet, Mr Lee, in a great measure if not totally, denies its sincerity. He has not hesitated to draw this inference. It is on this aspect of his theory, in so far as he applies it to a work that is, in a moral point of view, eminently typical of the Renaissance, that I wish to dwell here.

In accordance with this theory, Mr Lee sees in Sidney merely an imitator who writes " under the glamour of Petrarchan idealism, and holds that it is

the function of the 'lyrical kind of songs and sonnets'
to sing 'the praises of the immortal beauty,' and of no
more mundane passion.   Detachment from the realities
of ordinary passion, which comes of much reading
about love in order to write on the subject, is the
central feature of Sidney's sonnets."

The case is more complex than Mr Lee supposes.
I fancy he has confounded Sidney's methods with his
own.   If really he sees nothing else in the verse-novel
which is called *Astrophel and Stella*, this simply proves
that his very extensive reading has dulled his acumen.
If Sidney's sonnets be read, lost amid the endless
string of quatorzains Mr Lee has collected in his two
volumes, the first impression may be that of an artificial work, and it is doubtless the one Mr Lee wished
to produce.   But, on analysis, it fades away.

Every one has seen in the showcases of museums,
ranged shelf above shelf, the lacrymatories of Roman
funerals.   These vessels all look alike.   Each one is
now but a little iridescent clay, whose glaze is tarnish-
ing and chipping.   This reliquary, at present empty,
once held the surplus of a heart overflowing with
sorrowful emotion.   The tears may have evaporated
in the course of ages, but was the suffering that
caused them to flow less intense on that account?
The antiquary sees in each only such and such a
specimen, discovered at such and such a date, at
such and such a place.   But let a Keats one day
stop before the showcase,—there will be called up
before us the whole of the real tragedy of which

this urn is but a token, and thence perhaps he
will deduce one of the most poignant psychological
truths. Mr Lee plays a little too much the part
of the antiquary; without wishing to set up for a
Keats, I would like to show, by a somewhat close
analysis of the work in question, that, beneath the
affectation, the rhetoric and the idealism then fashion-
able, is hidden the story of a soul that suffers, struggles,
gives way, and recovers.

" My flesh and my heart faileth: but God is the
strength of my heart, and my portion for ever." Thus
spake the king of Israel three thousand years ago,
and before and since how many times it has been
repeated, this cry of human weakness which, on the
point of sinking, unable to struggle alone against the
billows, tightly clings to the eternal principles. Such
is the theme of the story that Sidney tells us in
*Astrophel and Stella*, and for the reader whose knowledge of Petrarch is not too deep, there can be no
doubt of the sincerity of its tone. The same feeling
is present, developing under conditions profoundly
modified by the hero's temperament and by the
religious and moral surroundings.

In Sidney's life the sonnets are of quite special
importance, for they enshrine the story of the only
moral trial in his short existence. He is twenty-seven;
he has not yet known love, and has not yet learnt to
know himself. Love will be the tuning-fork that
will test the truth of intonation of all the notes in
his soul. So far his character has remained rather

hazy. He seems to have, in moral matters, that amiable and grave indulgence, not without weakness, of which many a sign is found in Greene, and of which Shakespeare has fixed the type once for all in the character of Troilus. This ductile nature has been fashioned by an education which, in its severe simplicity, foreshadows the rigours of Puritanism and is not very far removed from the education of Milton[1]. While leaving indelible marks on his soul, it has not succeeded in permeating it through and through. It represses the instincts he has in common with the generality of sinners, but does not suppress them. This incongruity is not noticeable in the ordinary circumstances of life: an ordeal will alone bring it to light. The one he is soon to undergo will upset his whole moral being. While at rest, his soul resembled a glass jar full of clarified liquid, with a residue from which will now rise together all the saccharine sweetness and all the impurities.

The story may be recalled in a few words. He has known a child whom he has admired without loving; five years later he meets her again, grown a woman and married to another. The shock of this discovery awakens in him passion and, at the same time, the rebellious tendencies that were slumbering in his nature.

There is a small group of sonnets (Nos. 4, 5, 10, 14, 18, 21) all in the same key, although unequally

[1] For a confirmation of what I assert, see the chapters that Fox Bourne devotes to the child's education in the quiet of the paternal manor of Penshurst. (*Sir P. Sidney, Type of Elizabethan Chivalry.*)

spaced in the series.   These sonnets form the prelude
to the psychological drama.   In them the two great
motives appear, cross and interlace.

It is a dialogue, now respectful, now growing
more heated than it ought, between youth that
clamours for pleasure and reason that refuses it.
Spenser deals with the same situation when he shows
us Guyon, the Knight of Temperance, for a moment
escaping from the tutelage of the Palmer to give
himself up to the seductions of the Bower of Bliss.

Sidney, stung by the reproaches with which his
very sensitive conscience harasses him for having
desired a married woman, weary of contention, utters
a rebellious cry:

> Virtue, alas! now let me take some rest,
> Thou sett'st a bait between my will and wit;
> If vain love have my simple soul opprest,
> Leave what thou likest not, deal not thou with it.

Immediately after his tone changes to the almost
bashful complaint of a child that suffers at being
thwarted and yet dare not claim it is in the right:

> I do confess (pardon a fault confest!)
> My mouth too tender is for thy hard bit.

And Sir Philip, seizing the bit with his teeth,
bolts.  He repeats with jeering inflections in his voice
the ready-made phrases in which Virtue (i.e. his
conscience-keepers) utters its oracles:

> It is most true that eyes are form'd to serve
> The inward light; and that the heav'nly part
> Ought to be king...

. . . . . .

True, that true beauty Virtue is indeed,
Whereof this beauty can be but a shade;

. . . . . .

True, that on earth we are but pilgrims made,
And should in soul up to our country move.

The principles are in the right; all they say is true,
but instinct has just revealed to him a higher truth,
viz. that he must love Stella.

He literally sends Reason about her business:

Reason, in faith, thou art well serv'd, that still
Would'st brabbling be with Sense and Love in me...

. . . . . .

Leave Sense and those which Sense's objects be....

To his friends who want to bring him back into
the path of duty, he replies, in a fit of nervous
irritation:

Alas! have I not pain enough...

. . . . . .

But with your rhubarb words ye must contend
To grieve me worse, in saying that Desire
Doth plunge my well-form'd soul even in the mire
Of sinful thoughts which do in ruin end?

This excitement is too novel a thing to last, and
soon he has a crisis of repentance:

With what sharp checks I in myself am shent,
When into Reason's audit I do go,
And by just 'counts myself a bankrupt know...

. . . . . .

And, which is worse, no good excuse can show,
But that my wealth I have most idly spent....

My youth doth waste, my knowledge brings forth toys;
My wit doth strive those passions to defend
Which for reward spoil it with vain annoys.
I see my course to lose myself doth bend.

But forthwith the hopeless versatility of his character leads him to forget all these truths he has so wisely been repeating to himself. He again turns to his Mentor:

> you say well, my friend....
>
> .    .    .    .    .    .
>
> ...Plato I read for nought but if he tame
> Such coltish years....
>
> .    .    .    .    .    .
>
> For since mad March great promise made of me,
> If now the May of my years must decline,
>   What can be hop'd my harvest-time will be?
> Sure, you say well....
> Now tell me this:
> Hath this world aught so fair as Stella is?

Notice one thing of capital importance for the right apprehension of the drama. This nature, too weak to turn its principles to account, has not the strength to do without them. His early education has made too deep an impression on Sidney to be entirely disowned. The consequence is that, after each rebellious outburst, he is repressed by a power against which there is no fighting. The balloon may try ever so hard to escape to the clouds: a stout cable binds it to the earth.

This becomes still more noticeable when the actual struggle begins, when he has to face not only his own conscience, but the principles of the woman he loves.

Stella, more perspicacious in this respect than Mr Lee, soon discovers that the realities of ordinary passion have a perilous charm for her friend. She

honestly does her best to raise him to the idealism of
Petrarch, but, I am sorry to say, Mr Lee, with very
little success.  There is clashing, from the outset,
between love as understood by Stella and love as
understood by Sidney.  For her it finishes with
platonic friendship; for him it only begins there.
Each time he raises the delicate problem she would
ignore, she invokes the principles they both recognize.
Sidney reminds her that

> The love that binds us to eternal beauties
> Smothers not our love of temporal ones.

He does not succeed in convincing her

> That such a passion free from guilt may be.

She stands firm, despite the inclination his charms
and his assiduity are beginning to awaken in her.
It is the same struggle as that of the Princesse de
Clèves, who gives up a lover of whom she is fond,
in order to remain true to a husband she has never
loved.  She has need of all her virtue, for soon her
admirer's passion becomes disquieting in character.

The struggle shifts to other ground.  It is no
longer a debate between the two opposite feelings in
Sidney's conscience, but between his conscience well
nigh won over by desire and Stella's, as yet untouched.

In order to keep him in the path of virtue, she
has come by the notion of solemnly entrusting him
with the guardianship of her inviolate heart.  It is
the trial *par excellence* of the purity of his love, and
Sidney cannot stand the test.  Though he at first
utters a loud cry of joy

> I, I, O I may say that she is mine,

it ends in a little dissatisfied sigh.  He is irritated
by her granting him his joy *conditionally*: "while
virtuous course I take."  For the moment he submits: "No kings be crowned but they some covenant
make."  The charter weighs heavily on the young
monarch.  He who, somewhere, sets up for an
emulator of Edward IV can do with nothing short
of absolute power.  In the sonnets that next follow
there recurs and then loudly bursts forth the note
heard from the beginning in an undertone.  He has
just been celebrating Stella's beauty, which while it
"draws the heart to love As fast her virtue bends
that love to good"—

> But ah! Desire still cries, Give me some food.

He very well discriminates the two feelings that are
struggling within him; not for a moment does he
confound them, although he sometimes comes very
near doing so: "Desire...thou oft so clings to my
pure love that I One from the other scarcely can
descry."  Often he remonstrates with himself on the
folly of his wishes; he upbraids himself for not being
able to rest content with what Stella is willing to
grant him: "Those looks...That face...That presence
...That hand...Those lips...That skin...Those words...
That voice..."

> That conversation sweet where such high comforts be
>   As, constru'd in true speech, the name of heav'n it bears,
> Makes me in my best thoughts and quiet'st judgment see
>   That in no more but these I might be fully blest.
>   But...

But, Sir Philip Sidney, how fleeting are your best
thoughts.  Turn over the page and you light upon

the famous sonnet to Jealousy, Stella's husband, a
sonnet which ought to dispel all doubt as to the
nature of Sidney's feelings towards Jealousy's wife.

In order to get her love he runs the risk of losing
her friendship. Passion has carried him so far that
he is now ready to stake everything to satisfy his
desire. The ties between them are finedrawn as it
is : by his imprudence he snaps the threads that
sustain this frail spider's web.

One day he finds his friend slumbering without
any suspicion of danger. Great is the temptation to
touch those lips she has so often denied him. He
yields to it. Less fortunate than the kiss that awoke
the beauty with the sleeping heart, this one leads to
the rupture. Stella suddenly roused from her dreams
in the "hushed twilight of platonic shades," starts up,
with flashing eyes and threatening lips, while her too
daring admirer says to her with compunction :

Sweet, it was saucy Love, not humble I.

She forgives him, but from that day onwards she
keeps careful watch over herself. And she does well,
for, as soon as the recollection of the kiss has died
out, Sidney, emboldened by his first success, assails
her again. One evening, when " Night hath clos'd all
in her cloak," when "Twinkling stars love-thoughts
provoke," when "Jealousy itself doth sleep," he draws
closer to her with little insidious words: "Take me
to thee and thee to me." Ever comes the same
reply, affectionate but inexorable: "No, no, no, no,
my Dear, let be."

He has no better success at a meeting she grants
him

> In a grove most rich of shade,
> Where birds wanton music made,
> May, then young, his pied weeds showing.

In these favourable surroundings he makes a last
effort.   She gives him an answer, and it is a final one:

> all love, all faith is meant thee;
> If thou love, my love content thee.
>
> Trust me, while I thee deny,
> In myself the smart I try.
> Tyrant Honour doth thus use thee;
> Stella's self might not refuse thee.
>
> Therefore, dear, this no more move.

Only once more does he " move " it, with the consequence that she dismisses him.   Stella rightly judges
that absence is the only remedy.   After a few attempts
to renew their former intercourse, Sidney, wearied
by her denials, ends by forgetting the woman who, for
two years, was his sweet and helpful comforter, and
allows himself to be bound by new ties.   Desire, the
noisy child that played in his heart, tired with its
own frolics, falls asleep, leaving no other token of
its presence than the weight of remembrance.   For
the last time he turns to Stella in the sonnet

> Stella, since thou of right a princess art,

a respectful summons in which the subject asks his
sovereign to abdicate her power.

Sidney, having attained to the peace of mind he
longed for, looks back on his past life.   How empty

it now seems to him, even at its best,—how unworthy
of an immortal being in the hour of trial. He has
known religion without understanding it; he has
known right principles without caring for them. Did
he not forsake them at the first ordeal? He has
come out of the trial safe and sound, but not victorious.
Upon the intoxication of desire and defiance follows
a crisis of repentance, a true crisis this time—the
severest he had to go through. When he recovers
from it, he is filled with pitiless contempt for the
passions that lowered him and a yearning with all
his soul for the eternal truths he has disregarded.
Enraged, he turns on desire, to which he has sacrificed
two of the best years of his youth. For him desire
has been but the "delightful source fruitful in woe"
of Polyeucte. He would never have known all the
ignoble instincts of his nature if they had not been
called forth by this single passion, the "bond of all
evils." It is this passion that forced him to fathom
the depths of his soul, that revealed to him his hidden,
unsuspected weaknesses, and it is because it has
humbled him in his self-conceit, far more than because
it has wounded his heart, that he pursues it with such
intense hatred. His only consolation is that he recovered himself in time. His remorse, however cruel
it may be, has none of the poignant bitterness of
Shakespeare's cry after the fall. It is in vain that
Desire has sought his ruin; Virtue has come to his
succour and will now teach him to find his bliss,
not in earthly delights, but in the treasures of his
immortal soul.

But on renouncing desire, he at the same time

renounces love.   Why?   Because, for Sidney, the
two feelings, after the struggle, have become one.
Feeling the impossibility of ever making sensual love
and intellectual love agree, he determines to banish
both from his heart, leaving in it only eternal love.
He waves away all earthly passions, whether pure
or corrupt, to raise his eyes towards Heaven which
has now indeed become for ever his "country."

> Leave me, O love which reachest but to dust !...
> .     .     .     .     .     .     .
> Eternal Love, maintain thy life in me.

With this contrast *Astrophel and Stella* ends.
Sidney has reached quiet, not harmony.   The discord
is transposed, but there is no resolution.

Two centuries earlier another had had to face
the same problem.   Another while yet a child, had
loved a child to whom he was never to be united.
After she had been taken from him, he had continued
to worship her from afar till the day when, weary of
waiting, he married another, while at the same time
he remained true to the memory of his first love.

But, along with circumstances that are alike, what
a profound difference there is in feeling !  Love, which,
for Sidney, is an essentially discordant feeling, because
it continually clashes with the noble aspirations of his
nature, in the other becomes the harmonizing principle
that makes all the faculties of his being vibrate in
unison.

" Nine times since my birth," he tells us, " had the
heavens of light performed their revolution, when for

the first time there appeared before mine eyes the glorious Lady of my thoughts,—she whom some have named Beatrice....At that moment I may truly say that the vital Spirit, which hath its dwelling in the heart's most secret chamber, began to tremble so violently that I felt pulsations run through all the arteries of my body, and I had not left off trembling when my spirit said unto me: 'Here is a deity more powerful than I, that cometh to rule over me.' At that moment the animate Spirit, which dwelleth in that lofty chamber whither all the senses send their perceptions, was filled with wonder, and, speaking more especially to the Spirits of the eyes, said unto them: 'Your bliss hath been revealed to you.' At that moment the natural Spirit...began to weep, and weeping groaned: 'Woe is me! what torments I shall henceforth endure.'"

This love, which is at once of the heart, of the mind and of the body, is so complete that it keeps them all in harmony. Never in Dante does there arise any conflict between passion and duty, because for him duty and passion are one. "When she passes by," he says of Beatrice, "the love she inspires sends a mortal tremor through corrupt hearts, killing every impure thought in them. All who meet the brightness of her gaze are either ennobled by it, or else die under it." For him mortal love is not the opposite of divine love: it is only the beginning of it.

It will be felt how far Sidney is from this conception of love—no longer degrading desire, but an infallible guide, since childhood, to eternal bliss. He is able, by turns, to get the better of one or other of the two opposite feelings; never does he succeed in combining these discords in masterly polyphony.

In Sidney there is already perceptible that contrast between the love of earthly things and the love of heavenly things which will form the very basis of Puritanism.  Angelo in all sincerity believed in it; like Angelo, Sidney found it impossible to live up to the ideal; like Angelo, too, he fell.  In falling he repudiated his principles, and in rising again he had to repudiate his feelings.

In essence, it is the story of David over again.

Would it occur to Mr Lee to try to prove that the Psalms are idealistic confessions, detached from the realities of ordinary passion?  It was not very judicious to head the complete edition of the sonnets with such a fanciful legend: the mere reading of them is its refutation.

# THREE OF SHAKESPEARE'S
## *SONNETS* (59, 60, 61)

IN these three sonnets it is possible to distinguish pretty clearly the three *leitmotive* which, now salient, now veiled, give unity to the whole series. The feeling of the poet for "the master-mistress of his passion" passes again and again through three main phases. First there is the prostration before the idol, the absorption of his own individuality into that of the beloved one. Next comes the candid joy, without egotism and almost without personal pride, of having within himself the power of defying Death that may part them, of embalming the memory of their friendship in immortal verse. Lastly, and it is torture more cruel than happiness is intense, there is the doubt whether his love is returned—a doubt which will soon change into intolerable certainty.

### I.

If there be nothing new, but that which is
Hath been before, how are our brains beguil'd,
Which, labouring for invention, bear amiss
The second burden of a former child!

> O, that record could with a backward look,
> Even of five hundred courses of the sun,
> Show me your image in some antique book,
> Since mind at first in character was done!
> That I might see what the old world could say
> To this composed wonder of your frame;
> Whether we are mended, or whether better they,
> Or whether revolution be the same.
>     O, sure I am, the wits of former days
>     To subjects worse have given admiring praise.

Just as Mme. de Staël was "haunted by the fancy that Jesus Christ was everywhere to be seen," so the poet labours under the delusion that he can everywhere see the face of the beloved one. In many a passage he expresses the surprise every soul feels, after having discovered its ideal, to find it again in ideals already known. He asks his friend

> What is your substance, whereof are you made,
> That millions of strange shadows on you tend?
> Since every one hath, every one, one shade,
> And you, but one, can every shadow lend.
> Describe Adonis, and the counterfeit
> Is poorly imitated after you;
> On Helen's cheek all art of beauty set,
> And you in Grecian tires are painted new.
>                                   (*Sonnet* 53.)

The persistent repetition of this phenomenon awakens a fear in him. May not this being that he believed to be unique have had a prior existence in the person of an ancestor? Remember that these sonnets were probably addressed to a nobleman of ancient family, in whom a traditional resemblance had perhaps been perpetuated. If he may really be identified with

William Herbert, Earl of Pembroke, the second
quatrain would admit of a historical interpretation,
for the Herberts claimed descent from Herbertus
Camerarius, a companion in arms of William the
Conqueror, *five hundred years* before the time at
which Shakespeare wrote[1]. Be that as it may, the
poet seeks in history for the resemblance he suspects:

> When in the chronicle of wasted time
> I see descriptions of the fairest wights,
> And beauty making beautiful old rhyme
> In praise of ladies dead and lovely knights,
> Then, in the blazon of sweet beauty's best,
> Of hand, of foot, of lip, of eye, of brow,
> I see their antique pen would have express'd
> Even such a beauty as you master now.
>
> (*Sonnet* 106.)

Now arises the question whether in the evolution of
ages the ideal has not altered. But in which direction?
He does not hesitate an instant. Never has poet or
chronicler found a subject equal in beauty to the
beloved one.

### 2.

> Like as the waves make towards the pebbled shore,
> So do our minutes hasten to their end;
> Each changing place with that which goes before,
> In sequent toil all forwards do contend.
> Nativity, once in the main of light,
> Crawls to maturity, wherewith being crown'd,
> Crooked eclipses 'gainst his glory fight,
> And Time that gave doth now his gift confound.

[1] See *Dictionary of National Biography.*

Time doth transfix the flourish[1] set on youth
And delves the parallels in beauty's brow,
Feeds on the rarities of nature's truth,
And nothing stands but for his scythe to mow:
  And yet to times in hope my verse shall stand,
  Praising thy worth, despite his cruel hand.

But does his friend return his love? For a moment he tries to believe so. Soon, however, he recognizes the sad truth. At the very time when he is taxing his ingenuity to pay every honour to this being he worships, he is inwardly convinced that his friend is deceiving him with the woman he loves.

### 3.

Is it thy will thy image should keep open
My heavy eyelids to the weary night?
Dost thou desire my slumbers should be broken,
While shadows like to thee do mock my sight?
Is it thy spirit that thou send'st from thee,
So far from home into my deeds to pry,
To find out shames and idle hours in me,
The scope and tenour of thy jealousy?

---

[1] According to Blades (*Shakespeare and Typography*) Shakespeare was for two years a professional typographer. This ingenious hypothesis would explain the technical precision of the two lines:

    Time doth transfix the *flourish* set on youth
    And delves the *parallels* in beauty's brow.

"Flourish" would thus be used with reference to the ornamental figure that serves as a heading to a page. "Parallels" would imply the comparison of the wrinkles that furrow the brow to one of the marks of reference used by printers.

O no! thy love, though much, is not so great:
It is my love that keeps mine eye awake;
Mine own true love that doth my rest defeat,
To play the watchman ever for thy sake:
  For thee watch I whilst thou dost wake elsewhere,
  From me far off, with others all too near.

## A PARALLEL BETWEEN
## BEN JONSON AND SHAKESPEARE

THESE were two radically different natures whom circumstances brought together in the carrying out of a common work, where they had to correct and complete each other.

There have been few minds better balanced, in the ordinary acceptation of the word, than Jonson's. In this sense, balance means constant equilibrium between the moral and the intellectual qualities, an equilibrium whose very constancy suppresses the disturbing element of emotion. This definition applies to Jonson, a cold and rational nature, in whom emotion hardly appears in any form other than anger, and folly scarcely in any shape but that of almost incredible personal susceptibility. Leaving aside shortcomings due to irritation or wounded pride, there are few beings whose psychology is less disconcerting. He was a man of robust, almost brutal health, for which he had to pay the ransom. He was really not morbid enough. He knew neither great dangers nor great ecstasies. Through having escaped disease, he lacked sensitiveness; through having escaped delirium, he lacked enthusiasm; through having escaped madness, he lacked that acute penetration which it brings as a compensation. The crises of over-excitement are the most powerful motor-springs of normal life. Now, there is no trace of any moral crisis, either in the life or in the work of Jonson. This lack of vibration always prevented him from developing in the highest degree even the healthy and solid qualities with which he was endowed. In him intellect is the master faculty : so he venerates, above all things, reason ; on the other hand, he is almost totally deficient in emotion : so it is not before reason reasoning and acting that he bows down, but before reason established, consecrated by tradition. Hence his respect for existing things and for the rules that make them such. His conscience warns him of the slightest breach of the rules he recognizes ; his will-power gives him the strength to observe them himself ; his logic enables him to apply and extend them. His conscience does not strive after hyper-refinement, and consequently never falls into the hesitations of scepticism or the hair-splitting of casuistry ; his will never stiffens for too great an effort, and therefore never wavers in the tasks it undertakes ; his logic never carries its conclusions too far, and accordingly never allows itself to be perplexed by the contradictions of dialectic. Conscience, will, logic always keep on good terms, and on this tripod he poises himself. Thus he is able to attain a definitive result—a thing too rare not to awaken admiration and respect. He rejoices at it with naïve satisfaction poisoned by no misgivings as to the value of this result. Not the qualities of bellicose strength were lacking in him, but those of humility, sympathy, submissiveness—divine weaknesses which have regenerated the world. Liberality therefore, and along with it true moral vitality, was wanting in Jonson. There is not in him the stuff of a very great artist, but there is that of a good burgher and of a perfect gentleman. He conceives of his literary mission with the straightforwardness and assurance of a burgher, and fulfils it with the scrupulous probity of a gentleman.

It is not in this sense that Shakespeare's could be called a "well-balanced" mind. But let us cease to make use of this term in its current, common, worldly acceptation. When thus understood, it applies only to man in his relation to society. It expresses only in a very imperfect fashion the co-ordination of the qualities that make up the complete individual. There is no manifestation of human activity but what plays a useful part in the formation of the individual soul. Morbidity is as indispensable as health, delirium as necessary as sanity. The best-balanced soul, in this sense, is that which best knows how to counterpoise reason by folly, optimism by misanthropy, and so on. The ideal would be to incline in no direction. As far as is humanly possible, this is what is found in Shakespeare's soul. To attempt defining it is labour lost, for definition involves restriction, and as soon as, basing upon some passage in his work, an endeavour is made to settle the bounds of his nature, it is thwarted by the recollection of an opposite passage. Only one general remark can be made: to wit, that the impelling force of his nature is not intellect, but emotion—emotion comprehensive enough to absorb

all mental and moral qualities. The suppleness of
this emotion proves how fallacious are the usual
distinctions of psychology. It has enough consistency
to take the imprint of every influence; it is too ductile
to retain the stamp of any. His soul is like a pool
of mercury which becomes disaggregated with the
slightest motion and whose floating fragments unite
again when at rest. He seems able to pass through
all the phases of feeling without allowing any one
phase to be perturbed by the memory of another; he
describes and frequently takes pleasure in juxtaposing
libertinism, voluptuousness, chaste love, virginal freedom from passion, without allowing the colours of one
emotion to run into those of another, without making
licentiousness seem less brutal, or ecstasy less passionate, or the union of souls less pure, or isolation less
peaceful. He reaches almost unheard-of paradoxes
of feeling. His versatility of emotion is unexampled.
Mere friendship sets in vibration in his breast all the
chords of love. For a single being he exhausts all
the varieties of sentiment. He addresses his friend
now in a tone of paternal protection, now with almost
religious fervour, now with the confidence of a humble
and fearful mistress, now with the passion of a lover
for his lady. In none of his dramas has he made
a study whose psychological wealth equals that of the
*Sonnets*, for he never had to analyze a soul whose
complexity could vie with his own. Nothing gives
fuller insight into that suppleness of emotion which
forms the very basis of his nature. From it he
derived all it is able to give: sympathy, penetration,
tolerance, liberality, and also a certain amount of

unconstraint, some distrust of tradition, and not a little contempt for externals: in a word, a royal indifference to all rules save those of psychological truth. All qualities compatible with suppleness he had, but there are some, after all, which it precludes. Owing to its very nature, it has to forgo constancy, absolutely direct action, implicit self-reliance, unhesitating firmness, very close logical reasoning, and the support of established rules. These are appreciable advantages, which Shakespeare was better able to dispense with than any one else, but of which every human being must feel the need. It is in this especially that he differs from Jonson. He who can do most cannot always do least, despite the saying. He had all the superior qualities that go to make up the perfect individual ; he was deficient in a few of the elementary ones which bring these personal perfections to bear directly upon the consciousness of others. He did not take his mission to heart, as did Jonson; he fulfilled it with more nonchalance and without making as much noise about his name: he therefore did not attain as definitive a result or, at any rate, as evident a one, and he certainly exercised a historical influence very appreciably inferior to that of his rival.

This mission was, in essence, the same for both.

In the drama there are two essential factors: the living substance, which is psychology, and the art of presentation, which is technique. Everything else— imagination, fancy, lyricism, etc.—must be subordinated to these two fundamental necessities. Jonson and Shakespeare early understood this fundamental rule of the art.

To be just, they invented it. At the time when they began their stage career they found in the repertory of the sixteenth century a great variety of forms, a profusion of sketches, of rough draughts, of half-developed ideas, which both of them put under contribution, and a style already supple with practice—clear, fluent and, at times, sonorous and memorable. Literary qualities were not what it lacked : they could not be wanting in men like Kyd or Marlowe. But what must strike any one perusing, however superficially, the pieces representative of the time, is the deficiency of dramatic feeling they all betray. The drama has not yet taken shape as a form by itself. It proceeds from the mysteries and moralities of the Middle Ages. It has not yet managed to harmonize the incongruities it owes to its origin, in order to transform them into means of action or psychological motives. Despite its brilliant qualities of rhetoric and, in some cases, of pure poetry, it has thus far never succeeded in creating living beings, or even in acquiring the technical skill that would render the creation of living beings possible. The personages are too isolated ; they do not directly react on one another, and the interdependence of their actions is not made clear to the public. [Notice, for instance, the stiffness of the comic dialogues in *Damon and Pythias*; the unskilful interposition of the Vice in *Appius and Virginia*; the weak management of the scenes between the taxgatherer and the insurgents in *Jack Straw* ; the total lack of communion between Andrea and Bell' Imperia, the two so-called passionate lovers in *Hieronimo*. The same remark applies to a scene of far greater poetic scope: the death of Zenocrate in *Tamburlaine*.] Logic is lacking in their interconnexion; relief is therefore wanting in their presentment. Lack of psychology and lack of technique are, in reality, two sides of the selfsame defect.

The two knights who came riding towards each other could not agree as to the nature of the shield of which each saw but one side. It is against one and the same defect that Jonson and Shakespeare do battle, but it is not seen by the one under the same aspect as by the other. Jonson, like a good old pedant respectful of tradition, relying on his reading and proud of his science, attributes the dramatic weakness of the sixteenth-century stage to the neglect of certain rules consecrated by antiquity. The psychological instinct of Shakespeare—for it is an instinct like hunger and thirst—warns him that the more serious vice, to which, in a great measure, are due these external defects, is insufficient knowledge of the human soul.

How is this to be remedied?

Jonson—a scholar—looks back to the theatre of classical antiquity; Shakespeare, without paying much attention to Terence, casts his eyes about on his immediate surroundings. Authority imposes on the one what personal reflection suggests to the other. The starting-point of every reform must be the observation of real life. Jonson and Shakespeare seem to have made up their minds on this point. It is interesting to compare their declarations.

As might be expected, it is especially Jonson who is the propagandist. In the Prologue to his first comedy, *Every Man in his Humour*, he sounds the charge against the unlikelihoods, the impossible turns of fortune, the loosely-knit intrigues of the old school. He means to substitute for them a perfectly simple, plain form of comedy, a study of the "humours and manners of the time." With his characteristic vigour and faithfulness he hastens to carry out his project, so that in the Induction to *The Magnetic Lady*, one of his last plays, he was able with legitimate pride to sum up as follows the various stages of his life as a playwright:

" The author, beginning his studies of this kind with *Every Man in his Humour* and, after, *Every Man out of his Humour*, and since continuing in all his plays, especially those of the comic thread, some recent humours still, or manners of men, that went along with the times; finding himself now near the close or shutting up of his circle, hath fancied to himself in idea this Magnetic Mistress....And this he hath called *Humours Reconciled*."

Shakespeare's words are equally explicit:

"O'erstep not the modesty of nature; for anything so overdone is from the purpose of playing, whose end, both at the first and now, was and is, to hold, as 't were, the mirror up to nature; to show virtue her own feature, scorn her own image, and the very age and body of the time his form and pressure." (*Hamlet*, Act III, Sc. 2.)

These definitions resemble each other, but are not identical. To " study the humours and manners of the time" does not mean to " hold the mirror up to nature." Here again, there are two sides to the observation of life, one of which is called reality, and the other nature.

The latter is only reached *viâ* the former. Jonson starts from the direct observation of reality. But it is not in and for itself that he studies it. He only adopts it because it seems to him the sole satisfactory basis for drama. Before examining how he conceives of realism, the question must be asked to what purpose he subordinates it.

What Jonson condemns in the plays of his predecessors is the almost total lack of adaptation to the spectator. His dream is to establish direct communication between the actor and the public. "That is the most unlucky scene in a play which needs an interpreter." (Induction to *Magnetic Lady*.) His ideal is to get *snap-shot* effects.

This is the true principle that guides him in his observation of reality. He copies what he sees around him with absolute conscientiousness and fidelity. But he does not reproduce at random all he sees. He makes a strict choice from amid reality. What he seeks are striking traits, telling speeches. He fixes his attention on the most characteristic words and deeds only. In a certain man he notices a certain trait, a certain tendency, a certain defect, which he seizes and magnifies, eliminating every other element. He takes an interest only in the manias men are slaves to. This system leads him straight to the theory of "humours."

> For when some one peculiar quality
> Doth so possess a man, that it doth draw
> All his affects, his spirits and his powers
> In their confluxions, all to run one way
> This may be truly said to be a humour.
>
> (Prologue to *Every Man out of his Humour.*)

It is his playwright's instinct, strengthened by reasoning and reflection, which drives him to these all too simple conceptions, against which the psychologists of our days rebel—they who are fond of minute and complicated analyses. Jonson does not even claim to seek for psychological truth. The characters for him are not objects in and for themselves; they are means of action. The spectator must be able to recognize each one of them by means of a distinctive sign: an absorbing vice—avarice (Volpone); a dominant passion—the love of luxury and pleasure (Sir Epicure Mammon); a dialect (the witch in *The Sad Shepherd*); a professional jargon (Knockem, the horse-dealer in *Bartholomew Fair*), etc. Each of them is required to have a certain amount of summary, vigorously outlined individuality, serving to differentiate them one from the other, but that is all. That the spectator should be able to bear them all in his memory and that he should soon have become so familiar with them as to be able to foresee the action they are about to perform, the saying they are about to utter: such is Jonson's ideal. He does not allow them freedom of action, of development, of evolution. On the contrary, they have to remain stationary, to take the crease they are given, and not to ask to change. Not only does he simplify them: he congeals them.

For he wants them to form part, either as supports or as ornaments, of a vast architectural design which the slightest motion would upset. Grave or grotesque, they will never be anything for him but caryatids. This over-docile disciple of antiquity takes in its most literal sense Aristotle's aphorism: "In the drama action takes precedence of everything else." Action, for Jonson, means the skilful arrangement of facts, an operation altogether independent of the development of characters. This dove-tailing business gives his essentially logical mind more satisfaction than would the study of the inconsistencies and abrupt changes of the human soul. Making eight intrigues turn around a single pivot (*The Alchemist*) is a *tour de force* that gives him deeper joy than the creation of one complete living being. By his overwhelming will-power he suppresses in his personages every tendency to independent action, and to every objection that may be raised he can be heard answering:

"Interrupt not the thread or series of the argument. A good play is like a skein of silk which, if you take by the right end, you may wind off at pleasure on the card of your discourse; but if you light upon the wrong end you will pull all into a knot or elf-lock which nothing but the shears or a candle can undo or separate." (Induction to *Magnetic Lady*.)

So, in order to wind off satisfactorily the skein of action, Jonson does not hesitate to entangle in inextricable knots the psychological motives of his characters. There comes a time when, without his realizing such to be the case, his logic dulls his conscience. Jonson is very faithfully and very scrupulously a realist, but he subjects the materials furnished him by reality to a logical treatment which distorts their true purport. Unconsciously, he veers away from his first conception. If he is not aware of

the fact it is because his realism puts him on the wrong
scent. The sayings of his personages are mostly taken
from real life, but their actions he adapts to the needs
of construction. Words and deeds are very markedly
at variance in all Jonson's more developed characters.
The speeches of the braggart in the *Alchemist* are,
no doubt, copied from a living model, but why does
this "angry boy," who has no other word in his mouth
but that of "honour," wish to force his sister to prosti-
tute herself to a stranger? It does not appear that
Jonson intended this as a study of hypocrisy; nothing
explains this singular contradiction but the needs of
his plan. In the grave characters this defect is all
the more conspicuous because no superficial realism
of speech any longer deceives as to the lack of
fundamental truth. Corvino is exhibited, mad with
jealousy, picking a quarrel with his wife on a baseless
suspicion; a moment later he is seen, without scruple
and without reason, without even the allurement of
sure reward, itching to offer her to Volpone. All
psychological paradoxes are possible, but sudden and
groundless volte-faces are not.

Something of this defect is noticeable even in his
style. Dramatic appropriateness, beyond a certain
point, he lacks. He is like a captive balloon that
can rise to a fixed height only. Jonson, it is true,
admirably reproduces the Puritans' phraseology, and
we know what pains he took to learn the dialect
of the North-country peasants, before putting them
on the stage. But he makes his serious personages
speak in a uniform fashion. Volpone and Sir Epicure
Mammon express themselves in similar terms. It

is not Jonson who could imagine or would even be able to understand the difference between the ample and grandiose imagination of Othello and the mean, despicable and really ignoble and depraved metaphors of Leontes. This lack of delicacy in perception sometimes leads to his making very serious blunders. I spoke of the disagreement between the words and deeds of his characters. In the more or less lyric passages of his plays a similar disagreement may be observed between the sense and the sound of the words. Sir Epicure Mammon dreams of the splendours the philosopher's stone is to bring him:

> My meat shall all come in Indian shells,
> Dishes of agate, set in gold and studded
> With emeralds, sapphires, hyacinths and rubies....

and then, all at once:

> My foot-boy shall eat pheasants, calvered salmons,
> Knots, godwits, lampreys: I myself will have
> The beards of barbels served instead of salads....

Against the impression here produced it is superfluous to argue. Merely with regard to sound, the ring of these words is not true. And, to realize fully that such is the case, it will suffice to call to mind an analogous scene in *Dr Faustus*. Marlowe does not pride himself on realism, but his psychological imagination enables him to enter into the high-wrought feelings of his hero, and his lines are thrilled with the flutter and tremor of Faust in ecstasy at the vision

> of women, or unwedded maids,
> Shadowing more beauty in their airy brows
> Than have the white breasts of the queen of love.

The worst of it is that this defect, everywhere

patent, turns back upon Jonson, even in that science of construction to which he has sacrificed everything. The intrigues he elaborates with such close and pains-taking logic have no kind of basis. The building is usually impeccable in workmanship, but every moment threatens to collapse: the ground on which it is built is of too loose a consistency. It may be granted Jonson that his *Silent Woman* is a positively faultless masterpiece of construction, but it rests on nothing. Even Dryden, the most fervent of his admirers, was much perplexed as to how to defend the psychological conception of the taciturn Morose, and if this con-ception cannot be justified the play no longer has any *raison d'être.* It is a *tour de force* which consists in balancing an enormous weight on the tip of the little finger. The impression of inevitableness is what is always lacking in Jonson's plays. His much-vaunted construction reminds one of a hurdle-race. It is enjoyable to see the obstacles jumped, but the need for them does not appear very clearly.

Jonson, then, began by observing real life, but did not proceed very far on the way, which was soon closed to him by his logic. What he did take from real life he subjected to intellectual treatment which, while seeking to transform, ended by deforming. Shakespeare made no such ostentatious display of science. He was always less of a fault-finder. He accepted existing forms more good-naturedly. It would even seem that he groped longer than Jonson. At the beginning of his career he seems to have hesitated between the comedy of intrigue (*Comedy*

13—2

*of Errors*), the comedy of wit (*Love's Labour's Lost*), and the comedy of fancy (*Midsummer Night's Dream*). His first tendency seems to be diametrically opposed to realism. He at first dreams of giving "to airy nothing A local habitation and a name." But, from *Romeo and Juliet* onwards, that play which is of capital importance for the comprehension of his mind's development, he determines to take psychology as his guide. And having once entered upon this course, he never again allows himself to be diverted from it by external considerations. Carried far enough, it absorbs all Jonson's rules, all Jonson's formulas. In it Shakespeare finds not only the salvation but also the *raison d'être* of the drama.

For Shakespeare's supple soul dramatic form is not in itself an object: it is only a means. He never shows that subservience to the lack of memory, of delicacy of perception, and of feeling on the spectator's part, which Jonson practised till he took the point off psychology. Observe with what insistence, with what energy he opposes any emphasis, any exaggeration of the tragic "to split the ears of the groundlings," any caricature, any exaggeration of the comic "to make the unskilful laugh." Nor is this a mere sally, like the Induction to *Bartholomew Fair*; it is not the outcome of a hooted author's vanity disguising itself in clumsy bits of irony, which are the best proof of Jonson's servility, of his fear of giving offence, of his terror of the public. The comparison of the two scenes would make clearly manifest the difference between the ideal of the one, which is success of the play on the stage, and that of the other, which is psychological truth.

To this fundamental difference of purpose corresponds a fundamental difference of method. Jonson, allowing himself to be guided, in his observation, by stage necessities, seeks in life for exceptional effects only, and when reproducing them hollows and scoops them out yet further. Shakespeare's more catholic, more democratic mind does not set about hunting for the characteristic trait: he receives all impressions without rejecting any.

To keep to the mere observation of reality, Shakespeare will be found to carry the day even in Jonson's own special field. Each of Jonson's personages is, by definition, an incarnation of a particular "humour." Shakespeare is not so parsimonious: each of his realistic characters is made up of five or six different "humours" which hold each other in check, and whose mean must be taken, in order to form a true estimate. Nothing could better demonstrate the complexity of even his most summary creations than comparison with Jonson's.

One of the most living figures Jonson has drawn, one of those that best impress themselves on the mind, is certainly that of the fat pig-woman Ursula in *Bartholomew Fair.* There are few beings with more body, few standing out in stronger relief, few whose physical presence makes itself more distinctly felt. But what a mere daub in comparison with that paradoxical Falstaff, a character as complex as its creator's art! What a caricature, fit for a sign-board, beside that amazing old man, younger at heart than his ward, at once Atlas and Proteus, a quick intellect in a heavy body, stout, fat, brisk, waggish, paternal, a libertine, a coward, a liar, a braggart, a softened sceptic, a moralist at times—here I stop: enumeration only serves to convince one how well nigh impossible it is to find a formula for any one of Shakespeare's characters.

Perhaps it is not fair to Jonson to begin with Falstaff. Let us take a portrait more delicate, more subtle 'than Ursula's could be, the portrait of Lady Politick Would-be ( *Volpone*), the most successful of all his women. She is a typical representative of feminine frivolity; no kind of affectation is lacking in this voluble, giddy, coquettish creature, who thinks herself irresistible and who, out of mere want of judgment, out of sheer vanity, pays assiduous court to the unscrupulous Volpone: the most dangerous of games to play. She is one of Jonson's most complex characters; she is far more than a "humour," for not only has Jonson managed to accumulate in her, more felicitously and lavishly than in any one else, the traits that reveal the dominant passion, but, beneath this frivolity, he has very judiciously shown the fundamental purity of the lady, her evident unconsciousness of the infamy of the part she is playing, and her attachment, notwithstanding, to the home life, manifesting itself by an altogether gratuitous jealousy of her husband.

And yet, despite her complexity, how rudimentary in development Lady Politick Would-be seems in comparison with Shallow. She is an ephemeral being of rapid growth, who does not seem to have had a past, who had no existence before she appears on the stage, who fully exhibits herself within twenty-four

hours, on whose mind past events have left no furrow,
no trace, and future ones will leave none either.
Observe, on the contrary, by what slow gradations the
complete personality of Shallow has been formed;
notice the superposed layers in his nature. This
little, wizened, frivolous and talkative old man has
passed through the most varied experiences before
definitively setting up as justice of the peace. Of yore,
with other jolly fellows as boon-companions,—among
whom Falstaff,—he has heard the chimes at midnight.
Falstaff has left his stamp upon him, as on all whose
education he undertakes to perfect. This frisky little
man has, in his youth, been a pleasure-hunter. He
still smacks his chops at the thought of it, and nothing
can be more curious than to see floating up to the
surface of his learned and edifying conversation recollections of this life long since given up. Lady
Politick Would-be is amusing for a moment, but that
is all; "out of Shallow you may devise matter enough
for the wearing-out of six fashions and laugh without
intervallum."

Let us take one of Jonson's most important
characters, the one on whom rests the whole intrigue
of the *Silent Woman*. Morose is an old man who has
a horror of noise. This is his characteristic—the only
one. It is his sole claim to individuality. He has
broken all the bonds that connect him with ordinary
humanity, in order to cultivate this mania at his ease.
He knows neither human passions nor human preferences; he has lost all feeling of personal dignity (see
the divorce scene); he is not far from having lost all
feeling of honour and ridicule; he allows himself to

be scoffed at, bantered, insulted, without uttering a single complaint. He has but one preoccupation : to avoid noise ; and one sometimes even wonders whether it is sincere, for he is certainly the most garrulous personage conceivable, and the sound of his own voice nowise gives him umbrage.

Let us set over against him the most elementary, the most insignificant of Shakespeare's characters, Shallow's cousin Silence. *He* is the true taciturn one. On ordinary occasions he scarcely opens his mouth; in every dialogue in which he has a share, he merely approves; he retires behind his loquacious cousin, and by glorious Falstaff he is only too happy to be eclipsed. And yet in the depths of this shrivelled-up nature there still slumber some instincts that connect it with the great human nature. Animated by wine, Silence sets about being merry for the fourth time in his life. To show " an old man can do some-what," he begins in tremulous tones to sing drinking songs that bear the same relation to normal pleasure as does his shrill pipe, his falsetto voice, to the ordinary organ of mortals.

And these are but a few examples selected from the vast work of Shakespeare, ever teeming with life. No delineation in full has been attempted ; a few traits only have been singled out amid the incalculable diversity of each character. Moreover, it is as a realist only that Shakespeare has been viewed. In realism pure and simple, a science in which Jonson has specialized, Shakespeare, without apparent effort and without bluster, carries the day on every issue.

However, realism pure and simple hardly exists.

There comes a time when the individuality of the most inveterate realist awakes. No human being, save as a discipline, can be content to remain a mere sensation-machine. Intellect and emotion grow equally impatient of such constraint.

The critical moment comes: that of the awakening of the individuality. Jonson and Shakespeare have thus far proceeded together on the highway of realism, the one picking up the pebbles in the gravel, the other culling the flowers by the road-side, yet fellow-travellers, to all appearance bound for the same destination. But now comes a bifurcation: which road is to be taken?

We have seen the choice Jonson made. Guided by the intellect alone, he forsakes reality to turn towards logic. It is from thence onwards that he wanders from the right course. This fortuitous intervention of logic, external and ungrounded, points to a disdain of reality whose cause Jonson perhaps did not himself fully grasp. It is because, in itself meagre and naked, reality does not satisfy his vigorous mind, that he discards it. I know of no better argument against realism than the attitude of its most sincere and undoubting champion towards it.

Yet there is another solution, which Jonson with his cold temperament could hardly guess at. Shakespeare, guided principally by emotion, divines beneath this reality, which is a stumbling-block to Jonson, an inner and invisible life, wherein reside the deeper causes of those outward effects unexplained and inexplicable by the logic of the intellect. He goes down deeper into the study of realism; instead of turning away from it, he pushes forward his researches. Observation furnishes him with the means of illuminating his path on his exploring tour; with this feeble rushlight he finds his way into the hidden depths of the soul; forthwith the flame he bears is on all sides mirrored back by the stalactites hanging there undreamt of. Shakespeare makes use of realism with more true constancy and fidelity than Jonson, but he never allows himself to be enthralled by appearances, and therefore never feels the need of rebelling against them. It is curious to see how differently the two navigators double this formidable Cape of Storms.

It would be a mistake, however, to view this method of Shakespeare's as an extolling of emotion at the expense of logic. He has by no means renounced logic; he has merely delayed its application. For, by going ever deeper into the study of psychology, Shakespeare discovers in the hidden motives of souls the logic of facts. There comes a time that Jonson never knew: the moment of complete disconnection, the point at which the fruit of the author's invention, fully developed, slowly come to maturity, falls from the tree. His characters live as individuals, independent of their creator's will. They are masters of their own actions, and of the sum of these actions and of the reactions to which they give rise in their neighbours the total Action of the drama is the outcome.

It is relatively easy to build up, considering how very complex the characters are. Upon close inspection, it will be perceived that the true cause of the difficulty Jonson finds in arranging the succession of events lies in his rigorously simple system of "humours." The special character of each individual thus conceived of can only show itself under certain very limited conditions. Volpone, as an individual, has no existence outside of his small circle of flatterers and parasites, but Othello is equally true, equally life-like before the Senate, in the garrison of Cyprus, and in the chamber of Desdemona. It is for Jonson a true labour of Hercules to overcome the difficulties of his self-imposed system. Almost a superhuman effort is required to assemble under one and the same roof Subtle, Face, Doll, Dapper, Drugger, Kestril, Dame Pliant, Sir Epicure Mammon, Surly, Ananias, Tribu-lation Wholesome, and Lovewit. Jonson is almost forced to replace complexity of character by multi-plicity of personages. Whereas Shakespeare's person-ages put out their feelers in all directions. Falstaff can, without unlikelihood or effort, be brought into contact separately or simultaneously with the Prince of Wales, a band of thieves, the justice of peace, the Lord Chief Justice, Doll Tearsheet and Mrs Quickly. Thus the characters are not made to tally with a preconceived intrigue; the action evolves in accordance with natural logic—the only satisfactory kind—by the will of the actors and not by the will of the author.

Shakespeare now only has to collect and group together the scattered impressions, in order to make up the definitive drama. He intervenes personally only to determine the total effect. It is not he who prearranges the actions of Lear or those of Gloucester, but it is he who juxtaposes these two sufferings[1], who

[1] This remark is borrowed from Moulton: *Shakespeare as a Dramatic Artist.*

combines these two stories, so as to form the complete drama of ingratitude. His plays have their unities just as Jonson's have theirs, but, instead of being the unities of time, place and action, they are the unities of psychology, logic and ethics.

Such is the import of the reform accomplished, and in this work it is thus that the individuality of each of the two poets manifested itself. The one starts from the exterior, the other from the interior. Jonson asks himself how the drama is to be built up; Shakespeare asks himself what its purpose is. The one uses his lucid intelligence to apply rules already established, whose wording he understands but whose true signification he does not grasp. The other uses his supple emotion to search for psychological truth, which in his hands spontaneously assumes artistic shape. The one comes to a result precise and definitive, but full of inherent contradictions. The other carries out a reform deep and still, whose principle never varies.

# ADDISON'S HUMOUR:
## ITS MATTER AND ITS FORM

THE word "humour" is one of those fortunate vocables which, while continually changing in meaning, have never passed arbitrarily from one sense to the other. By a phenomenon rare in the history of languages, its development can be reconstituted phase by phase, so that not a single important transition appears to be missing in the series.

*Humour* was, originally, a medical term which corresponds exactly to the French word *humeur*. Having become a metaphor, it acquired figuratively the sense of peculiar disposition of the moral temperament. In consequence of the narrowing process to which are subjected all words when once they have entered into common use, it acquired the meaning, at once more limited and more intense, of a characteristic carried to eccentricity. It is the most decided and uncompromising expression of individuality. This meaning appeared in the sixteenth century and is not yet obsolete. It gained a firm footing in current speech, as its derivatives "humorous" and "humorist" show. Indeed, it corresponds to a still living reality.

"The English are a nation of humorists," says Emerson, and it is quite certain that in no country individuality is in greater esteem than in England. Every mania that dare assert itself is respected. "In all companies each one has too good an opinion of himself to imitate anybody. He hides no defect of his form, features, dress, connexion or birthplace, for he thinks every circumstance belonging to him comes recommended to you. If one of them have bow legs, or a scar, or mark, or a paunch, or a squeaking or a raven voice, he has persuaded himself that there is something modish and becoming in it and that it sits well on him." (*English Traits*, Cockayne.) It is a point of honour with them to uphold their individuality against fashion, against criticism, against satire, against reason itself. They exaggerate their defects for independence' sake. Some time ago, a certain lord accused the Eton schoolboys of having an ungraceful gait; immediately by common consent they began cultivating a peasant slouch; the illustrated papers published photos of it, and every one applauded this trait of national spirit. This might pass for a boyish freak, but it is a tendency which becomes confirmed in the grown man. All the more so, because he prides himself on remaining true to his prejudices. At no price and under no circumstances would he consent to abdicate the personality he has acquired. This grave and dignified humour reaches its apogee in the dialogues of Charlotte Brontë (Rochester and Jane Eyre, Crimsworth and Frances Evans, Mr Emanuel and Lucy Snow), where those who love each other with the strongest and deepest love that has ever been,

those who are frightened neither by physical defects
nor moral faults, those who are repelled neither by
age, nor plainness, nor misconduct, nor poverty, nor
disease, nor infirmity, yet spend the greater part of
their time in abusing each other, in order to better
defend their individuality against the fondness that
seeks to unite them. But, save in these exceptional cases, the humorist is by no means aggressive.
He grants others the liberty he claims on his own
account. When he finds a number of people of his
opinion he founds a club, but no one is obliged to
belong to it. This feeling of mutual tolerance from
the outset limits humour within bounds that should
not be forgotten. It makes humour an innocent
mania, or at least an unrepulsive one, which does not
degenerate into a fixed idea, does not lead to crime,
is not amenable to any tribunal, which at last solves
the great social problem of developing the liberty of
the one without detriment to that of the others.—Such
is the serious humorist as he has existed for centuries,
and the type does not seem likely to disappear soon.
To attain its full development it above all needs tranquillity and isolation. It is a plant that grows in damp
nooks, in the chinks of old creviced walls, too wild to
prosper in the flower-beds of ornamental gardens. It
is not found in hot-houses or floral exhibitions; it
must be sought for in remote country places or in the
blind alleys and still closes lost in the tumult of great
cities. But now imagine our humorist taken away
from his favourite sphere, sent forth into the world,
brought into contact with his fellow-men, induced to
reflect about his individuality, to see it from without,

learning to judge it without therefore renouncing it: a new variety is obtained, of which Falstaff could be taken as the type. The latter, who might be called the conscious humorist, knows reason without in the least recognizing it. It brings home to him his own absurdities; its part extends no further. It throws light on his character without attenuating it. A hardened sinner like merry Jack will take particular pleasure in quizzing it, in defying it. Reason proscribes the abnormal development of personality; so, for his Epicurean palate, humour acquires the zest of forbidden fruit. All those who are in a similar case like him manifest their individuality without fear of ridicule; only, each exaggeration now becomes a conscious infraction of the laws of reason. From a cross between madness and sanity at last springs modern humour.—Those who have, once for all, been convicted of a defect are usually not slow to see it in others. In the light of reason, the whims and manias of his neighbours will stand out before our humorist in strong relief. He judges them as he judges himself. But, if he has any memory, the remembrance of his own weaknesses will always come and stop him in the height of ridicule. Mockery will be balanced by sympathy which, though selfish, is none the less sincere. Justice, at every moment, gives place to mercy. According as the observer allows a larger share to ridicule or to sympathy, he inclines to satire or to pathos. When he balances them, he is not far from the truth.—Such is the state of mind that may give rise to literary humour.

So, it will be seen, humour in literature is no artificial growth. It is the spontaneous reflex of the
national temperament. It always retains something of
its first meaning; accordingly it can exist only in a
country where individuality is greatly encouraged. A
people that is swayed by fashion knows nothing of
humour. That is why humour so readily gained a
footing in Germany and in England, and also why, as
it seems to me, it was so slow to appear in France. To
this condition must be added another, inconsistent with
the first: the knowledge of reason, which suppresses
the errors and excesses of the individual and makes
him conform to an ideal and uniform standard. From
the clashing of the two springs the divine spark.
Humour in literature is nothing but the psychological
study of individual exaggerations, made in a sympathetic spirit, guided and enlightened but not attenuated
by reason. Such is the humour that was, if not
created, at least revived, renewed, reinstated and
definitively established as a literary form by Addison.

Addison had the good fortune to be brought up
apart, outside the general movement of the time. He
was born in the very midst of the Restoration, but, as
a child, escaped the deleterious influences of the great
anti-Puritan reaction. He grew up far from London;
he knew the country before he knew the town, a point
it is essential to note. The grandson and son of a
clergyman, he was himself intended to have a religious
career. Assuredly there was in him the stuff of a
preacher: his essays are there to prove it. His serious
and contemplative turn of mind leads him to take all

the advantage possible of a simple and healthy education directed but not dominated by religion. He sees Christianity in a pleasant and smiling light. Addison never liked Puritanism (see *Spectator*, No. 494), on account of its sullen severity. He is no more a bigot than a freethinker. I do not believe he was enthusiastic enough to be inclined to excessive fervour. His goddess, whom he never ceased to worship till the last, was indeed Spenser's "sweet Cheerfulness,"

> Whose eyes, like twinkling stars in evening clear,
> Were decked with smiles that all sad humours chased,

surrounded by her companions Modesty, Obedience and Courtesy. The essence of his nature is this feeling of kindly content, of serene playfulness, the result of a clear conscience never sullied by crime, or even disturbed by doubt. I do not know whether it has been remarked, but Addison is really a Dr Primrose in embryo. There is an essay in the *Spectator* (No. 500) where he seems to express his own ideal. Well, it is almost word for word that of the Vicar of Wakefield. It is the innocent and naïve dream of the good pastor. That worthy "Philogamus," born in wedlock (he does not fail to emphasize this point), brought up according to the precepts of morality and religion, has married as a duty, and out of patriotism has founded a numerous family. In his old age he busies himself with preaching marriage to young people and with giving his children a pious education. Near to death he can rejoice that he has all his life defended the cause of morality and rendered service to his country : "In short, Sir, I look upon my family as a sort of

patriarchal sovereignty in which I am myself both king
and priest....As I take great pleasure in the administration of my government in particular, so I look
upon myself not only as a more useful, but also as
a much greater and happier man than any bachelor
in England of my rank and condition.

" There is another accidental advantage in marriage
which has likewise fallen to my share: I mean the
having a multitude of children. These I cannot but
regard as very great blessings. When I see my little
troop before me, I rejoice in the additions which I
have made to my species, to my country, and to
my religion in having produced such a number of
reasonable creatures, citizens and Christians. I am
pleased to see myself thus perpetuated ; and, as there
is no production comparable to that of a human
creature, I am more proud of having been the occasion
of ten such glorious productions than if I had built
a hundred pyramids at my own expense, or published
as many volumes of the finest wit and learning."
(*Spectator*, No. 500.)

Addison need only have continued in the path
that had been traced for him : he would have come
to a like result. It is not what he did, it is what
he might have done ; and *late in life*[1] he perhaps
regretted not having done so. And this ideal is
not only his own; it is that of all the respectable
people about him. It is the simple and indulgent
moral basis on which rests the strength of the
country gentry. Nothing better than this letter

---

[1] This essay appeared in 1712, seven years before his death, when
he was forty.

seems to me to show the temper of the sphere in which Addison was brought up. He is not the man to want to break with his surroundings. His peaceable nature, with its horror of paradox and conflict is very well satisfied with this manner of life; he merely adds to the faith of his fathers a stronger dose of rational conviction. The conception of his youth is the conception of his mature years; he remained faithful to his motto all his life; in any case, if he had ever had for a moment the idea of abandoning it, he would have been revived by the warm if somewhat vacillating spirit of his friend Dick Steele.

Perhaps neither Addison nor Steele would have noticed anything ridiculous in the conduct of their neighbours if they had not learnt to look upon them from a new point of view. Their studies being finished, the two friends are sent forth, the one into the military, the other into the political world. Addison gives up his first plan of life and accepts the post of Under-Secretary of State. Over the preacher is fitted the diplomatist. In the sphere in which he now moves there prevails a very different conception of morals. Never at any time in England were polite, literary and artistic circles so completely under the sway of fashion. It has frequently been asked what the Restoration really borrowed from France; I believe simply the respect for fashion, which now takes the place of the old national respect of individuality. It is hardly just to render the court of Louis XIV responsible for the excesses of Charles II's court. In France the worship of reason has always been carried much further than in England, and the external uniformity that fashion imposes is only the reflex of the moral uniformity imposed by reason. But to transplant this respect for fashion to England is to run counter to the genius of the people. The English nature, more robust, more brutal and, in general, less intellectual than the French nature, with difficulty accepts the standard of fashion, or, if it accepts it, it is without well understanding its object. So, this short interregnum, during which individuality dethroned had to give place to fashion, was filled with the wildest excesses. When Addison reaches London, although the Restoration properly so called is over, although William III, a sovereign whose conduct, if not exemplary, at least always remains decent and measured, now wears the crown, he finds all the barriers of former morality thrown down. Atheism is openly professed; if the Decalogue is still read it is only, as Addison says, in that famous edition called the Immoral Bible (*Spectator*, No. 579); the women are giddy coquettes when they are nothing worse; the men fops and coxcombs when they are not professed libertines. This society, always useless, often dangerous, lives only in accordance with the precepts of fashion, and fashion, for the moment, declares ridiculous in principle all religion and all morals. It is easy to imagine the reception that awaits the new comer still countrified enough to have personal convictions and to utter them aloud. It may be readily fancied what a shower of sarcasms will fall on all the shoots of originality that have sprouted in country seclusion.

Our good Philogamus of a little while ago feels some embarrassment in confessing himself a legitimate child and a married man ; a spirit of bravado may be felt in such phrases as these : " For my own part, I was born in wedlock and I don't care who knows it....Nay, Sir, I will go one step further and declare to you before the whole world that I am a married man, and at the same time I have so much assurance as not to be ashamed of what I have done." It is an age when more courage is needed to be moderate than to be excessive. The only sayings and writings still deemed proper are improper ones, as the comedies of the time sufficiently show. The provincial who, without any very extraordinary asceticism, still retains a few instincts of decency is called a " queer fellow " or a " country put," a greenhorn or an old fogey as the case may be. All without exception, for their hobbies or crotchets devoid of malice, are placed in the category of those the Spectator calls " whims or humorists " and as such become the butts of public raillery. Let them bear with this a while : a saviour is at hand, about to deliver them from the pillory.

Addison has too much good sense to deny that there is a portion of truth in this pitiless mockery. His town education seems to have given him what he might have lacked : the brilliancy, the polish, the varnish which can hardly be acquired in the country. He borrows from this factitious and frivolous society its only quality : its wit. The great harvest of the Restoration is over, but there is the aftermath :

Addison cuts his sheaf from it like the others. But he borrows nothing further.

Now imagine Addison as joint-editor of a journal that will find its way into all the drawing-rooms and even reach the remotest country seats. As a good Christian he must seriously reflect on the nature of the influence he will exercise. In concert with Steele he draws up a moral code, of which the following is the first article: Relentless warfare against fashion which extols atheism and libertinism; the second being: Honour to all those who by their example still uphold the cause of morality and religion. Never, and the rule admits of no exception, never will contempt be allowed to touch the things they believe in. They will hold out against raillery; they will not allow themselves to be influenced by custom; they will make no concessions to public taste. We have almost all of us sinned in this respect, especially if we pride ourselves on liberalism. We venerate sincerity, but this does not prevent our thinking deceit ingenious; we have the highest ideal of love, and yet a gay anecdote is very amusing; in our hearts we respect above everything modesty, and we listen to indecency without frowning. At every moment, the lips profane what the heart holds sacred. Addison vowed he would not be guilty of this inconsistency, and, without venturing to make too daring a generalization in such a delicate case, I believe he kept his word.—" I have resolved to refresh my readers' memories from day to day till I have recovered them out of that desperate state of vice and folly into which the age has fallen." (*Spectator*, No. 10.)—"The great and only end of these my speculations is to banish Vice and Ignorance out of the territories of Great Britain." (No. 58)—etc.

It is thus that the *Spectator* challenges fashion. The latter has the advantage, for it has the choice of weapons. It knows how to handle wit and satire only; so it is by satire and wit that Steele and Addison answer it. They add sermons, sentiment, allegory; they employ all means, in accordance with Beecher's principle: "When you are fighting the Devil shoot him with anything." But there is no doubt that wit is their great resource. If they had not been men of the world as well as preachers they would not have definitively carried the day. Addison himself very well feels that his great triumph lies in having changed the standpoint of ridicule. "I have new pointed all the batteries of ridicule. They have been generally planted against persons who have appeared serious rather than absurd; or at best have aimed rather at what is unfashionable than what is vicious. For my own part I have endeavoured to make nothing ridiculous that is not in some measure criminal. I have set up the immoral man as the object of derision: in short, if I have not formed a new weapon against vice and irreligion, I have at least shown how that weapon may be put to a right use which has so often fought the battles of impiety and profaneness." (*Spectator*, No. 445.)

So much for the negative part and it is relatively easy. It is always possible to find the vulnerable

side. There is no need of superior genius to cover
with ridicule the pretentiousness and the swagger
of the rakes, the patches, the paniers and the inordi-
nately large head-dresses of the women of fashion;
only a little sense and wit are requisite. No great
philosophical acumen either is needed to show up the
hollow frivolity of their feigned atheism, of their
lukewarm libertinism; only vigorous morals and a
fixed determination are requisite. The aberrations
of fashion almost expose themselves.

Once this task is performed, there comes the
positive part, which is incomparably more delicate.
The second article of the code says: Honour morality
and religion and all who uphold them. The things
that are despised must be brought back into favour.
The maxims that used to be put into the mouth
of the Cassanders of comedy must be advanced as
serious propositions. "Religion is a beautiful thing,"
and it is not Sganarelle who must any longer be
made to say it. "Marriage is a holy and sacred
thing," and it is no longer Gorgibus who must be
allowed to proclaim it so. After having covered the
libertines with ridicule, their victims must be cleared
from it. All who out of good nature allow themselves to be deceived and scoffed at, all who out of
ignorance of fashion employ language that has fallen
into disuse, or wear a somewhat singular costume,
all who for lack of a society education have developed
their instinctive tendencies till they have turned
into crotchets or manias, all that race of "whims and
humorists" must be reinstated in the good opinion
of the public. For it is in these people, however

naïve and contemptible they may seem, that the
moral strength of the country lies, and it is high
time their banterers should become aware of the fact.
The captain, the clergyman, the squire, all those who
exercise honourable functions must take precedence
of the noxious and evil-doing rakes. But how can
he openly take the part of the gulls ? Even nowa-
days it is not easy, and yet the taste of the public
has greatly changed ; imagine Addison's perplexity
at the beginning of the eighteenth century. None
of the literary forms current meet this need. Wit
does not go with sympathy, preaching ill agrees with
merriment. And a hostile public has to be allured.
The comic side of respectable things has first to be
shown, in order afterwards to make the respectable
side of comic things better felt. It is driven by this
moral impulse that Addison, as a Christian and also
as a man of the world, creates for his own use a new
manner, of which he discloses the secret neither to
Steele, nor to Hughes, nor to Budgell, nor to Tickell,
and this manner, entirely his own creation, is humour[1].

If the double origin of Addison's humour be
considered, no surprise will be felt at the complexity
of the manner he creates and the infinite possibilities
that are latent in it. Humour, as he conceives of it
and as it has remained since, is not a study of the
deeper motives of the human soul in general ; it is

---

[1] Steele attempted it, but, in my opinion, was not successful. His
is a warm and manly nature ; he errs on the side of too great energy in
a manner that especially calls for discretion. His touch is too heavy ;
he always carries humour towards burlesque or towards pathos.

the reproduction of the little weaknesses, the little
eccentricities of each individual shooting up from a
common ground of humanity with which we are supposed to be familiar. Very deep, refined psychology
does not come within the scope of humour. It is a
lancet, not a scalpel. But precisely because it plays on
the surface of things, or, if it sinks deeper, takes care
not to seem to, humour has an advantage peculiar
to itself. When, like Molière or like Balzac, an
author probes the soul to its depths, he divines beneath
the particular trait the general truth, and the nature
of generalities leaves no room for doubt. A thing
is decidedly tragic or comic ; it provokes tears or
laughter. Arnolphe, as an old man in love, is at
times amusing, at others touching, but he is such by
turns, not at one and the same time. When he
preaches the duties of marriage to Agnès, he is
comic ; when he beseeches her on his knees to love
him, he is pathetic ; even that unfeeling little creature
does not think him ridiculous (despite what has
been said to the contrary): she is cold, not scornful.
Molière's touch is absolutely frank ; so is Balzac's ;
so likewise Shakespeare's at essential moments. But
it is because they scrutinize human nature as it is
underneath convention, because they study it in crises
where all the ordinary trammels of society are
shaken off. When the soul in its natural condition
and in a state of intense excitement is exposed to
view, the spectator is carried away against his will.
There can be no doubt as to the nature of the
interest awakened by listening to the delirium of
Père Goriot on his death-bed, or the inarticulate cries

of Othello foaming while Iago lashes him to fury.—
Addison, on the contrary, assumes the existence in
his humoristic personages of a common basis of
religion and morals. If they did not all believe in
the same principles, they would not awaken in him
feelings of respect. The Spectator, Will Wimble,
the Chaplain, the Butler, Sir Roger de Coverley,
despite social and individual differences, are members
of one and the same church and obey the laws of
one and the same moral code. They are essentially
the children of convention and civilization. Addison's
congenial personages all belong to the category of
honest people. Not a single black sheep could be
found among them[1]. They are above all respectable.
It is in virtue of this connecting link that is supposed
to exist between them and us that they first attract
us. In all the important actions of their lives, they
take a middle course. We know them to be incapable of crime, of cowardice, of meanness, of deceit
of any kind. We have confidence in them. It is
this confidence that is the essential element in the
feeling we experience in regard to them. Once this
sympathy is well established, we shall be able to
follow them, without any shock or disillusion, through
all the comic adventures into which they may be
drawn by the excess of their very qualities. All
their laughable weaknesses will have their roots in
their virtues or, to say the least, if they are not their

[1] The portrait of Will Honeycomb is more than half satirical: that
is why I hesitate to take him into account. He is humoristic on the
occasions where Addison shows him as more naïve than the simple folks
he is deriding. (Essay on Pedants.) And again at last when he returns
to the path of duty and becomes steady.

immediate consequences, will at least not contradict
them. Merriment, at every moment, plays like a sun-
beam on the surface of respect, but directly sympathy
intervenes and softens its glare. Addison expresses
in a charming fashion the mixed impression left by
humour, in the preface to an anecdote which illus-
trates all its best qualities (*Spectator*, No. 245):

" There is nothing which one regards so much
with an eye of mirth and pity as innocence, when it
has in it a dash of folly. At the same time that one
esteems the virtue, one is tempted to laugh at the
simplicity which accompanies it."—And, as a proof,
he tells the following story about St Francis :

" The Cordeliers tell a story of their founder
St Francis, that as he passed the streets in the dusk of
the evening he discovered a young fellow with a maid
in a corner ; upon which the good man, say they,
lifted up his hands to heaven with a secret thanks-
giving that there was still so much Christian charity
in the world. The innocence of the saint made him
mistake the kiss of a lover for a salute of charity."

Is it St Francis who is ridiculous, or is it we who
are cynical? Addison has a quiet way of turning the
blame against the reader. We laugh at the little
mistakes of these good people, but it is with the
underthought that they are much better than ourselves. The author sometimes hints this very cleverly:
Sir Roger, as a good Christian solicitous about morals,
exercises an active superintendence over the conduct
of his tenants :

" I was yesterday very much surprised to hear my
old friend, in the midst of the service, calling out to

one John Matthews to mind what he was about and
not disturb the congregation. This authority of the
knight, though exerted in that odd manner which
accompanies him in all circumstances of life, has a
very good effect upon the parish, *who are not polite
enough to see anything ridiculous in his behaviour....*"

Addison excels in this art of chiaroscuro. He
has a way of preserving the dignity of serious things
in the very midst of ridicule, of recalling the estimable
side of virtue in the height of raillery, of touching
the chord of pathos in the middle of comedy. His
humour requires the co-existence and the union of
these two opposite elements. They occur in all
degrees, incongruity varying according to intensity.
Sometimes it is conscious, serious and dignified originality which, supported by the feeling of its own
merit, resists raillery with imperturbable gravity: it
is from this variety that the conception of the Spectator himself proceeds. Sometimes it is the spirit of
malice that amuses itself for a moment with discovering the selfishness that lies hidden beneath solemn
appearances : this is what gives all its zest to the
account of the Grinning-Match. [In a small English
town a prize is founded, which will be awarded to
the cleverest grinner. A Frenchman enters the lists,
makes strenuous efforts, and seems to be on the point
of carrying off the prize; the judges at first take fright
at the notion that a foreigner should be the victor,
"*but upon a farther trial they found he was master
only of the merry grin.*" *Spectator*, No. 173.] Sometimes, and this is much more usual with him, he
exhibits in a light at once affectionate and smiling

a personage whose absurdities are not concealed, but who at every moment is seen to have, amid his eccentricities and in virtue of his very eccentricities, an inexhaustible fund of kindness and delicacy, which changes raillery into compunction; it is in this spirit that the whole of Sir Roger de Coverley's part is conceived. Better still, he once attains to an exquisite degree of sensibility amid greatly subdued comedy, viz. in the account of Sir Roger de Coverley's death. (*Spectator*, No. 517.) His most refined humour is an indeterminate feeling the precise definition of which must not be attempted; it is the silent smile of eyes filling with tears. The new manner essentially differs from all known manners by the impression it seeks to produce. The pleasure afforded by tragedy, comedy, pathos, burlesque, and wit is the pleasure of certainty; the pleasure afforded by humour is that of uncertainty.

This is the first impression produced by Addison's humour and it is the definitive impression. It is a question of temperament rather than a question of art. Coming to the study of reality with a fund of sympathy due to his education and a feeling for the ridiculous quickened by his society life, Addison must in all sincerity have felt puzzled by the incessant oscillations between pathos and burlesque that are seen in average characters. It is this hesitation, this perplexity that he spontaneously expresses in literary form. His is the scruple, moral rather than artistic, of a moderate mind. To every too direct question he must have answered, as he answered Sir Roger,

*That much might be said on both sides.*   Pope declares
him

> Alike reserved to blame or to commend,
>> (*Imitations of Horace*)

and Pope knew him better than we can.

This impression is still further confirmed by a close
examination of the form of his humour.   No author
shows less artistic prepossession.   The humour of a
very self-conscious writer, like Sterne or like Daudet
at times, on analysis gives up its secret.   But the
study of Addison teaches no *device*; it only at every
moment recalls the great fundamental rule: True art
consists in sincerity along with moderation.   It is like
the pathos of *Manon Lescaut*; no other explanation
of it will be found.   Addison is one of those rare
artists who are content to see aright, and to express
without insistence truths that we ought to have felt
for ourselves and that our lack of acumen alone deems
paradoxical.   The best humour has this peculiarity:
while it dazzles at first sight, it may be reduced to the
simplest and most literal expression of the truth.   It
is a glow-worm that ceases to shine as soon as it is
touched ; it may be examined at leisure : it is nothing
but a small, dull, grey body which, however, retains
the faculty of glowing again as soon as the observer
retires to a distance.

Yet this absolute sincerity gives him a manner
which, in an inferior man, would be the acme of art,
a lightness of touch that none of his imitators have
been able to equal, to which none of them can even
faintly approximate.   When a thing is believed with
the whole heart it is said in an undertone.   To urge, to

lay stress, to expound, to make a rhetorical display is distasteful to a sincere soul. Addison has none of such quackery in him. He never raises his voice. He would allow his most delicate touches to pass unobserved rather than explicitly call attention to them. Consequently Addison must be read in a state of mind at once attentive and disengaged, without soaring and without attempting to fathom, for his fun is so delicate and passes by so quickly that it is barely noticed. Take e.g. the scene at the club where the man of wit, the merchant, the lawyer, the baronet, and the captain criticize the Spectator, each from his own point of view:

"I last night sat very late with this select body of friends, who entertained me with several remarks which they and others had made upon these my speculations, as also with the various success which they had met with among their several ranks and degrees of readers.

"Will Honeycomb told me, in the softest manner he could, That there were some ladies (but for your comfort, says Will, they are not those of the most wit) that were offended at the liberties I had taken with the Opera and the puppet-show: That some of them were likewise very much surprised *that I should think such serious points as the dress and equipage of persons of quality proper subjects for raillery.*

" He was going on when Sir Andrew Freeport took him up short and told him That the papers he hinted at had done great good in the city and that all their wives and daughters were the better for them....In short, says Sir Andrew, *if you avoid that foolish beaten*

*road of falling upon aldermen and citizens,* and employ
your pen upon the vanity and luxury of courts, your
paper must needs be of general utility.

"Upon this, my friend the Templar told Sir Andrew
That he wondered to hear a man of his sense talk after
that manner; that the city had always been the province of satire and that the wits of King Charles's time
jested upon nothing else during his whole reign....
*But after all, says he, I think your raillery has made
too great an excursion in attacking several persons of
the Inns of Court;* and I do not believe you can show
me any precedent for your behaviour in this particular.

"My good friend Sir Roger de Coverley, who had
said nothing all this while, began his speech with a
Pish! and told us That he wondered to see so many
men of sense so very serious upon fooleries.  Let our
good friend, says he, attack every one that deserves it:
*I would only advise you Mr Spectator,* applying himself to me, *to take care how you meddle with country
squires;* they are the ornaments of the English nation;
men of good heads and sound bodies; *and, let me tell
you, some of them take it ill of you that you mention
fox-hunters with so little respect.*

"Captain Sentry spoke very sparingly upon this
occasion.  What he said *was only to commend my
prudence in not touching upon the army,* and advised
me to continue to act discreetly in that point.

" By this time, I found every subject of my
speculations was taken away from me by one or
other of the club...."

And the scene ends with an anecdote.

Addison, when he unexpectedly wheels about, has

something of the flight, at once abrupt and graceful, of the swallow, like whom he skims over his subjects, extracting from them their humour with a single wing-flap: the water that has thus been swept undulates but for a moment, almost immediately becoming smooth again; close attention is required to notice its sparkle. Addison, and in this lies his great quality, has the art of veiling the fun: he does not throw it into relief as would a less discreet humorist. Read the scene between Sir Roger and the gipsies and observe how each time the comic touch is disguised:

"As I was yesterday riding out in the fields with my friend Sir Roger, we saw at a little distance from us a troop of gipsies. Upon the first discovery of them, my friend was in some doubt whether he should not exert the justice of the peace upon such a band of lawless vagrants; *but not having his clerk with him, who is a necessary counsellor on these occasions, and fearing that his poultry might fare the worse for it,* he let the thought drop; but at the same time gave me a particular account of the mischief they do in the country," etc.

Despite his contempt for these fortune-tellers, he goes and speaks to one of them. After having examined his hand she told him:

" That he had a widow in his line of life. Upon which the Knight cried Go, go, you are an idle baggage, *and at the same time smiled upon me.* The Gipsy, *finding he was not displeased in his heart,* told him, after a farther inquiry into his hand, that his true-love was constant and that she should dream of him to-night: My old friend cried Pish! *and bid her go on.* The Gipsy told him he was a bachelor but would not be so long; and that he was dearer to Somebody than he thought: The Knight still repeated She was an idle baggage and bid her go on. Ah Master, says the Gipsy, that roguish leer of yours makes a pretty woman's heart ache; you han't that simper about the mouth for nothing—*To be short, the Knight left the money with her that he had crossed her hand with* and got up again on his horse.

"As we were riding away, Sir Roger told me *that he knew several very sensible people who believed these gipsies now and then foretold very strange things*; and for half an hour together appeared more jocund than ordinary. In the height of his good humour, meeting a common beggar on the road who was no conjuror, *as he went to relieve him he found his pocket was picked*; That being a kind of palmistry at which this race of vermin are very dexterous."

The fun in Addison is supple and unseizable like jelly; it glides into the throat and melts there before there has been time to swallow it. Is it artlessness, as some would say, is it supreme art as others would maintain, or is it refined sincerity, as I am myself inclined to believe? I cannot say; the fact remains that Addison, out of ignorance or out of disdain, avoids every kind of display and flourish. He never begins with a loud burst of laughter and never ends with a clap-trap saying. The most successful of his humorous scenes stand between calm and serene sermons, mostly illuminated by no gleam of wit. He never hesitates to add the moral to the dramatic fable. It is perhaps a defect, but the humour is fresher and more spontaneous through not being made to suit the purposes of construction. The surrounding seriousness possibly obscures, but also protects it. Thence it half emerges, all moist and glossy, like a fruit out of its gaping shell.

Addison is not a humorist by profession; this is what it is especially important to remember. Humour occupies but a very small place in his literary performance. It is with him the very flower of wit and morals. Created partly, no doubt, by artistic instinct, but also, be it not forgotten, to meet a social requirement, his humour possesses the quality common to all spontaneous creations: homogeneousness. Its essential principles may be summed up in a few words:

It is the study of the average man in his individual eccentricities.—So much for its matter.

This study is undertaken with a broadly sympathetic intent, ever accompanied by a feeling for the ridiculous.—So much for its spirit.

It must be made without prepossession, with an appearance of unconsciousness.—So much for its form.

Addison counts less for what he has done than for what he has suggested. He is the first in date of a long line of humorists. He himself has left only cartoons: his successors have made finished pictures of them. But they have changed nothing in his principles. Addison set the key of humour; he determined its limits; he circumscribed the field of its subjects; he suggested its form. Afterwards, there could be added to his baronets and his clergymen the business men, the governesses, the clerks, the missionaries—all the creations of nineteenth-century England; the scale could at will be inclined towards pathos or towards comedy; impassibility of form might be turned into conscious phlegm, or into sham depth; but these are merely developments: they are not radical changes. Fielding, Sterne, Scott, Dickens, Thackeray, Douglas Jerrold, George Eliot, Jerome K. Jerome, all, in reality, draw upon the methods of Addison.

# SWIFT'S POETRY

SWIFT's poetry is not the instinctive expression of an artistic temperament; it is the putting into practice of a certain preconceived theory of art, the explanation of which must be sought in his philosophy.

Swift imposed upon himself a mission: that of proving the deep-seated baseness of mankind. Man, in his eyes, is a Yahoo, a perfectly immoral being, uniting in himself the most noxious instincts of the foulest animals: "it is doing him too great an honour to equal him with certain brutes, even when the vilest are chosen: the wolf, the ass, the swine and the ape." (Preface to *The Beasts' Confession*.) He has acquired this conviction by the direct contemplation of reality: "It argues no corrupted mind In him; the fault is in mankind." (*On the Death of Dr Swift*.) The moralist's duty "in verse and prose" is to cure the vices of mankind (*Ibid.*), or rather, for the enterprise would be too ambitious, to strip man of the covers which hide his own deformities from him, leaving it to others to apply the whip. (*To a Lady*.) Such is the theory he has always professed in his prose; it will not only reappear in his verse but will determine his conception of poetry.

The poet is a Yahoo like the others, but a Yahoo whom the folly he calls inspiration has led to forget his mortality. Shrewd folks well know to what cause to attribute this elation in which he glories. He takes his flight only at times when a purely physical giddiness has so far turned his brain as to make him lose sight of reality. See the *Progress of Poetry* for the analysis of this madness of which Shelley, the representative of idealistic poetry, has given the definition in the apostrophe to the skylark "That singing still dost soar and soaring ever singest." Shelley's own words are used by anticipation. It is here that Swift declares war against poetry itself. Born of an unhealthy state of mind, it has no other purpose than to propagate illusion. Its effect on mankind is to pervert the sense of reality. Therefore the duty of the philosopher is to react by his own example against this pernicious influence. To put things back in their true light again, by destroying, one by one, all the illusions with which poetic tradition has clothed certain ideas and certain sentiments, such is very frankly Swift's object in all the negative part of his work in verse.

Fairly considerable in extent it depends for its effect on a device always the same, viz. the faithful reproduction of an idea recognized as poetic, followed by its extra-poetic counterpart, for the purpose of associating the two in the reader's mind, to the detriment of the former. A single example will suffice to illustrate the application of the principle. It is the one in which the device is most clearly seen, in which it seems to take pleasure in displaying itself, in reducing itself to formulas.

Which is the pre-eminently poetic subject? Love, and love at its culminating point, celebrated in the form of an epithalamium. The transcendent effort of poetic imagination has always borne upon the triumph of love. It is a subject hallowed by tradition, a subject, therefore, fit to be profaned. Swift eagerly sets about to do so. He will make his epithalamium like the others, but an epithalamium reversed. His system is very simple. It consists in starting in a serious tone, leading up to the central subject with all the customary caution, then suddenly evading it, in order to substitute another which poetry has always disowned, and, from the clashing of the two, deducing this moral: In order to retain one's illusions, the realization of high-flown sentiment must not be examined too closely. So he announces his subject with all the obligatory ostentation : "*Imprimis*, at the temple porch Stood Hymen with a flaming torch, The smiling Cyprian goddess brings Her infant loves with purple wings"...thence, by a skilful gradation of the incidents, he leads it forward to the point where, thanks to this device of substitution, these same Loves fly away scared [" The little Cupids, hovering round (As pictures prove) with garlands crowned, Abashed at what they saw and heard, Flew off, nor ever more appeared "] ; there, his purpose being attained, he strikes up the triumphal hymn of disillusion :

> Adieu to ravishing delights,
> High raptures and romantic flights, etc. ;

then, without swerving, presses it vigorously forward
to the moral :

> For fine ideas vanish fast
> While all the gross and filthy last,

a distich which might serve as an epigraph to the
whole of his philosophy.

Such is the device in all its simplicity.    Swift
never tires of repeating it under the same form and
applied to the same subject, for the opportunity is
really too good not to be taken advantage of, but it
must not be imagined he confines himself to it.   Without seeming to, he, in the same manner, goes the
round of all, or nearly all, the great poetic sentiments.
—After the Progress of Love comes the Progress of
Beauty.    There is only the change from the concrete
idea to the poetic metaphor.    We know what use the
poets have made of the moon as a symbol.    It suffices
to name her, in order to recall the apostrophe of
Coriolanus to Valeria : " The noble sister of Publicola,
the moon of Rome," or a similar idea.    There will
therefore be a delight in associating her with the
name of Celia who, like the luminary, "her sister-star,"
shines at night, "when sober folks are all a-bed."—The
psychology of dreams is the very realm of poetry.    It
is there that imagination has free play ; it is there
that it is difficult to call it to account for the pranks
it plays with reality.    Set over against the high
soarings of fancy the nocturnal visions of those
respectable but unimaginative beings whose existence
our aristocratic poets ignore.    Drive Queen Mab's

chariot first through the dreams of the king, as behoves, and thence through those of Tom the nightman, "Who rakes the city filth in search of gold." There is little idealism that can resist such treatment.

It suffices to point out the device. We see what its systematic application leads to. It means universal disenchantment and disillusion.

Many pessimists have gone further than Swift and have nevertheless succeeded in producing poetry of the highest order. Many have sung the absolute nothingness of human things and by the expression of this disillusion have added something stable and abiding to literature. Leconte de Lisle may exclaim as much as he likes : "O Brahma, everything is but the dream of a dream"; the very tone of that line clearly proves that style is no dream. James Thomson may put on the most mournful air to assure us that "The spheres eternal are a grand illusion, The empyrean is a void abyss"; the only thing he will show is that he knows how to write harmoniously. Never do these naïve pessimists come by the idea of attacking the poetic form—a frivolous amusement of the human mind which ought, logically, to sink, like all the other illusions, into the eternal gulf. Swift, more consistently, has vowed quite particular hostility to it.

"The most delicate faculty of a writer," Michelet has said, "is the sense of rhythm" and, it may be added, that of sonority. It is the most instinctive faculty, the one that takes precedence of all theory in every man of artistic temperament. Nothing better shows how deep-rooted in Swift is the hatred of poetry in its essence than his relentless animosity towards the sonorous form. The idea that the intelligence should ever have been at pains to combine certain sounds to the exclusion of certain others, for the greater pleasure of the ear, seems to him ridiculous in the last degree. He several times scoffs at the melodies transmitted by Spenserian tradition:

> Melancholy, smooth Meander
> Swiftly purling in a round....

> Limpid rivers, smoothly flowing,
> Orchards by those rivers blowing....

And why? Because these lines depend for their fluid sonority on the skilful blending of vowels and liquids. The poets, without knowing it, have had a foible for liquids and vowels, a foible that has often led them to stick at plain words bristling with consonants; whence a suppression of truth; therefore an illusion which must be destroyed. "Smooth your words to fit the tune," he says in the advice he gives the official poets of George I's court. (*Directions for Making a Birth-day Song.*) Suppress all the ugly German dissonances you will have to deal with in singing the Hanoverian dynasty: "*Hesse-Darmstadt* makes a rugged sound, And *Guelp* the strongest ear will wound." This is another way of saying: "I am familiar with all your sonorous euphemisms; you do not deceive me." A moment later he goes into ecstasies at the name of Caroline.—" Hail, queen of Britain, queen of rhymes!—Too happy were the poets' crew If their own happiness they knew: Three syllables (Ca-ro-line) did never meet So soft, so sliding and so sweet "—

> Behold three beauteous vowels stand (a-o-i)
> With bridegroom liquids hand in hand (r-l-n)
> *No jarring consonant betwixt.*

If he despises sounds that are productive of illusion, what would he replace them by? In accordance with his usual method, by the deformities they conceal.— " A skilful critic," he remarks, "justly blames"

> Hard, tough, crank, guttural, harsh, stiff names.

So it is in the use of harsh, stiff, hard, guttural, crank words that he makes his own poetic art consist. He takes such pride in them that the most flattering compliment that occurred to Sheridan, an intimate friend who must have been well informed concerning the dean's tastes, was to praise him for his "harmonious sets of clinks." These clinks, of which he may have found the secret in Skelton and in Butler, consist of a frantic alliteration of the harshest, the most self-conscious, one might say the most realistic consonants; those that involve smacking of the lips and percussion of the palate....

> Not beggar's brat on bulk begot
> Not bastard of a pedlar Scot.
> 
> (*On Poetry.*)
> 
> So rotting Celia strolls the street.
> (*Progress of Beauty.*)

> Queen of wit and beauty, Betty
> ( *To Betty, the Grisette.* )

> Now jealousy my grumbling tripes
> Assaults with grating, grinding gripes.
> ( *Love-letter from a Physician to his Mistress.* )

This is replacing lyre and pipe by Jew's harp and castanets. And he does this everywhere, without intermission. Never in Swift is any more delicate instinct revealed. Yes, once. In the middle of a parody and blending with it these lines break forth:

> When lo! Vanessa in her bloom
> Advanced like Atalanta's star
> But rarely seen and seen from ·far.

Their beauty is undeniable. Three lines in three volumes are not too much. With this reserve, Sheridan's dictum may be accepted: " Thy verses produce on me the deafening effect of the echo of Galway "—

> And every couplet thou hast writ
> Concludes like *Rattah-whittah-whit*;

and this is not meant as criticism, but as praise.

He is then a man who in theory uncompromisingly despises all the elements of poetry, both as to form and as to matter. What kind of artist can such a man make?

This theory believes itself hostile to art, and, at first sight, one would be inclined to deem it so. Swift disowned art as he understood it, but art, in the widest acceptation of the word, will not disown Swift. The poetry so far considered is the idealistic poetry, lyricism in its essence, the purely æsthetic part of art. From that sphere Swift debarred himself and in so doing believed he was shutting himself out from all poetry. With his narrow conception of poetry, as a nurse of illusions, a deceptive comforter whose only purpose is to close our eyes to reality, he could hardly think otherwise. It is not thus that the best poets have understood it. If it ends in idealism, it starts from reality. It has need of truth as a basis: it starts from reality;—to go beyond it—but it starts from it. It is possible to disown the end without disowning the beginning.

That is what Swift does. If he were only a vulgar profaner, out of pure malignity attacking the consolations of others, powerless to construct a new building on the ruins of the one he has demolished, his work would long since have fallen into oblivion. But no. The basis of his doctrine, however brutal its manifestations may be, is the love of truth. If he sincerely cares for reality, there will be in him the stuff of an artist. No one has less desire to appear so than Swift; few have been so more conscientiously.

His gifts may be summed up in two words: the faculty of correct observation and the rarer one of reproducing, without exaggeration, but with the maximum of effect, what he has perceived.

His sensations are sound, his imagination is sound

and his psychology is correct, all in correct proportion. This is not saying little.

This art lies all in details; it is by detailed analysis that we shall best succeed in understanding it.

His Sensations:—He is a man whose senses are always on the alert. Whether he walks through the streets of London, saunters over the estate of Sir Arthur Acheson, the country gentleman, or goes the round of his room, it is always note-book in hand, jotting down his impressions as they come and shading them in as he advances.

He describes the waking of the city at daybreak: he hears the distant rumbling of the hackney-coaches heralding the "morn's approach"; then he sees the slip-shod 'prentice come out of a shop, "pare the dirt" that has dried on the steps and "sprinkle round the floor"; a little further on, Moll, the servant-girl, on the threshold whirls her mop before scrubbing the entry and the stairs; then the street-cries strike his ear: first is heard the "cadence deep" of the coal-man, soon "drown'd in shriller notes of chimney-sweep"; yonder "at his lordship's gate" the duns are beginning to meet, while through the peep-hole of the prison the turnkey watches for the return of his flock, "let out a-nights for fees"; the bailiffs "take their silent stands," and a few school-boys "lag with satchels in their hands...."

Just as he excels in depicting this almost still life, so he successfully paints the broad, lively scene of the Irish feast, which puts one in mind of Rubens's Kirmess.

Better still, he will make this observation of external details serve to prepare, to accentuate a state of mind. He requires to depict the dejection of the student, the "Soph" who has lost his illusions concerning his mistress. The Soph has just discovered the brutal reality of even the most divine creatures (this is a well-known theme with Swift); he is about to unbosom himself to a friend who is more of a philosopher, but before the dialogue begins the personage must be introduced to the reader:

> He seem'd as just crept out of bed;
> One greasy stocking round his head,
> The other he sat down to darn,
> With threads of different colour'd yarn;
> His ragged shirt exposing wide,
> Embrown'd with dirt, his hairy hide.
>
> . . . . .
>
> A rug was o'er his shoulders thrown,
> (A rug, for nightgown he had none,)
> A vessel stood in manner fitting
> Between his legs, to spew or spit in;
> His ancient pipe, in sable dyed,
> And half unsmoked, lay by his side.
> Him thus accoutred Peter found,
> With eyes in smoke and weeping drown'd;
> The leavings of his last night's pot
> On embers placed, to drink it hot.

Might not this be taken for a leaf torn from the *Scènes de la Vie de Bohême*? Swift is a naturalist come before his time.

His Imagination:—An imagination that rises from reality to return to it immediately, an imagination that distrusts itself, hardly dares to leave the sphere of ascertained and verifiable fact and which, through this very scrupulousness, is very powerful in its effect. He will make us witnesses of, say, the transformation of the hut into a church in *Baucis and Philemon.* First he notes the precise form of all the objects in the hut, next that of all the objects in the church; then, having fixed the terms of comparison, leaves to fancy only the care of making the latter evolve out of the former. Even then there is nothing but what seems within the bounds of possibility. First it is the roof of the hut which has to change into a vault; in logical progression will come the rafters and, last, the wall:

> fair and soft
> The roof began to mount aloft,
> Aloft rose every beam and rafter,
> The heavy wall climbed slowly after....

The verse here moves like a lift. Then comes the arm-chair which, by a slight alteration, is transformed into a pulpit.

> The groaning-chair began to crawl
> Like a huge snail along the wall.

Lastly, the ballads affixed to the wall, which become texts, but not before he has informed us of the precise subject of each one:

> The ballads, pasted on the wall,
> Of Joan of France and English Moll,
> Fair Rosamund and Robin Hood,
> The little children in the wood...

for it is only thus that these inanimate objects can acquire the concrete life the faculty of transformation presupposes.

His Psychology:—If he knows how to communi-
cate this intense life to things, he will render still more
intense that of living beings. While he is making
sketches he at the same time records scraps of conversation, he analyzes himself and he analyzes the sayings
of those he is talking with, singles out telling sentiments, speeches and gestures, and reproduces them.
He knows how to conduct a dialogue in the right key,
without deviation or weakness, putting each word in
its place,—never too soon, never too late,—without
requiring it to be divined and without emphasizing
it. He overhears an interview between former lovers
in a coffee-house, or from a window strains his ear to
enjoy the idyll of Sir A. Acheson's two weeders,
Dermot and Sheelah,—an idyll for a moment disturbed
by jealousy. He perceives and gets us to perceive
the change from caress to threat. Sheelah, at first
loving, becomes jealous. Prayer is followed by insult.
We hear the voice coaxing, and then becoming
hoarse; we see the motion of the weeding-hook:

> Dermot, how could you touch these nasty sluts?
> —I almost wished this spud were in your guts.

Or we have the mute dialogue of hearts, without
tenderness, without emotion even, but as surely as
delicately drawn. The masterpiece in this style (and
the masterpiece from many other points of view) is
the central part of *Cadenus and Vanessa*, from "But
now a sudden change was wrought" to "But what
success Vanessa met...," the study of the transformation by which master and pupil exchange parts.

His Construction:—This psychological intuition
he turns to account for the purposes of construction.
This art, carried to a rare degree of perfection in the
eighteenth century (think of Dryden's *Fables*) was
handled by no one more skilfully than by Swift. His
construction is of the best quality, because it results
from the psychological data of the subject: it depends
almost entirely on sudden changes of feeling. The
dénouement of the piece, the clue to the enigma are
led up to with never-failing logic. All the poems of
which the analysis has been given, however various
their qualities, are remarkable for this close construction, carrying to its extreme consequences the idea
set forth at the beginning.

His Style:—These qualities are thrown into relief
by the most unpretentious and most efficacious style
in the world. Swift speaks in verse the same language
as in prose, save for the rhymes ; it is unnecessary to
dwell on it at length. A quick ear is the only indispensable quality in a poet; he never had it. This is
an advantage for the object he has in view. Rhythms
that are too inspiriting, melodies that are too seducing
have the defect of obscuring the meaning or of causing
it to be forgotten. To express his meaning in a form
neither falling short of nor overshooting his thought is
Swift's sole ambition. That is why he makes use of
so few images, why he so carefully avoids neologisms ;
it is also the reason why he does not proscribe them.
He knows that now and then a metaphorical expression may condense without blurring an idea. To say
that the white lead with which a woman paints herself

cools the passion of her lover is not striking, but to
say that

> Love with white lead cements his wings

to fly away arrests attention and at the same time
elucidates the thought. He has the gift of finding
the right phrase which, without any artifice that can
well be defined, with a pin-prick fixes the idea in the
mind. The dancing-master teaches his pupil love at
the same time as the polka :

> And oft the dancing-master's art
> Climbs from the toe to reach the heart.

He will even, on very rare occasions, to express a
new idea, instead of a periphrasis, coin a new word.
Death has need of a wife who shall give him children.
What specific name shall be given to these little beings?

> The interest of his realm had need
> That Death should get a numerous breed,
> *Young deathlings*, who might stock around
> His large dominions underground.

The fact is that the only quality of style, in Swift's
eyes, is that it should tell.


These observations all lead to the same conclusion.
In this subordination of personality to the necessities
of the subject is manifested, perhaps unconsciously,
the dramatic instinct. This tendency, which was
already apparent in a few little scenes scattered through
*The Battle of the Books* or *The Tale of a Tub*, developing in Swift's verse, gives it its only artistic value.
From his poetry there might be derived a *Théâtre en
Liberté* of Lilliputian dimensions, but complete—

scenery, dialogue, actors and chorus all in harmony. On turning away from lyric poetry he went towards the drama. He went towards it, partly driven by instinct, but also because in the drama his feeling for reality was not offended by the continual illusion which, according to him, forms the basis of lyricism. This is still art. It is even poetry, for poetry enlists reality in its service.

Only poetry does not stop with reality. The true artist starts from reality to rise to the ideal. This Swift did at no time in his career. That is why he is voluntarily an incomplete poet. Penned up in reality, he never attempted to escape from it.

We have seen with what fidelity he knows how to express it, but is this reproduction complete? Is it life broad and complex, with all its misery, all its ugliness, and also with all its elements of joy and beauty that Swift wishes to exhibit? No, it is only a part of it, a very limited part. His mission was to expose the infirmities of the Yahoo. At the very time when art has sharpened his eyesight, philosophy provides him with blinkers that prevent him from turning it to account. All the artist's gifts are to serve only to voice the distressing philosophy of the moralist. Accordingly, this power of observation is brought to bear only on the diseases, disgraces and vices inherent in mankind. In the poems in which the artist has freest scope this dominant preoccupation is noticeable.

He is walking on a rainy day in the street, in

quest of sensations. He notes them down one by one, as usual. Guess what he observes most curiously! The meeting of all the gutters laden with household refuse: "Now from all parts the swelling kennels flow," bearing "Filths of all hues and odours," in which Swift's eyes and nostrils seem to take real pleasure. First there is mere waste matter: sweepings from a butcher's stall, dung, guts, blood; then death itself: drowned dogs, dead cats, mixing with vegetable refuse; then decomposition: fish already stinking;—all of which soaking in mud:

> Sweepings from butchers' stalls, dung, guts and blood,
> Drowned puppies, stinking sprats, all drenched in mud,
> Dead cats and turnip tops come tumbling down the flood.
> *(Description of a City Shower.)*

This, transposed into the sphere of mankind, gives him, as his only subjects, the morbid, the ghastly, the obscene, and even the fetid. Psychology will serve only to disclose the baseness of the soul, keenness of sight to note physical deformities, imagination to awaken ideas that might be thought unavowable, the art of construction to lead up to the broad joke at the end.

Analysis is unnecessary, but, in order to better feel this prepossession, compare Swift for a moment with a poet like Rossetti. He, occasionally, has treated subjects analogous to Swift's. His eye is not less keen, his philosophy is not more cheerful. He is an accurate observer, incurably pessimistic, but he is above all a lover of beauty. He seeks it by instinct, just as by instinct Swift avoids it. Rossetti censures the corruption of great cities symbolized in Jenny's frivolous and thoughtless little person. He takes Jenny at a time when satire can have its full moral force, but when there still remains an element of beauty to satisfy the imagination. Jenny is young; she is not much purer on that account, but she is infinitely more poetic. She is the Magdalen of Guido Reni, by whom Rossetti might be thought to be inspired. What is her soul?

> Jenny's desecrated mind
> Where all contagious currents meet,
> A Lethe of the middle street.

Her body remains beautiful; from this external beauty proceeds the poetry. While picking her to pieces, the poet notes with the joy of an artist the smooth eyelids, the transparent skin, the clear-cut outline of the chin, —above all, the glory of the hair "All golden in the lamplight's gleam." This hair is a kind of halo for her which, in spite of all, protects her from insult, for is it not the same with which the masters have crowned the Madonna?

Swift, too, has drawn his Jenny—Jenny twenty years later, Jenny without a halo, Jenny faded and worn out, with body as artificial as her soul. Now she is called Corinna, pride of Drury Lane, "a battered strolling toast." She wears crystal eye, plasters, paint, artificial teeth, etc.—we are spared no detail. Swift makes us witnesses of her toilet. As if the hideously artificial were not sufficient, these artificial things are made to enter into decomposition. So there is a detailed description of the transformation of all these objects during the night. And Swift lets us go only when he thinks he has brought us to vomit:

> Who sees will spew, who smells be poisoned.

Such is the device in his positive poetry: he eliminates every element of beauty, in order to leave only the repulsive elements, and submits these to an imaginative treatment carrying them beyond the bounds of all conceivable repulsiveness. To this job Swift has devoted by far the most considerable part of his work. It at least serves to prove that man is a Yahoo.

Ought it to be said that Swift's work is only an instance of the perversion of fairly considerable gifts under the influence of a paradox? Swift is above all a logical being; at least so he would wish to believe. He did not remain so to the end. Under an opposite influence—one only—his philosophy belied itself. One day, lying sick, after having, as usual, vented his spleen in insults and imprecations, he felt the need of being consoled, helped, loved. A woman there chances to be who listens to him with sympathy. She tends him like a humble slave; when he raves indecently, when his brutish passions break out, with gall in every word he utters, then her " soft speech " cheers his anguish, or her tears melt his wrath. Perhaps at that moment he remembered a former time when

> on my sickly couch I lay,
> Impatient both of night and day,
> Lamenting in unmanly strains,
> Call'd every power to ease my pains;

> Then Stella ran to my relief,

as she has always done, as she will always do. Contact with this influence causes light to flash upon him. Is he not himself a brute? Elsewhere he may have set himself up for the impeccable censor of the vices of mankind; now he feels that the only Yahoo in the world is he and that he has no one but himself to render responsible for it.

In his way, Swift has confessed and repented. When Stella is by his side he tries to amend. In her honour he composes the only lyric poetry he has written. Stella may have her deformities, but he will not see them. In order to examine her wrinkles this pitiless scrutinizer "would be ashamed to use a glass." For her he marshals forth all the best qualities of his mind and style. His imagination, but now ghastly or morbid, softens and changes into tender playfulness tinged with fancy. Stella is the angel whose charm age cannot alter, an angel at thirty-six as at sixteen. In the expression of this quiet affection, which was never love, Swift found his true lyric strain. It is to his credit that he at this time puts one in mind of Cowper singing the glorious old age of Mary Unwin.

Is it likely that he could approach lyricism with the freshness of inspiration of a man who had never tried to profane it? Does not the inveterate habit he has given his mind render him incapable of feeling real inspiration? Not quite, but it prevents him from keeping at the height he has reached. He now speaks the right language, with intelligence and conviction, but still with a slight accent and, at times, slips of the tongue that would be incomprehensible if it were not known to what a process of deterioration he had subjected his soul. He wishes to celebrate Stella's virtues; the theme inspires him; he writes eight fine lines running: "Heroes and heroines of old By honour only were enrolled Among their brethren in the skies, To which, though late, shall Stella rise. Ten thousand oaths upon record Are not so sacred as her word. The world shall in its ashes end Ere Stella can deceive a friend,"—all at once the evil influence comes over him again and what bid fair to be a lyric continues as a parody:—"For Stella never learned the art At proper times to scream and start: Doll never flies to cut her lace Or throw cold water in her face"

> Because she heard a sudden drum
> *Or found an earwig in a plum.*

Such is Swift's poetry: limited but very real gifts, degradation of these gifts by a philosophy which is the very negation of art, attempted amendment in moments of repentance and, in the end, discovery that it is too late.

# WORDSWORTH'S "IMAGINATION"

> Our birth is but a sleep and a forgetting,
> The Soul that rises with us, our life's star,
>  Hath had elsewhere its setting
>   And cometh from afar....

To understand the origin of Wordsworth's "Imagination" it is necessary to start from this affirmation where he expresses more clearly than anywhere else the conviction that animates all his poetry. The theory of the *Ode* is not new: it is, as may be seen, the Platonic theory—the belief in an ideal type which precedes all the forms of reality and to which all these forms must be referred. Wordsworth felt with quite particular intensity the illusion which leads us to think, on first seeing a new object, that we have already seen it elsewhere. It is this same feeling which makes Shelley say, when speaking of the odours, beams, and tones of the enchanted isle:

> They seem
> Like echoes of an ante-natal dream.

According to Wordsworth, in this ante-natal dream we have distinctly seen in all their perfection these things which on awaking we only find again confused and imperfect on earth.

On issuing from its sleep, the child still retains the faculty of comparing reality with the ideal, the remembrance of which yet remains unimpaired in its memory. But, before he has been able to realize its value, this power grows weaker—

> Shades of the prison-house begin to close
> Upon the growing boy....

This first way of feeling does not, however, become entirely obliterated. On growing aware of the inconsistencies of reality, the child feels perplexed. He soon notices the weakness of the senses as organs of perception. There is a very brief period during which he enjoys the simple pleasures of sight and hearing, the time of "glad animal movements" (*Tintern Abbey*)—accepting the world of sensation as it is, without seeking beyond. But this unconscious pleasure does not last long; these superficial impressions do not satisfy the heart of the youth. In moments of elation the spectacle of nature sinks down deeper into his being, so deeply that he is frightened:

> In that silence while he hung
> Listening, a gentle shock of mild surprise
> Has carried far into his heart the voice
> Of mountain-torrents; or the visible scene
> Would enter unawares into his mind
> With all its solemn imagery....
> > ("There was a boy....")

He soon feels the need of prolonging these moments of ecstacy. It is then only that he seems to see things in their true light. When, purified, calmed by his peaceable love of nature, he succeeds in repressing every physical sensation, to live only in soul, then he

sees looming through reality the forgotten ideal the
senses could not reveal to him:

> that serene and blessed mood
> In which the affections gently lead us on—
> Until—the breath of this corporeal frame
> And even the motion of our living blood
> Almost suspended, we are laid asleep
> In body and become a living soul:
> While, with an eye made quiet by the power
> Of harmony and the deep power of joy,
> We see into the life of things.

Even in *Tintern Abbey*, however, Wordsworth expresses the fear this supernatural penetration may be
an illusion…"If this be but a vain belief…."  In reality,
these moments become so rare and are so fleeting
that he can no longer believe in them.  How then
shall he call them back and fix them?

Wordsworth does not wish to reach the ideal by
abstracting from reality.  He does not want to with-
draw his gaze from the world of sensation, but he
wishes to sharpen his faculty of vision, in order to be
able to scrutinize things until his eye succeeds in
distinguishing, through all material envelopes, the
ideal.  His peaceable and sleepy nature has perhaps
too great a tendency to indulge in the charm of
sensible things, to slumber too securely in reality.
There is a moment, delightful, but through its very
stillness unsatisfactory to the mind, in which he
yearns for

> The silence that is in the starry sky,
> The sleep that is among the lonely hills.
> (*Song at the Feast of Brougham Castle.*)

It is then that he becomes filled with

> the silence and the calm
> Of mute insensate things.
> (" Three years she grew in sun and shower.")

"A slumber did my spirit seal," he says then, and in this lethargy his spirit forgets its own independent existence to identify itself with rocks and stones and trees...

> No motion has she now, no force,
> She neither hears nor sees,
> Rolled round in earth's diurnal course
> With rocks and stones and trees.
> ("A slumber did my spirit seal.")

This torpor which lulls the soul to sleep, in order that the senses may, without remorse, enjoy Nature, is the very negation of that first activity which made everything the reflex of a preconceived ideal, an ideal half veiled, but which persists in the depths of memory and which all the faculties of the man must make it their study to revive. The direct observation of reality obscures rather than reveals this ideal. The ascendency of the world of sense is too great. Wordsworth understands that his first duty is to get free from it.

It is at this moment that creative Imagination steps in to effect a kind of transposition of reality. In an *Evening Voluntary* Wordsworth describes this process of transformation. At eve, by the side of a lake, he listens to the owlet's scream. The landscape is reflected in the water, the shadow of the bird seems to be suspended in it and, at the same time, he fancies

he hears rising up out of the depths of the water the
*echo* of the hooting:

> then, ('mid the gleam
> Of unsubstantial imagery, the dream
> From the hushed vale's realities transferred
> To the still lake,) the *imaginative* bird
> Seems, 'mid inverted mountains, not unheard.

It must have been noticed that Wordsworth has a
preference for a landscape seen in the mirror of a lake
or a stream rather than in reality[1].   This idealizing
effect which deprives reality of its tangible character,
without taking away any of its charm, appears to
Wordsworth as the symbol of imagination.   The too
direct impression, by acting too forcibly on the senses,
dazzles him.  He needs time to collect himself, in order
to find the ideal again in the depths of memory and
to suit reality to it.  This need for perspective is very
clearly marked in the *Daffodils*.   No doubt, the sight
of the flowers gives him pleasure, but while he is
looking at them how far he is from feeling their value.
What is of consequence is not the sight of the daffodils,
but the impression they are able to leave on the
memory.

> I gazed and gazed but little thought
> What wealth the show to me had brought....

It is only after a certain lapse of time that the physical
impression changes into spiritual vision.   Then, the
flowers pass again before the mind's eye clothed
with new splendour:

> They flash upon that inward eye
> Which is the bliss of solitude.

[1] See : " There was a boy "....*Airey-force Valley...The Prelude.*

Wordsworth thus forms the habit of looking at nothing
without a mental reserve. He always asks himself in
what form the thing he is momentarily looking at
will reappear later. Its beauty will no longer be
judged by the immediate impression, but by the impression it will leave on the retina of the imagination.

> Here I stand, not only with the sense
> Of present pleasure, but with pleasing thoughts
> That in this moment there is life and food
> For future years....            (*Tintern Abbey.*)

So, imagination must start from reality. The shock it
receives from the sight of sensible things must awaken
in it the remembrance of the ideal. It is dangerous
for it to get too much accustomed to contemplating
an ideal as yet unrealized, for later, on comparing this
abstract ideal with its counterpart on earth, it might
suffer a disillusion. This is what happens to the poet
in the case of Mont Blanc, of which he has too much
fostered in advance a purely idealistic image :

> That very day
> From a bare ridge we also first beheld
> Unveiled the summit of Mont Blanc, and grieved
> To have a soulless image on the eye
> That had usurped upon a living thought
> That never more could be.      (*Prelude*, Bk VI.)

It is this disillusion he fears for Yarrow, and that is
why, the first time, he refuses to go and see this river,
of which he has formed too precise an idea in his
imagination.

> We have a vision of our own,
> Ah ! why should we undo it ?
>                 (*Yarrow Unvisited.*)

But the deception he feared he does not experience. Wordsworth, with that strong feeling for reality which always saved him, goes and seeks a new joy in the direct sight of Yarrow:

> But thou that didst appear so fair
>   To fond imagination
> Dost rival in the light of day
>   Her delicate creation....

Consequently, he carries away with him a remembrance which retains all the charm of the preconceived image, adding to it the satisfaction of reality:

> I know where'er I go
> Thy genuine image, Yarrow,
> Will dwell with me—to heighten joy
> And cheer my mind in sorrow.
>
>                 (*Yarrow Visited.*)

And the sight and remembrance of Yarrow so well fulfil his expectations that he does not fear to come back to it a second time, in order to put his impression to the test. He receives but a new confirmation of it—a conviction henceforth unshakable :

> To dream-light dear, while yet unseen,
> Dear to the common sunshine
> And dearer still, as now I feel,
> To memory's shadowy moonshine.
>
>                 (*Yarrow Re-visited.*)

Lastly, memory is the most powerful auxiliary of imagination. Sensible things seen in the distant prospect of remembrance are divested of all that is accidental or ephemeral about them, retaining only their essential attributes. When the poet has succeeded, by means of this process of reflection, in seeing them in their inmost truth, consistent with the ideal type he ever carries in himself, he may again compare remembrance with reality, of which now *he will be able to see only the essential feature.* Thus, reality and the imaginary type, found again in the depths of remembrance, strengthen and complete each other. Perhaps the poem of Wordsworth's which most clearly shows the stages through which his mind passes again and again, before finding the satisfaction it seeks, is "She was a phantom of delight." The beloved, first vaguely perceived in the twilight of imagination, little by little gains more consistency, as the poet approaches nearer to the woman as she exists in reality,—but reality does not yet suffice: the poet must penetrate to the inmost essence of her soul, and then, having found the ideal, there will come and settle on the head of the beloved the pristine halo that hovered about the phantom preconceived by the imagination.

First, the phantom :

> She was a phantom of delight
> When first she gleamed upon my sight....

Next, the woman :

> I saw her on a nearer view,
> A spirit, yet a woman too....

Then, the spiritualized, ideal being :

> And now I see with eye serene
> The very pulse of the machine....

In the last place, the union of all three :

> A being breathing thoughtful breath
> A traveller between life and death...
> A perfect woman nobly planned
> To warm, to comfort and command—
> —And yet a Spirit still and bright
> With something of an angel-light.—

It is thus that Wordsworth comes back to his
starting-point. The initial theory is not disowned by
him,—the belief in the preconceived ideal remains ;
all his efforts had but one aim : the transmission to
reality, or rather the learning to see through reality,
of this first ideal. But, in order to be able to come
back to this ideal of his youth, in order

> to beget
> That golden time again
> *(Cuckoo)*

he must submit the impressions received by the
senses to the action of memory, which obliterates
whatever is useless in them, to retain essentials only.

This is how Wordsworth comes to think he may
define his as

> a mind sustained
> By recognitions of transcendent power
> In sense conducting to ideal form.
> *(Prelude,* Bk XIV.)

Lastly, this is why he thinks he may claim for
Imagination the highest place among the human
faculties, for, to him, Imagination is nothing but
Reason under its poetic aspect, Reason whose sole
object is to discover, under all the forms of reality,
the ideal :

> Imagination............in truth
> Is but another name for absolute power
> And clearest insight, amplitude of mind
> And Reason in her most exalted mood.
> *(Prelude,* Bk XIV.)

# THE HOUSE OF LIFE

THIS work occupies a place by itself, outside the sphere of the great normal development of English literature. Begun about 1848, published between 1870 and 1881, it revealed to the public, in poetic form, the principles of a small circle of artists and men of letters, very little known and very exclusive—the new Pleiad founded under the name of "The Pre-Raphaelite Brotherhood." It is then the work of a *coterie*. Nothing in the general tendencies of the century foreshadowed it. It satisfies no instinctive need of the time. Its origins are more remote. It is a reconstitution as well as a creation. It is suggestive of æsthetics both new and renewed, which, while inspired by ancient methods, have, with quite modern materials, known how to shape out an individuality of their own.

*The House of Life* is a late blossom of the Renaissance, or rather it is a Renaissance refined, harmonious, self-conscious, transposed into the very heart of the nineteenth century. It would be a mistake to take it for a mere historical evocation such as many before Rossetti had accomplished; his distinctive achievement is to have divined the vital

principle of that forgotten art and then to have known
how to utilize it for the exhibition of the joys, struggles
and speculations of his own life. It is a principle
already known that he adopts, but he assimilates it
so perfectly that he succeeds in deriving from it
a personal and original art. And precisely because
he is so thoroughly imbued with the *spirit* of the
time, it is not the Renaissance at a given moment
that he reproduces; no, it is through all the great crises
of the epoch that his soul passed, thus leaving on the
work traces of progressive development. In twenty
years (1860–1880) he condensed and transposed into
another key the yield of four centuries.

Rossetti was born at a time when life was becoming disaggregated, as a consequence of an ever
more marked tendency to specialization. During
his youth the energies of society are exhausted by
continual internal strife. Religion has lost its omni-
potence as a political influence; ethics become more
and more the affair of the laity; art, in its turn, pro-
claims its independence of ethics and the arts become
clearly differentiated; lastly, science declares war
on all and already bids fair to be mistress of the
future. True, on both sides conciliation is attempted,
but the very effort points to the feeling of division.
This general tendency of civilization makes itself
felt in literature. The vital forces of art are frittered
away in perpetual analysis. Drama is, so to speak,
no longer extant—a sure sign of lack of cohesion
in the creative spirit; the novel, a pre-eminently
analytical form, holds supreme sway; the poetry of
the day, in the hands of Browning, of Tennyson and

their disciples, is chiefly concerned about making the novelist's methods its own. To this poetry, which has already shown all its qualities of minute fidelity, of finish in details, and which ceaseless vivisection is beginning to exhaust, Rossetti again sets the example of the above all homogeneous art of the Renaissance.

It is instinctively that he enters into the spirit of that epoch, whose ideal was the holding in equilibrium of all the faculties of the individual, the perfect distribution of all the forces of society—an epoch when religion directed the sum-total of human activities, when ethics had not yet thought of disowning their natural origin, when art conformed to the requirements of ethics, when, especially, the arts recognized their kinship, when, above all, the essentially analytical spirit of science had not yet sowed discord. In him it is not the outcome of conscious effort, it is not the triumph of highly-developed historical penetration : it is the result of the accident which caused him, an Italian, to be born on British soil, and to be brought up in the society of the masters of yore,—those universal and encyclopædic intellects whose names are Leonardo, Michael Angelo, Chaucer, above all Dante. Of this accident he knows how to take advantage, and this is seen when his double vocation of painter and poet becomes manifest. It allows him to throw himself literally heart and soul into the life of that great movement which may be said to exert all its powers of cohesion with a view to but one object, viz. the conciliation of the material world and of the invisible world. The education of Rossetti, whose sentiments and sensations progress side by side, becoming ever more refined, causes him to feel with the force of personal conviction the equal importance of the two sides of the problem. At once poet and painter, viewing his feelings with a painter's eyes, reproducing external objects with the soul of a poet, the happily harmonized dualism of his vocation inclines him instinctively towards that broad conception of art that the profane term symbolism, and the faithful, with a more correct comprehension of its meaning, naturalism. Its characteristic feature is the insisting upon the indivisibility of mind and matter, under whatever form the union may appear, whether it be in man, in nature, or in art. In the most general fashion, it may be said that the spirit that animates the Renaissance is the spirit of synthesis, as opposed to the spirit of analysis. Rossetti's merit consists in having known how, in an analytical age, to instil this synthetic spirit into his art, both in its main outlines and in its details.

The principle, then, is borrowed from another epoch, but the modifications Rossetti causes it to undergo, in the conception as well as in the execution of the poem, are so perfectly calculated as to give it the appearance of a novelty.

Its central subject is the celebration of that complete ideal of love of which the men of the Renaissance sang so much, based on the Platonic ideal of beauty. The fundamental theme, on which he sings all the variations of hope, ecstasy and regret, is the equal satisfaction of the senses and of the soul in physical beauty inseparable from moral beauty. Rossetti makes this well-known conception his own and transforms it into something absolutely original. He refines upon the work of the Renaissance. What distinguishes him is his much more intense feeling of the blending. By a more delicate instinct of condensation, he raises his own conception above all those that may have served him as models. The heroine of his prolonged epithalamium, like her sisters, unites spiritual and physical perfection; in her, as in the others, outward beauty is accepted as a symbol of inward beauty; but this is not all. She is body as well as spirit, if you will, and yet, on close inspection, she is neither one nor the other. In the blending, something of the essential quality of each has evaporated. You might think she was vacillating between the two. She appears to us in a kind of indecision, living yet immaterial; it is Rossetti's triumph to have succeeded in arresting and rendering this character of hesitation, in divining the connexion between the body, always quivering as with the electric thrill of the spirit that animates it, and the spirit, always soaring above the form in which it is pleased to become incarnate for a while, like one of those delicate transparent flames that play about a jet of smoke without ever settling on it. She produces the impression of motion amid calm—like lights that cross in the depths of still waters. She is only clearly seen when but half seen. " When do I see thee most, beloved one ? " asks the lover. It is not in the full radiance of day, it is in the veiled and fugitive light of the gloaming

> When in the dusk hours—(we two alone)—
> Close-kissed and èloquent of still replies
> Thy twilight-hidden glimmering visage lies.

Her changeful eyes

> > like water brimming with the sky
> > Or hyacinth-light where forest-shadows fall,

her "glances' sweet recall Of love," her long lithe throat, the thrilling pallor of her cheek, the delicate love-lines of her mouth,—these things are so much spiritualized by the motion in which lies all their charm that they seem to have existence only on the confines of the invisible.  Even her hair has a meaning ; it is loved not so much for its deep golden masses as for its soft touch, living like a caress. All her life seems an unconscious effort to transform her physical beauty into spiritual beauty.  Her uncertain kiss, as soon as it succeeds in settling, lingers on the mouth like a thought.  "Her tremulous kisses faltered "...but soon she recovers herself " And, as she kissed, *her mouth became her soul.*" (*Secret Parting.*)

This oscillation in the object will give rise to a corresponding oscillation in the soul of the lover. In the same degree as the connexion between the spirit and the body of the woman seems unsettled, does the lover feel perplexity concerning the relative importance to be attached to the two sides of love, *Passion* (of Love) and (Love's) *Worship*.  Her physical perfections first attract him :

> Sweet dimness of her loosened hair's downfall
> > About thy face ; her sweet hands round thy head
> > In gracious fostering union garlanded ;
> Her tremulous smiles ; her glances' sweet recall

Of love ; her murmuring sighs memorial ;
  Her mouth's culled sweetness by thy kisses shed
  On cheeks and neck and eyelids, and so led
Back to her mouth which answers there for all :—

What sweeter than these things ?

But at the moment when he asks himself this question, the feeling that these things owe not only the value but the very existence of their beauty to a higher beauty, which though invisible is none the less powerful, gives him an inkling of the answer : Nothing is sweeter than these things

                              except the thing
  In lacking which all these would lose their sweet.

As may be divined, this mysterious beauty is

  The confident heart's still fervour : the swift beat
  And soft subsidence of the spirit's wing,
  Then when it feels, in cloud-girt wayfaring,
    The breath of kindred plumes against its feet.
                              (*Love-Sweetness.*)

There is indeed an oscillation, but an oscillation which will soon settle down into perfect equipoise. This hesitation will not be resolved by choice between alternatives, but by harmony.   Rossetti is on the way to the most complete and most elevated definition of love ever discovered.  A time will come when spiritual beauty will have so thoroughly permeated physical beauty, when physical beauty will have become so perfectly spiritualized that love will no longer be able to distinguish them.  The soul and the body of this woman correspond as do meaning and word, but in absolutely sincere, absolutely true speech, word and meaning join in one:

> Her speech Truth knows not from her thought
> Nor Love her body from her soul.
>
> (*Love-Lily.*)

Nothing better shows the superiority of Rossetti's conception over all that preceded as over all that surrounded him, than this indissoluble union between the two aspects of love. We are far from the pseudo-scientific analysis that modern psychology has made use of to kill and dissect every normal sentiment. Rossetti makes emotion healthier by freeing it from morbid speculation, a result no less important from the moral than from the æsthetic point of view. And in doing so he improved upon the Renaissance conception. What is slightly painful in all the work of the Renaissance is the feeling of division which persists beneath all these efforts at mediation, even in its greatest men. The poet of the sixteenth century appreciates spiritual beauty to the same degree as physical beauty, but not at the same moment. He celebrates both, but not in the same work. He writes a Hymn to Earthly Beauty and another to Heavenly Beauty. But Rossetti carries the love of both to that degree of exaltation where extremes meet.

The best proof of the solidity of a philosophical conception is perhaps the ease with which it subordinates the imaginative form. Feeling so direct and intense seeks a form of expression equally direct. But how can such an immaterial thing as feeling succeed in assuming a concrete form without becoming chilled? According to our modern conceptions it is difficult to raise feeling to imagination, because we always wish to see them as distinct things. All our system of images, metaphors, etc. depends on comparison, but the division implied in comparison suffices to deprive the things compared of their vitality. A living and acting whole will never be the result. The poets of yore were clearer-sighted. They well understood the necessity of a more coherent imaginative conception. This boundary-line between the essential thing and the point of comparison is fatal to the life of the whole; it must be suppressed. This can only be done when feeling shall have succeeded in transforming itself of its own accord into a real person, master of its impulses changed into actions. It is this principle, very human, much anterior to the Renaissance and which reappears at all the great imaginative epochs, that was transmitted to Rossetti. The artistic education of the poet is here not without influence. He is not content to examine his emotions with the intellect; he wants to see them besides with the eyes. How are the feelings in question to be represented on canvas? Every kind of comparison is impossible; there a direct imaginative form is required. It is as a painter as much as as a poet that Rossetti accepts symbolism under the aspect of personification. So, each of his feelings will assume corporeal shape, will become a living being with special attributes—Love, Passion, Worship, Death-in-Love, Death, etc. He recreates a whole mythology for his own use.

I say that he recreates and not that he creates

or adopts. It is certain that for his method Rossetti is indebted to his precursors, but only very superficial reading of his work could lead to the conclusion that he is content to reproduce, without modification, conventional types. It is a case of the novel application of a principle already known, not of the servile appropriation of results obtained previously. The allegorical figures that live in *The House of Life* have only a racial connexion, without marked personal resemblance, with their ancestors of the Renaissance or antiquity. Each of them expresses by its external appearance one of those very subtle changes of feeling we had noticed in the general conception. The comparison might be made in the case of all the personages, but the modification that has most interest, since it bears upon the central subject, is the one the poet causes the god of Love to undergo. Nothing better evidences his power of adaptation than the fashion in which this little Cupid, blindfolded, shooting arrows at random according to his mischievous or cruel caprice, becomes transformed into a Christian angel with earnest look and feeling voice, neither light-headed nor evil, pensive, merciful, helpful, beneath the halo that gilds his head like the glory of a saint. (See *Bridal Birth, Love's Lovers, Love's Baubles, Death-in-Love*, above all *Willowwood*.)

Feelings endowed with this independent individuality are able to converse quite freely without any intervention of the author's. This clearness of artistic presentation, whatever our difficulty in getting accustomed to it, better fulfils the conditions of objective art than all the cynical impassibility with which our contemporary masters handle the scalpel. Rossetti continually starts dialogues, in which the speakers are differentiated and stand out in perfect relief, either between himself and an embodied emotion or between two opposite feelings: Love and the two lovers, Passion and Worship, etc. He endows his feelings with as much reality as the personages of his ballads.

This construction in dialogue form would seem to carry the work in the direction of drama, and we are tempted to ask why, with his instinct for scenic effect, Rossetti did not produce his work in the form of a lyric tragedy. It would, however, be going too far to set Rossetti up for a dramatist. He has one of the principal qualifications required, viz. the power of seeing his personages and feelings in an objective and coherent form, but he did not possess in a sufficient degree the gift of animating his synthetic creations with motion. It cannot be denied there is in his work that kind of still motion contained in fluctuation, and even a power of progressive development which is at times very effective; what is lacking is suppleness. This is probably why he did not attempt dramatic composition; but he had sufficient feeling for construction to seek in lyric poetry for the form best adapted to dialogue or to the ebb and flow of feeling. He found it, like so many others before him, in the sonnet.

His task was to reform rather than to revive it. The sonnet had not fallen into disuse, but it had lost all its original cohesion. As might have been expected, in the hands of the dreamy, contemplative romantics, inclined rather to meditation that dilutes than to passion that condenses, the form of the sonnet had gradually become more and more lax. Rossetti's mission was to re-establish it on its former basis. On the question of form he proved almost invariably uncompromising, for, with his conception of construction, he needed a very steady framework with very definite outlines in which to place his dialogues between feelings. Without entering into a full technical study, Rossetti's various efforts may be summed up under a single heading. His ideal is to restore the balance between the two halves of the sonnet, without allowing either to trespass on the department of the other. The romantics, under the influence probably of Shakespeare, had forgotten this fundamental rule: Rossetti calls them back to order. He emphasizes the boundary between the octave and the sestet, but this division in form aims at bringing back unity of thought. It tallies with his usual method of construction—question and answer—as may be seen by the following example. (Love is upbraiding the poet with having forgotten his first beloved, and the poet defends himself):—

*Question.*

"When that dead face, bowered in the furthest years,
    Which once was all the life years held for thee,
    Can now scarce bid the tides of memory
    Cast on thy soul a little spray of tears,—
    How canst thou gaze into these eyes of hers
    Whom now thy heart delights in, and not see
    Within each orb Love's philtred euphrasy
    Make them of buried troth remembrancers?"

*Answer.*

"Nay, pitiful Love, nay, loving Pity! Well
   Thou knowest that in these twain I have confessed
   Two very voices of thy summoning bell.
   Nay, Master, shall not Death make manifest
   In these the culminant changes which approve
   The love-moon that must light my soul to love?"

                                        (*The Love-Moon.*)

This sonnet, which may be taken as typical, fulfils the conditions the poet lays down in his definition of the sonnet:

   A Sonnet is a coin; its face reveals
   The soul, its converse to what power 'tis due.

In a word, the analytical sonnet was losing itself in a parabola: Rossetti, by reinstating the synthetic sonnet, clenches it into a circle.

All these modifications tend towards a firmer construction, but, in the building up of the materials, will Rossetti be able to make the great effort of synthesis implied in the cohesion of the parts in the whole? Before deciding about the result, it is well to recall what we have said about the circumstances under which the work was composed. We have seen in what way it differs from the century in which it appeared and, on the other hand, how great is the advance it had made on the forgotten art by which it was inspired, but to this first great change is superadded an internal change. As we have already said, it is not by any particular phase of the Renaissance that Rossetti was influenced. He examines it from all sides, he studies it at all the essential moments of its development. During the twenty years he

devoted to the elaboration of this volume, which he
intended to be both a chronicle of his life and the
crowning of his art, his mind passed through all the
stages of the movement.    And, now that we have
determined in what way Rossetti's method differs from
that of his contemporaries and, on the other hand, how
he grasped the general result of the Renaissance and
made it his own, let us scrutinize the subject more
closely and ask what new modifications will need to
be made in this general modification owing to the
changes that took place in the development of his art.

Rossetti began his literary life by the study of the
greatest precursor of the Renaissance : Dante.    Thus
he became imbued with all the vigour and all the
sincerity of a primitive epoch which has not yet
succeeded in defining itself and is still groping its
way.    Under the influence of Dante and his circle,
he remodelled his soul into that of a mediæval artist.
He sets to work painfully, laboriously, without being
clearly conscious of what he is going to do ; he has
only one anxiety, viz. to adhere to truth.    He seeks
the highest and most refined expression of his inner-
most feelings, without much heeding the demands of
the public.    Working only for his own satisfaction, he
subjects his emotion as well as his art to a filtering
process which leaves only what is choicest, most
exquisite and most precious.    He writes his sonnets
one by one, under the impulse of pleasure or pain,
without thinking of collecting them in a volume.
Having no fixed plan, he is free to give to each one
of the constituent parts its maximum density, without
troubling about their interconnexion.    He is guided in

his work by an artist's sense of honour, which prevents him from exhibiting anything but the quintessence of feeling. Accordingly he manages to enshrine in some fifty sonnets and a dozen songs all the significant moments of his moral life, and they are so many blood-drops wrung from his heart by prolonged meditation. He has now material wherewith to make a pendant to his beloved *Vita Nuova.* So he decides to publish these fragments provisorily, while he is waiting to have discovered a plan for the whole work. This was the first version of 1870 entitled *Sonnets and Songs towards a work to be called " The House of Life."*

From this first sketch the framework of the whole may be divined. Its outlines are already drawn, albeit with an unsteady hand. The poem is vaguely divided into two parts, the one devoted to the story which properly speaking forms its subject, the second to the speculations to which it gives rise in the poet's soul. There are few facts, no explanations, no attempt at connexion: nothing but phases of feeling. Rossetti knows how to exhibit them with a brevity that does equal credit to the delicacy and to the power of his emotion. For him, the veil that hides the most delicate feelings is like the sheet of tissue-paper that protects a rare engraving amid the pages of a much-read book. It is with an infinitely dexterous hand that he lifts the sheet without crumpling it, exposes the engraving to view for a moment and then covers it again before its freshness is soiled. It is with such candour and such exquisite taste as this simile suggests that he describes the essential moments of

his private life : the awakening of love in the heart
of his lady, the hope of early union, the evenings
spent together, the kiss, the nuptial sleep, the spouse's
cogitations about his sleeping love ; then, all the
minor and yet significant circumstances of their daily
life in common ; and next, described with ever the
same good taste, the first fears of separation, the
foreshadowings of death, the death of the beloved ;
lastly, his regrets, his solitary suffering, the anguish
which seeks to lose itself in art and meditation, the
resigned expectation of death.

This first version teaches nothing, proves nothing,
does not hold together as a whole, but it has a more
subtle charm, the charm of perfect feeling exquisitely
if incompletely expressed. In reading it we feel the
same pleasure as in hearing a voice absolutely pure
and true sing scraps of old forgotten tunes. It is, in
another key, what the *Vita Nuova* would have been
without the prose commentary. If it is not without
defects, it is free from incongruities.

And if it contains no incongruities, it is in virtue
of its very defects. It is homogeneous in feeling
because it is of pure breed, and it is of pure breed
because it owes its origin to a primitive age. The
Italian art from which Rossetti drew his inspiration
had not yet been deteriorated by the cosmopolitan
spirit which was later to take possession of the Renaissance. The poet had really only to sift Italian feeling,
in order to convey it into English, but as is the case
with every exclusive art, it was deficient in the detachment, the suppleness of technique which contact with
other nations confers. It is technical skill that Rossetti

next borrows from the later Renaissance, with a view to modelling the complete work.

Twelve years elapse before the definitive poem is published. In the interval Rossetti has had time to realize what he wanted or rather what he should have wanted. The design of the work has become clearer, the indistinct outlines have become firmer. The poem is now divided into two distinct parts, with a general introduction, prologues and epilogues. The fifty sonnets of the first version, with some changes and suppressions, still stand foremost, fifty other explanatory and connecting sonnets being added. The fragments have fallen into line in a series; the poem, as to construction, forms a complete whole.

It no longer forms such a whole in the matter of feeling. The additions are not in the same style as the first sonnets. They belong to the end of the Renaissance, when the universal spread of primitive art had greatly deteriorated its quality. Italian feeling and English feeling no longer form a true blend; the addition of extraneous influences has diminished their intensity. Both seem to have been filtered through French feeling, and from the point of view of technique this is an advantage, but it has appreciably cooled and diluted the emotion. And worse still, what in Sidney and Lodge would have been additional grace and point, in the hands of Rossetti, whose mind was subtle but not acute, becomes a *marivaudage* both awkward and childish. In the combination what was most personal in Rossetti has been volatilized. The first version is the true work of a Pre-Raphaelite, not out of affectation but out of excess of artistic conscientiousness ; the second is the weakened echo of an exhausted age. It would be very little above the level of the contemporary English volumes of poetry, were it not for that fund of true feeling it has retained from the first work.

Rossetti was endowed with the acumen needful to enable him to enter into the spirit of an age already remote in feeling if not through lapse of years ; he had, besides, an instinct for assimilation sufficiently powerful to be able to follow and reproduce the evolution of the whole age ; what he lacked was the suppleness that would have allowed him to come back on the work when once finished, to clench its two ends together and to leave the whole vibrating with the emotion of the beginning, still fresh in feeling, intense in thought, concise in expression, with the mastery of technique, the freedom of style, the clearness of presentation and of connexion of the subsequent age.  He has given us a pleasing commentary of the Renaissance ; he has not given us what he was qualified to give us, what we had a right to expect of him, sufficiently contemporaneous in feeling to enter into the most obscure intentions of the movement, sufficiently disinterested to judge its defects and correct its faults—viz. the clear and conscious realization of what his predecessors had vaguely sought.  *The House of Life* contains the fragments of a masterpiece ; through lack of unity in workmanship it falls just below the standard of the great examples of this form of composition.

# THE CHARACTER
# OF JOHN INGLESANT

"I SHOULD not hate to be delivered over in trust to a rational person and to be governed by him in all things, absolutely, and always," La Bruyère confesses in one of his communicative moods. This longing, although purely human, appears to me to set the key of the feeling that inclines to religion a soul in which emotion is predominant. It is the need of finding in the depths of conscience a friend to whom one can unreservedly give oneself up, a friend who, while making allowance for all weaknesses, shall serve as a guide through all temptations to good. This feeling, in general, remains a mere vague aspiration; under favourable circumstances it rapidly develops into an all-absorbing preoccupation. When this influence has come to take possession of the whole of one's life, it is time to set it up as a principle, to be expressed by a symbol. In John Inglesant's case it takes the name of the Divine Light.

He in early youth conceives the project of devoting his life to the search for this distant Light, somewhat after the manner of Sir Galahad seeking the Holy Grail. The loneliness of his childhood, spent in a house haunted with visions and phantoms of the past, inclines him to mystic dreaminess. His readings in Plato, mixing with the surrounding influences of Christianity, lead him little by little to this idealistic conception of life regulated by the sole voice of reason speaking in the stillness of the soul. And so he is prepared to wait indefinitely for the revelation of the sound of this Voice or the shining of this Light ; so he can say with his master : " There is nothing in the world of any value but the Divine Light " ; so he is content to remain in ignorance, convinced " That it shall reveal itself when the time shall come."

This time is not to come yet. Between the moment when John Inglesant as a child vows to seek the unknown Light and the moment when the Light itself is revealed to the grown man, the youth's character develops. Unawares a subtle, penetrating influence, impalpable like an atmosphere, envelops him, enters into him, radically modifying all the faculties through which he will be able to perceive or put in practice the counsels of the Divine Voice. A man appears to him "as an angel of light" (p. 122). How can he help believing this angel is commissioned to lead him towards the Divine Light ? And he does lead him to it, but in a peculiar manner.

Father Sancta Clara himself has no independent will : he belongs to the vast organization of the Society of Jesus ; it is his duty to develop in the direction of the interest of his cause the nascent powers of young Inglesant. In the latter he divines a nature of exceptionally fine grain, which needs delicate hand-ling. He takes an artist's pride in shaping it. Soon

becoming aware to what a degree the spiritual ideal
has already absorbed the power of emotion in his
pupil, he makes no effort to thwart it, but subordinates
it to his own purposes. To attain his object, he begins
by allowing the youth unlimited liberty of speculation. He shows him his idea under all its aspects.
John Inglesant, through continually hearing this principle which he calls the Divine Light upheld or debated
under all kinds of names, ends in losing himself in the
multiplicity of systems. Owing to their discrepancies
or their hesitations, their first effect is to produce in
him a lack of moral resolution of which the jesuit
knows how to take advantage. Inglesant is not and
never will be self-confident ; in the state of continual
doubt in which he lives, his conscience, grown hyper-
sensitive like all his other faculties, forbids him to
disseminate his own theories which, unfortunately,
are anything but convictions. Besides, his master
gives him to understand that proselytizing would be
improper: "You have taken a wise course," he says
in answer to the young enthusiast who has just been
setting forth his conception of the Divine Light and
the difficulty he experiences in finding guidance;
"this is the most useful study you can follow, and
the most harmless to yourself, if you keep your own
counsel and gain knowledge without imparting it"
(p. 43). So Inglesant has to remain shut up in himself without projecting his personality outwards, and
to renounce translating his aspirations into actions.
Liberty of speculation limits liberty of action. And
besides not communicating his idea he is required not
to obey it personally. In his perplexity concerning

the nature of the Divine Light, he feels the need of support. While waiting for the manifestation of the Divine Light, some rule of conduct, whatever it may be, is indispensable. If the divine will delays making itself heard, he must seek for a substitute in a human will. The jesuit opens his arms. Inglesant throws himself into them. Liberty of speculation kills liberty of initiative.

Thus he becomes the slave of an alien will, and by this will will be all the more surely subjugated to certain habits of mind which no will, human or divine will be able to overcome. In a nature so fraught with emotion, after the mind has absorbed all it is able to contain, there remains over a residue which serves to feed the senses: very delicate, very refined senses, purified from all coarseness by the dominant intellect, but still senses calling for pleasure with an insistence as firm as discreet. Inglesant's education complacently develops the æsthetic side of life. The priest who directs him is at the same time a man of the world; by inculcating moral truths through the writings of antiquity he gives him the taste for form ; these truths in turn are echoed in the trifling civilities of polite society ; in the very religion he provisorily accepts while waiting for revelation, that religion intermediate between Catholicism and the faith of the Church of England, the ceremonial is evidently as full of charm as the doctrine. For Inglesant is meant to become not only an honest man, but more and less than an honest man,—a courtier. He has every aptitude requisite. As soon as the jesuit thinks him fit for court he takes him there, still keeping him in leading-strings. The influence of these luxurious surroundings definitively confirms Inglesant in this tendency of his nature. The Beautiful takes precedence of the Good. The former does not preclude the latter, but henceforth it conditions it. The Divine Light will only be able to shine behind the cloud of earthly enjoyment. As long as the two principles keep on good terms they serve as foils to each other, but in case of rupture there is already no doubt as to the issue. " He was a sincere believer in a holy life, and strongly desirous of pursuing it : he endeavoured conscientiously to listen for the utterances of the Divine Voice ; and provided that Voice pointed out to him that path which his tastes and training prepared him to expect, he would follow it, even at a sacrifice to himself ; but he was not capable of a sacrifice of his tastes or of his training " (p. 103). And, as if to show beforehand the dangers that might follow a rupture, lo, there rises up before John Inglesant his exact counterpart, his twin brother Eustace, a soul in which the need for pleasure has left no room for spiritual concerns and into which, in their absence, creep courteous weaknesses it would take but little to convert into vices.

Such is the progress made by the youth's mind since the day when he set out to seek the Divine Light. He has not yet found it and, what is worse, he has rendered himself incapable of turning it to practical account, when he shall have found it. For he has, without displeasure, abdicated his will. He is caught in the network of a great system. Attracted by the personal charm of one man, he has bound himself to a society which owes its power to the encouragement it gives to aspirations not always compatible with those of conscience. And even if he succeeds for a moment in so far conquering himself as to make pleasure give way to duty, this triumph is solely in feeling; it will be able to prompt him to no independent action, for, at the slightest sign of indocility, that higher will will crush him without mercy. He is like a swimmer who has unawares allowed himself to be carried away among weeds. As long as he floats on the surface without making any motion beyond what is required to keep him from sinking, immersed in the luxury of the tepid water titillating him on every side, the weeds do not molest him. But if a wish to get back to land arises in him, a thousand velvety hands detain him; while trying to extricate himself he only becomes entangled yet further; and at last, if he persists, an irresistibly gentle and gently irresistible power drags him down to the bottom.

Such is the struggle that looms up ahead, but before it begins a moment's respite is granted him.

He will be told later that God wished to win him by love. And it would indeed seem the Divine Light had taken the most graceful form in which to make itself manifest, while waiting for the most favourable occasion. John Inglesant is carried away, for a moment, into other surroundings. All the bonds that hold him are gently loosened. Withdrawn from all his temptations, delivered from the influence that hypnotizes his will, John Inglesant is free for the last time. The quiet that prevails about him in the

religious house, almost the convent, of Gidding
purifies all his being. A great stillness comes over
his soul. It is then that the revelation of the Divine
Voice comes by the mouth of the grey nun, the
Patient, the revelation of the Divine Light in the
peaceful eyes of Mary Collet. In her the author
seems to mean to symbolize pure Christianity, in
which alone he recognizes the true light. Beautiful
in itself, this religion has no need of the æsthetic
veil the jesuits throw over it. Mary Collet lives a
continual life of self-sacrifice, finding, in this very
power of self-sacrifice, freedom, since she is subject
to the influence of no worldly pleasure. (Observe,
even in the very "discourse" she repeats, the absence
of music and poetry...p. 57.) And Inglesant, a being
without personal will, since he has given up his not
only to a man but to a party, and not only to a party
but to the seductions that party has at its command,
is yet allowed, for a brief space of time, to enjoy this
liberty. Under the sweet impulse of the divine love
of which this mortal love is only the symbol, he is
drawn towards the Light. In the splendour of the
Light he at length beholds the Friend he has sought.
Under the eyes of Mary Collet, in the church of
Gidding, he fancies he perceives, behind the Christ
on the stained window, Jesus. For the first time he
sees him face to face.

He is saved or, at least, he has caught sight of
salvation. He sees the Divine Light, he knows how
to follow it ; just then the fatal influence encompasses
him more closely. The Light attracts him, speaks to
him lovingly in the gaze of Mary Collet, becomes

gracious, caressing, almost coaxing ; he goes towards it
...he cannot surrender to it : " I am not my own," he
tells her, " I am but the agent of a mighty will, of
a system which commands unhesitating obedience—
obedience which is part of my very being. I cannot
even form the thought of violating it " (p. 85). There
is a moment's hesitation in which the two principles
struggle for mastery, an inkling of rebellion against
the task-master, a dash for the Light. " If even for
me the gates of heaven may still be open...do with
me what you will, if there is anything in me worthy
of you, take me and make it more worthy." The
divine intelligence knows it is but a flash and can no
longer accept the sacrifice. Afterwards it is too late.
He henceforth remains under the beneficent spell, but
the Light is powerless to influence him. On his knees
in that church where he beheld the Friend at the words
" Lighten our darkness," his eyes seek Mary Collet
in a flood of sunlight and rest instead, in the shadow,
on the incarnation of the powers of darkness—the
messenger of the jesuit who comes to call him back
to the world's highway. There can be no more hesitation. " He got up quietly and went out. From his
marriage feast, nay from the table of the Lord, he
would have got up all the same had that summons
come to him " (p. 121).

He has turned from the Light and for a long time
he will not see it again. When he does come back
to it, he will be yet less able to follow it. For, as
soon as the truce of God has come to an end, the
conflict begins anew. The ties that bind him to
the world are drawn closer ; the jesuit involves him

in a political intrigue whose effect is to endear to him
yet more those pleasures which were already dangerous,
to render impossible any return to the life of abnega-
tion offered him by Mary Collet. He comes out of it
deteriorated both physically and morally. With his
conscience sullied by untruth, his body effeminated
by suffering, the lack of resolution which had already
prevented him from taking any personal decision
develops in a terrible degree. His brain grows weak :
he is not very far from mental alienation. In this
state of mind any preoccupation would become a fixed
idea. If the Divine Voice could speak to him, he
would change into a fanatic. But, although it is not
forgotten, in the life he leads it only reaches him as a
distant murmur. The personality of the Friend is ever
present. In his sufferings he can only attain to quiet
by repeating the name of Jesus (p. 155). He has but
little influence on Inglesant's life. In lieu of the
Divine Light the dangers of a worldly life creep in.
Not the ordinary dangers : John Inglesant is still
pure at heart, pure enough to see the future in the
magic crystal; no, but an exceptional danger, a
kind of fanaticism reversed, the outcome not of
his pious education but of his gentleman's training :
instead of religious fanaticism the fanaticism of
honour. Mary Collet disappears from his life ;
Eustace, that twin brother in whom he saw himself
from a gentleman become an accomplished *roué*, comes
on the scene again. Alive, Eustace would have but
little influence over him. But it suffices that he
should die by an assassin's hand for the principle of
which he was the incarnation to be transmitted to his

brother, i.e. the world's code of honour as opposed to
Christian honour. This code prescribes, as his first
duty, vengeance. Once this thought has entered his
unsettled brain, it becomes a perfect obsession. The
Society he serves does not forbid him to carry out
this idea; on the contrary, it helps him to do so.
Thus he is carried away by his life as a gentleman,
a courtier, a diplomatist far from the religious pre-
occupations of his early youth. With his ill-balanced
faculties it is almost impossible he should not founder.
Just then the Light reappears.

Alas! only to die out immediately after. He is
summoned to Mary Collet's death-bed. Her last
words for a moment stop him in his slippery descent.
She again points out to him the path he should
follow. "Will you serve your heavenly Master as
well as you have served your King?" she asks. He
swears he will, but is he any longer in a position
to keep his promise? The infinite pity still throws
its flood of light on him in the hour of temptation.
Before his eyes she who first brought him to see the
Friend seems to change into an emanation, a white
flame that loses itself in the Divine Light. "His
heart ceased to beat and he lay, as in a trance, to
behold the glory of God."

This glory does not last, but it does at least
make him realize how holy and solemn life ought to
be for him, and inspires him with the desire of finding, if not following, the path pointed out by Mary
Collet.

Feeling dizzy, powerless to act, and, since his
reason has begun to give way, incapable of judgment,

he goes and consults the Benedictine monk Serenus
de Cressy, who explains to him the true cause of his
distress. "You seek to follow Jesus, and have, to
begin with, the advantage of knowing Him. You
have seen Him face to face. He is your dearest
friend. Why then, knowing all His perfections, do
you find such difficulty in following Him? You
are like the young man who came to Jesus and
whom Jesus loved, *for you have great possessions.*"
And he explains to him how these very possessions
prevent him from following Jesus. "You have been
taught all that men desire to know, and are accomplished in all that makes life delightful. You know
the reality of men's power, and wisdom, and beauty.
But although everything in your mind is beautiful,
although all your acquirements are valuable, these
tendencies are too various. They will never be able
to harmonize.—You remind me of the rich oratories
I have seen of some of our Court ladies, where everything is beautiful and costly, but where a classic statue
of Apollo stands by the side of a crucifix, a Venus with
our Lady, a Cupid near St Michael, and a pair of
beads hanging on Mercury's Caduceus." The solution
is very simple. He must go and sell his possessions.
Only two alternatives are now left him. Will he let
himself be guided by the pure Light of faith, or is he
only willing to contemplate it through the prism of
human wisdom and philosophy? He must choose.
He already knows the worldly life: it does not
satisfy him. But what of the other life? De Cressy
describes it to him in the following terms:—"Intellectual study to you is fatal: you must renounce it.

You must engage in no study that is any delight or effort to the intellect. Come with me to Douay : there you shall teach the smallest children in the schools, and visit the poorest people, and perform the duties of the household—and all for Christ." That is to say, Inglesant must renounce the speculative life, in order to take part in the active life. If he consents to make this sacrifice, to undertake this new task, de Cressy promises him that in this course he will find the satisfaction he seeks :—" You shall walk with Jesus day by day, growing ever more and more like him ; and your path, without the least fall or deviation, shall lead more and more into the light, until you come unto the perfect day ; and on your death-bed—the death-bed of a saint—the vision of the smile of God shall sustain you, and Jesus himself shall meet you at the gates of eternal life."

Inglesant is convinced ; how could he fail to be ? Has he not seen this ideal realized in Mary Collet's life ; has he not just come from her death-bed ? He is convinced, but he is not converted. He is asked to renounce the world and pleasure, and not only the world, but intelligence too. Has not the latter taught him that the ways to salvation are infinite ? Why not see the others before settling his choice on this one ? He is convinced of the truth of all de Cressy tells him, but he is not convinced Jesus wishes him to accept this mode of life and follow him and find him in this single fashion, to the exclusion of every other. Oh, how open to suspicion is this nicety of reasoning. Is it not rather the shudder of the flesh recoiling before the idea of giving up all the luxury with which it surrounds itself and which now seems to it more indispensable than ever; is it not rather the cry of intelligence which dare not offer itself up for sacrifice; is it not rather the insuperable dread of positive action?

No, it is none of these things. It is solely the reply of conscience. But whom could he get to believe it when, the day after, he allows the old influence to recover its sway over him and, at the jesuit's request, undertakes a political mission in Rome, a mission which will give him the opportunity of satisfying all his amateur's and artist's tastes— a point Father Sancta Clara does not fail to dwell upon? Whom will he get to believe it when he is seen throwing himself into that life of luxury and pleasure, with the secret notion of being thereby enabled to carry out his plan of revenge, which has become more besetting than ever?

Not even he himself believes it. It was for a pure motive that he refused Serenus de Cressy's offer: it is for quite another motive that he accepts the jesuit's. As Inglesant is in the habit of analyzing himself, he reconsiders his own feelings: the first motive rises up indignantly against the second, and, through this very indignation, comes to doubt its own sincerity, to condemn itself, to identify itself with the other. Then Inglesant is inclined to think that he refused out of cowardice; if this is so, it is not Jesus who willed it. Then...then there creeps into his mind the notion that the Friend has forsaken him. He thinks he is possessed of the devil. All his intellectual culture, all his philosophical meditations have led him to the same conclusion as that poor ignorant Bunyan in *Grace Abounding*. But he has not, like Bunyan, that strength of exclusive belief which would enable him to struggle. To what purpose? In this frame of mind he starts for Italy.

It is easy to imagine the effect produced by the enervating pleasures of the South on this brain weakened by suffering, vaguely troubled by remorse for the crime he is about to commit, convinced that the Enemy has taken Christ's place. During this period of moral relaxation the senses regain the upper hand. There is food wherewith to satisfy them. The artistic splendours of Rome, the picturesque contrasts between the brightness of the sky and the darkness of the churches, the air heavy with incense, above all the music,—that music of which he would make a fifth element (p. 281),—little by little soften him, and in softening demoralize him. It is not that he has disowned the Friend: in calm moments he feels the Friend come back to him, but day by day he feels less able to follow him. "Communion after communion I find Christ and he is gracious to me, gracious as the love of God himself, but month after month and year after year I find not how to follow him" (p. 298). It is the logical consequence of his choice. For does he not always hear a voice saying to him: "The pleased acquiescence in life as it is, with all its follies and fantastic pleasures, is surely incompatible with following the footsteps of the Divine Ascetic who trod the winepress of the wrath of God" (p. 286). In the moments when, in the midst of his entirely æsthetic and intellectual life, this voice drives him to despair, what wonder is there that, seeing the impossibility of making his aspirations and actions agree, he should believe in a scheme spiritually directed against his soul's salvation? (p. 295).

Since such is the case, why reject the pleasures that are within his reach? Especially when there exists a philosophy that explains them. The Cardinal's arguments seem to him irresistible:

"It is more philosophical to take in the whole of life, in every possible form, than to shut yourself up in one doctrine which, after all, is dependent for its very being on that human life from which you have fled.— Human life, in all the phases of its beauty and its deformity, is instinct with the divine nature.—Even in the excesses of orgies I see traces of this general truth, for the renouncing of all bound and limit is in itself a truth when a good, though only sensual, is thereby perfected.—Nothing in human life comes amiss or is to be staggered at, however voluptuous or sensual, for all things are but varied manifestations of life" (pp. 289, 290).

Inglesant thinks he can accept this doctrine without danger: "Your doctrine is delightful to the philosopher and to the man of culture, who has his nature under the curb and his glance firmly fixed upon the goal," he answers, thus showing how well it satisfies his own desires; it is only "to the vulgar" that "it is death": for the vulgar Christianity is yet necessary. Dangerous casuistry, and how well this aristocratic distinction shows the relative esteem in which he holds the two tendencies that struggle for

the mastery of his soul. When there rises up before
him the representative of this religion of the vulgar,
the descendant of Luther, a phantom of the Reforma-
tion who comes and haunts the splendours of the
Renaissance, Inglesant has no better way of answering him than to invoke the Cardinal's arguments.
Under its brutality of expression the stranger's
doctrine does not appreciably differ from that of
Serenus de Cressy. Not only does Inglesant refuse
to accept it, he no longer believes in its intrinsic
value. The voice of the stranger thunders: "I see
around me a land given up to idolatry and sensual
crime, as if the old Pagans were returned again to
earth."...And Inglesant, like a docile pupil of the
Cardinal, answers: "You speak too harshly of these
things. *I see nothing in them but the instinct of
humanity.* The more I study humanity through all
its ramifications, the more enlarged my view becomes
of its trials, its struggles and its virtues. All things
that ever delighted it *were in themselves* the good
blessings of God" (pp. 315, 316, 317). And when
the other insists with ill-bred vehemence, a smile
plays on Inglesant's lips; he courteously declines to
hear more. Really, the enthusiast of the beginning
very rapidly changes into a sceptic.

The truth is that his own weakness drives him to
the extreme bounds of despair. In fact, in the unreal
state of mind he is in he exaggerates it. He in
good faith believes himself irresponsible, and he
believes it all the more willingly as it furnishes him
with an excellent excuse for not attempting to govern
himself. The fulfilment of his revenge for him marks

the term of his life, the moment when Christ will in his turn take vengeance for his infidelity by abandoning him to the devil. And although he indefinitely delays the hour of this revenge, as Hamlet did his ("Surely if the devil can afford to wait, much more can I," p. 349), it is less out of scruple than out of horror for the *action* implied in the carrying out of the project.

How he vegetates in the meanwhile matters little. Providing life is agreeable and luxurious, that he suffer no bodily pain, he is ready to perform all kinds of jobs, pretty well indifferently. His dulled conscience forbids none, his weakened judgment almost deprives him of the faculty of discriminating good ones from bad ones. The Society he is serving involves him in a plot which would formerly have been painful to him, since it is a question of trafficking in what were once his dearest beliefs, in order to procure for himself and the Society a purely temporal good. He obeys without any very great remorse. In this affair, as Malebranche would say, he does not act, he *is acted upon*. That suffices to relieve him of responsibility. He may enjoy in peace the advantages that his compliance, almost his neutrality, procure for him. Discreet scepticism leads him in the direction of hypocrisy.

From passive compliance to sin there is but one step. Especially when the sin harmonizes with the æsthetic surroundings. In this enervating atmosphere does not Lauretta appear as one of those manifestations of the principle of life—the most beautiful perhaps, the most perfect of all? Does he not know that "Nothing in human life is to be staggered at, however voluptuous or sensual..."?

Yes, but the sin that tempts him is an action. It is, besides, a present action which he has the opportunity of accomplishing once only, under special circumstances: it must be performed or abandoned; it is not possible to defer it to a distant future, like the *act* of vengeance. So it requires an independent effort; whether he yields or resists, his own will is in question. The Society is no longer there to direct him; he must act, for or against.

He must act....Ah, the enemy who came by the thought of laying that trap for him is in reality his saviour. What has so far been Inglesant's misfortune is that he has seen only the neutral side of the theories he professes. He has remained their passive exponent; let him but see their brutal realization under his own eyes: all his feelings are revolted. So he will act, since act he must, but *against.*

All the æsthetic temptations which had such a hold on him may unite to render sin agreeable and beautiful; he now has the strength to resist them. In the pavilion in the farthest depths of the forest wrapped in shade, amid silence, sin is preparing. Lauretta is waiting for him. But lo, at the moment when he turns round to pass from the verandah into the dining-room, on the horizon there rises a light, white and solemn. Symbol of a symbol, does not the dawn that is beginning to break in the east announce the return of the Divine Light[1]?

[1] Did Inglesant at that moment understand that, even leaving aside all question of principle, the pleasure offered by Lauretta would not in

It is the first decisive victory in his life, a victory that opens the way for another. The individual will awakes. So long subservient to an alien object, it was unconscious of its own strength. Through this independent action he has already half redeemed the great mistake, almost the crime, of his life—the fact of having given himself up without reserve to a cause imposing certain habits of mind on him which it did not seem possible he should overcome. He has known how to save himself from the first tangible temptation : the salutary influence of this action on his mind will be to restore to him hope, to a certain extent. Having caught sight of the Light again, that Light which in his dejection he believed to be but a will-o'-the-wisp, having seen it shine, bright and serene, in the moment of danger, a portion of his former enthusiasm comes back to him. In order to follow it he would now make every sacrifice, even unto that sacrifice formerly declared impossible: the sacrifice of his tastes

---

reality have been one for him? It is under the influence of unhealthy stimulants—the wine, the dizzying sights he has just witnessed, above all the "overpowering closeness of the air," that he may have thought so for a moment. His nature full of emotion, of emotion that will always need to expend itself in certain æsthetic pleasures such as music, has never shown the faintest symptom of passion. For most men this kind of emotion leads to passion or proceeds from it ; for Inglesant the two things are quite distinct. "By the peculiarity of his temperament he was enabled to resist," says the author, which is not very satisfactory. Shorthouse speaks more clearly elsewhere. The Viscount de Lys, in the same situation as J. Inglesant, hears a voice saying to him : " The pleasures you fancy you will have to renounce are not pleasures, *are not even such as you yourself really covet*. The pleasures you are formed to enjoy are of good report; they are all compatible with the Divine will : there is no voice that will call you to renounce these." (*Sir Percival.*)

and education. For, in order to recover the liberty
he has caught a glimpse of, it is needful to confirm
the success of the first victory by a second, perhaps
more difficult to win. After having resisted the
passing and, to him, novel temptation of desire, he
must repudiate the anti-Christian instinct which
has so long been urging him to take revenge.
His gentlemanly honour is at stake; in order to
become a Christian again, he must silence it. When
the moment comes he has so long awaited, so long
dreaded, the moment when he stands face to face
with his brother's murderer, he feels that the final
battle between Christ and Satan is about to take
place. On the outcome of this battle his future
salvation depends. And, as he had foreseen, it is at
first the principle of evil that seems destined to
carry the day. But, at the moment when he raises
his hand to strike, the principle of good, by the
mouth of his enemy, reclaims him. Malvolti for
his defence invokes the name of Jesus, that adorable
name which used formerly to lull his pain like a
monotonous lullaby. In the eyes of Inglesant the
sinister light of revenge dies out. He understands
that, in order to recover the confidence of the Friend,
it is necessary not only to worship but to follow him.
By this second action the redemption is completed.

He feels free now, free as at the time when
Mary Collet revealed the Divine Light to him. Now
he is able to accept the explanation that Molinos
gave him of the *raison d'être* of his life. "It seems
to me," the father of quietism said to him, at a time
when consolation could do him no permanent good,

"it seems to me there are some men whom God is determined to win by love. Chastisements are fit for others, but these are the select natures. Believe me, God does not lay traps for any....If He lavishes favours upon some it is because he knows that their nature will respond to love....God will win you, and He will win you by determined and uninterrupted acts of love" (p. 275).—He now feels the truth of those words. They afford a rational interpretation of the temptations through which the Friend has led him without indelible stain. Above all, they save him from the "terrible blasphemy" of having believed that Jesus had forsaken him. Peace comes back into his heart.

Need it be wondered that he should find in the doctrine which brings him this consolation a rule of conduct better than that offered him by the Society of Jesus? Since he has become accustomed to the free exercise of his will, the power that has dominated his life has lost much of its moral hold on him. He dare conceive the project of detaching himself from it; more than that, he imparts his views. Finding all his aspirations better realized in quietism, he does not hesitate to propose to the Society an essential change in the dogma; offering rupture as an alternative. The pupil of Father Sancta Clara is making progress. For he feels that he will be able to follow the Divine Light, to put into practice the counsels of his Master, only by breaking all the old bonds which, by restricting his will, benumb it. There can be no doubt that, had John Inglesant been able at that moment to gain his material freedom as he had already gained his moral freedom, he would have been definitively saved.

Just as he is taking his flight, a silken net is cast over him. "We call ourselves lords of our own actions and fate, but we are in reality the slaves of every atom of matter of which the world is made and we ourselves created," a friend had said to him formerly. However independent he may think himself in the new strength of his moral liberty, in this world he is the slave of the Society. The engagements he has entered into, or that he has been made to enter into, bind him till death. Serenely inexorable, the Society gives him to understand, by the mouth of its General, "that he must definitively choose between individual licence and obedience to authority....The Society would be loath to employ violence against an agent and inestimable friend, a gentleman of unstained reputation, etc. But...."

Inglesant understands that it is useless to struggle. So, when the General advises him "as a friend" to go back to England where Father Sancta Clara awaits him, he has no choice but to accept the yoke again with the best possible grace.

Thus it is that the young enthusiast, who started free and joyous in search of the Divine Light, in the end comes to be transformed into a disappointed philosopher, who spends his time in dreaming because he cannot act, and who does not even take an interest in his dreaming (p. 438). Only at the recollection of his past struggles does the flame revive in him that is so well hidden beneath the ashes as to be thought dead. Then he takes as an exponent of his feelings

his violin, causing it to express, through a plaintive
melody, in which cruel discords strike the ear, regret
for his broken, languid, useless life.

———————

It is not always possible to disentangle the *moral*
personality of the hero from the religious polemics
for which it furnishes a pretext. At times Shorthouse
seems entirely to lose sight of John Inglesant as an
individual, and to see in him only a mouthpiece for
his theories. This is the cause of serious deficiencies
in the delineation of his character, especially towards
the end, deficiencies it is not easy to fill in by reference
to the uncertain data of the beginning and the often
faltering development, particularly in the coming back
of the character on itself, the motion without advance,
which gives the impression of uncertain construction.
For this reason I have thought it better to borrow
but little from the last chapter, the most important in
the novel from the point of view of the philosophical
thesis, the most disconcerting from the point of view
of character. For another reason I have said nothing
of the part played by Inglesant in the episode of
Malvolti's death. This episode seems to me to ratify
the forgiveness scene, but not to show appreciable
progress in character.

# INDEX OF PROPER NAMES
# CHARACTERS AND TITLES

N.B.—In the last sentence of p. 117 MATTER is a conjectural interpolation. The original reads: *Already in sensation was attempting*, a noun evidently being omitted either *before* or *after* SENSATION.

. . . . . .

The *Keats Shelley and Shakespeare Studies* were written in English, the *Essays in English Literature* originally in French. The latter have been translated since the death of MARY SUDDARD.